# A DICTIONARY OF
# FLOWER, FRUIT AND STILL LIFE
# PAINTERS

# A Dictionary of
# FLOWER
## FRUIT, AND STILL LIFE
# PAINTERS

*by*

## SYDNEY H. PAVIÈRE
F.S.A., F.M.A., F.R.S.A., A.R.D.S.

*Author of 'The Devis Family of Painters'*
*'Flower, Fruit and Bird Prints', etc.*

## VOL. III—PART II
### 19th Century
(Artists born 1841-1885)

## F. LEWIS, PUBLISHERS, LTD.
PUBLISHERS BY APPOINTMENT TO THE LATE QUEEN MARY
### The Tithe House, Leigh-on-Sea, England

PRINTED AND MADE IN ENGLAND

*First Published 1964*

PRODUCED BY F. LEWIS, PUBLISHERS, LTD., AND PRINTED AT
THE DOLPHIN PRESS, BRIGHTON, ENGLAND

# ABBREVIATIONS USED IN THIS VOLUME

| | |
|---|---|
| b. | Born |
| Bazin | *Impressionist Paintings in the Louvre* |
| Benezit | *Dictionaire des Peintres, Sculpteurs, Dessinateurs et Graveurs,* 8 volumes, 1948–1955 |
| Bouquet | *Bouquet* by G. S. Whittet |
| B.I. | British Institution (1806–1867) |
| Blunt | *Catalogue of Flower Books*, London, 1950 |
| Bryan | *Bryan's Dictionary of Painters and Engravers*, 5 volumes, 1905 |
| Chaffers | *Marks and Monograms on Pottery and Porcelain* |
| coll. | Collection of |
| d. | Died |
| exhib. | Exhibited |
| Frankenstein | *After the Hunt*, 1953 |
| Gilhespy | *Crown Derby Porcelain*, 1951 |
| Graves | *Dictionary of Artists who exhibited in London*, 1760–1880 |
| G.G. | Grosvenor Gallery |
| H.M. & A.G. | Harris Museum & Art Gallery, Preston |
| Hardie | *Flower Paintings*, 1947 |
| lit. | Literature |
| N.E.A.C. | New English Art Club |
| N.G. | New Gallery |
| N.W.C.S. | New Water Colour Society, London |
| O.W.C.S. | Old Water Colour Society, London |
| op. | Operating |
| R.A. | Royal Academy, London (1769–    ) |
| repr. | Reproduced |
| R.H.A. | Royal Hibernian Academy (1823–    ) |
| R.I. | Royal Institute of Painters in Water-colours |
| R.S.A. | Royal Scottish Academy |
| R.S.W. | Royal Scottish Water-colour Society |
| Richter | *Floral Art—Decoration and Design*, 1932 |
| Salon | Paris Salon |
| s. and d. | Signed and dated |
| Sotheby's | Sotheby & Co., Auctioneers, London |
| V.E. | Various Exhibitions |
| Wilenski | *Flemish Painters*, 1960 |

ABBATT, AGNES DEAN
American School.
b. 1847, d. 1917.
Member of the National Academy. Painted flowers, land-scapes and coast scenes.

ABBEMA, LOUISE
French School.
b. Étampes 1858 (30th October), d. Paris 1927.
Pupil of Chaplin, Henner and Carlus Duran. Bronze medal Universal Exhibition 1900. Chevalier of Legion of Honour 1906. Painted flowers, portraits, and was a sculptor and engraver.
*auct.* Paris, 20.11.1925, flowers; 15.12.1927, flowers.

ABEL-TRUCHET
French School.
b. Versailles 1867 (29th December), d. 1918 (9th September).
Pupil of Jules Lefebvre and B. Constant.
Painter and engraver.
*auct.* Paris, 1.7.1943, Fleurs des Champs.

ABIT, ARMAND
French, 19th century (*see* Vol. 3, Part I, p. 7).

ABRAHAM, MISS LILIAN
British School.
*op.* 1880–1886.
London address.
*exhib.* Suffolk Street (2); N.W.C.S. (3), flowers.

ABRAHAMS, ANNA
Dutch School.
b. Middleburg 1849, d. The Hague 1930.
*coll.* The Hague, Mesdag Museum.

ABSOLON, JOHN DE MANSFIELD
British School.
*op.* 1862–1868.
London address.
*exhib.* Suffolk Street (4), still-life.

ACKER, FLORIMOND
Flemish School.
b. Bruges 1858 (6th April).
Studied Antwerp Academy and at Brussels under Portaels.
Known as FLORI MARIE VAN ACKER
*auct.* Brussels 30.12.1942, market still-life.

ACOCK, W. W.
British School.
*op.* 1870–1871.
Croydon address.
*exhib.* Suffolk Street (2), fruit.

ADAM, JOSEPH DENOVAN, R.S.A., R.S.W.
British School.
b. Glasgow 1842, d. there 1896.
London address.
*exhib.* R.A. (25); B.I. (6); Suffolk Street (6), fruit; R.S.A. Centenary Exhibition 1926, cattle.
*auct.* Sotheby's, 28.2.1962, game and fruit, signed and dated 1861.

ADAM, PATRICK W., R.S.A.
British School.
b. Edinburgh 1854 (12th October).
Studied Royal Scottish Academy.
*exhib.* R.S.A. Centenary Exhibition 1926, interior with three vases of flowers on tables in centre, lady at piano in distance, illustrated in Memorial Catalogue, pl. 76; R.A. (12), 1878–1892, domestic.

ADAM-KUNZ
German School.
19th and 20th century.
Painted still-life.
*auct.* New York 1905, still-life.

ADAMS, THOMAS
British School.
*op.* 1865–1879.
London address.
*exhib.* B.I. (1); Suffolk Street (4), fruit.

ADAN, F.
British School.
*op.* 1878.
London address.
*exhib.* Suffolk Street (2), flowers.

ADDENBROOKE, MISS ROSA
British School.
*op.* 1891–1892.
Salisbury address.
*exhib.* R.A. (1); Suffolk Street (1), still-life, fish.

ADLINGTON, MISS E. C.
British School.
*op.* 1893.
London address.
*exhib.* R.A. (1), still-life.

AERT, BERTHE (*see* ART)

AFFLECK, WILLIAM
British School.
b. Rochdale 1869.
Painted flowers and landscape.
*exhib.* R.A. (3); Suffolk Street (3); N.W.C.S. (5), land-
    scapes, 1890–1898.

AIRY, MISS ANNA, R.I., R.O.I., R.E.                    (*see* PLATE I)
British School.
b. 1882 (6th June).
Only child of Wilfrid Airy, M.INST.C.E., grand-daughter of
Sir George Biddell Airy, K.C.B., Astronomer Royal. Studied
at the Slade School 1899–1903. President Ipswich Art Club,
Vice-President the Artists' General Benevolent Institution.
Painted portraits, flowers, hedgerows, etc., and etched.
Married G. B. Pocock.
*coll.*    Auckland; Birkenhead; Blackpool; Ipswich;
    Lincoln (2); Liverpool; London, British Museum,
    Victoria and Albert Museum, Imperial War
    Museum; Newport; Rochdale; Sydney; Van-
    couver; Wanganui.
*exhib.* R.A. 1905–1956; Montreal; Milan; Ottawa; Paris
    Salon; Pittsburgh; Rome; Toronto; Venice, etc.
*repr.* *Floral Art* (H. Davis Richter); *Studio Magazine,
    Colour, Drawing and Design,* etc.

ALBERT, A. MILES, MRS.
British School.
*op.* 1900.
*exhib.* R.A. (2), flowers.

ALCAIDE, J.
Spanish School.
19th and 20th century.
Painted still-life.
*exhib.* Brussels 1910.

ALEXANDER, EDWIN, R.S.A., R.W.S., R.S.W.
British School.
b. Edinburgh 1870, d. Musselburgh 1926.
Eldest son of Robert Alexander, R.S.A. Studied art at
Edinburgh and under Fremiet in Paris. Visited Egypt in
1895 and 1902. Painted flowers, birds, animals and landscape.
*coll.*    Edinburgh; Glasgow; Preston, H.M. and A.G.
*exhib.* R.S.A. Centenary Exhibition 1926 (5), illustrated in
    Cat. No. 91; R.S.A.

ALEXANDER, HENRY
American School.
b. San Francisco 1862, d. New York 1895.
Studied in Munich at 14 years of age. Returned to San
Francisco in 1880's and remained till 1887. In New York
1887–1895. Painted still-life.
*coll.*    New York, Metropolitan Museum.
*repr.* 'After the Hunt', Frankenstein 1953, pl. 123.

ALEXANDER, JOHN
British School.
*op.* 1878.
Balham address.
*exhib.* Suffolk Street (1), fruit.

ALEXANDRE, EVA
French School.
19th century.
Working at Limoges.
*coll.*    Limoges (3), flowers.
*exhib.* Salon, 1908.

ALFORD, AGNES
British School.
*op.* 1881.
London address.
*exhib.* Suffolk Street (1), flowers.

ALHEIM, MME ALEXANDRINA (*née* PUSCHKIN)
Russian School.
19th century (*see* Vol. 3, Part I, p. 7).

ALHEIM, JEAN D'
French School.
d. Paris 1894.
Painted flowers and landscapes.
*exhib.* Salon 1866, 1875–1878.
*auct.*    Paris, 22.12.1898, landscape and flowers.

ALLAN, MRS. A. F.
British School.
*op.* 1866–1870.
London address.
*exhib.* R.A. (2), Suffolk Street (11), fruit.

ALLAN, MISS E.
British School.
*op.* 1863–1865.
London address.
*exhib.* B.I. (1); Suffolk Street (4), fruit.

ALLCHIN, J. HERBERT
British School.
(*See* Vol. 3, Part I, p. 7.)

ALLEN, MISS ANNIE C.
British School.
*op.* 1881–1883.
London address.
*exhib.* Suffolk Street (2), flowers.

**ALLEN**, MRS. CHARLES (*see* KATHERINE ALLMOND HULBERT)

**ALLEN**, L. JESSIE
British School.
*op.* 1881–1886.
London address.
*exhib.* Suffolk Street (7), flowers.

**ALLOUARD**, EDMOND
French School.
19th century.
Studied at School of Decorative Arts.
*exhib.* Artistes Francais 1881.
*auct.* Paris 1895, still-life.

**ALLSOP**, C.
British School.
*op.* 1864–1865.
London address.
*exhib.* B.I. (4), fruit.

**ALT**, THEODOR
German School.
b. Dohlau 1846 (23rd January).
Worked in Nuremberg and Munich.
Painted still-life.

**AMAN-JEAN**, EDMOND FRANCOIS
French School.
b. Chevry-Cossigny 1860, d. 1935.
Studied Ecole des Beaux Arts. Visted Rome. Painted still-life, engraved, and produced lithographs.
*coll.* Dijon, still-life.
*auct.* Paris, 10.5.1926, still-life.

**AMANS**, LOUISE
Swiss School.
b. Bale 1860 (5th June), d. there 1897 (10th February).
Pupil of Boulanger and J. P. Laurens and B. Constant in Paris. Painted flowers and portraits.
*exhib.* Bale 1889; Berne 1890.

**AMBLER**, MISS ESTHER
British School.
*op.* 1891.
Handsworth address.
*exhib.* N.W.C.S. (1), fruit.

**AMEN**, MME JEANNE
French School.
b. Belleville-sur-Saone 1863 (20th May), d. 1923.
Pupil of A. Grivolas.
Painted flowers and landscapes.
*coll.* Langres, Pontoise.
*exhib.* Artistes Francais 1911 and 1923. Silver Medal 1914.

**AMERIGO**, Y. MORALES, RAMON
Spanish School.
19th century (*see* Vol. 3, Part I, p. 7).

**AMIARD**, MLLE H. E.
French School.
19th century.
Painted flowers and genre.
*exhib.* Salon 1898.

**AMOR**, MISS E.
British School.
*op.* 1870.
London address.
*exhib.* R.A. (1), flowers.

**AMOUROUX**, JOSEPH
French School.
19th century.
Pupil of Gleyre. Working at Perpignan.
Painted still-life and portraits.
*coll.* Perpignan Museum.
*exhib.* Salon, 1879–1880.

**AMPHOUX**, ETIENNE PAUL
French School.
19th century.
Working at Havre. Painted still-life and portraits.
*exhib.* Paris 1877–1878.

**AMYOT**, MRS. (*see* CATHERINE CAROLINE CATHINKA ENGELHART)

**ANDERS**, MARIE JOSEPHINE (*née* HESEQUE)
French School.
19th century.
Pupil of Redoute. Working in Paris. Painted flowers.
*exhib.* Salon 1875, 1879 and 1880.

**ANDERSON**, MISS C.
South African School.
*op.* 1866.
Working at Swellendam, South Africa.
*exhib.* Paris Exhibition 1866 (£10 prize for 'Best drawings illustrative of Colonial subjects').
*lit.* *Pictorial Art in South Africa*, A. Gordon Brown, 1952.

ANDERSON, MISS S.
British School.
*op.* 1863–1870.
London address.
*exhib.* R.A. (2), still-life.

ANDON, F. D'
French School.
19th century.
Painted flowers and landscapes.
*exhib.* Salon 1891 and 1893.

ANDRE, ALBERT                                              (*see* PLATE 1)
French School.
b. Lyon 1869 (24th May).
Studied under Julian and Bouguereau. Visited Paris and
London.
*exhib.* Salon des Independants 1894; Cologne, Abels
Galerie 1963, flowers and fruit.
*repr.* Benezit, Vol. 1.4, flowers.
*auct.* Paris, 12.12.1921, 1.7.1943, still-life.

ANDRE, GASTON
French School.
19th and 20th century.
Painted flowers, still-life and landscapes
*exhib.* Salon des Independants 1910 and 1939.

ANDREASEN, SIGNE
Danish School.
b. 1853 (21st August).
Pupil of O. A. Hermansen. In Paris 1887. Painted flowers.

ANGELL, MAUDE
British School.
*op.* 1888–1897.
Hendon address. Painted flowers.
*exhib.* R.A. (8); Suffolk Street (7); N.W.C.S. (5).

ANGELL, MRS. THOMAS WILLIAM (*née* HELEN CORDELIA
COLEMAN)
British School.
b. Horsham 1847, d. Kensington 1884 (8th March).
Pupil of her brother, William Stephen Coleman. Married
1875 T. W. Angell, Postmaster, S.W. London district.
Painted flowers, fruit and birds and decorated ceramics at
Mintons. Associate of the Royal Water Colour Society.
Graves gives her as Mrs. *John* Angell.
*coll.* Preston H.M. and A.G. (2), flowers
*exhib.* R.A. (6); Victoria and Albert Museum (2), flowers;
O.W.C.S. (58); N.W.C.S. (25); G.G. (4).
*auct.* London, 28.11.1908, 19.3.1910, water colours of
flowers; Sotheby's, 20.12.1961, flowers.

ANKCORN, J.
British School.
*op.* 1864–1868.
London address.
*exhib.* R.A. (4); B.I. (8); Suffolk Street (5), still-life.

ANTROBUS, A. LIZZIE
British School.
*op.* 1882.
New Oscott address.
*exhib.* Suffolk Street (1), flowers.

APARICI-SOLANICH, ANTONIO
Spanish School.
19th century.
Working at Valence in 1878. Painted flowers.

APPLEYARD, FRED
British School.
b. 1874 (9th September).
Painted portraits, landscapes and flowers.
*coll.* Newcastle, Laing Art Gallery, roses.

ARADY, AUREL
Hungarian School.
19th century.
Working in Paris. Painted still-life.
*exhib.* Salon des Independants 1909.

ARCHER, C.
British School.
*op.* 1873.
Birmingham address.
*exhib.* Suffolk Street (1), flowers.

ARIZMENDI, ROSALIA
Spanish School.
19th and 20th century.
Pupil of Felix Iniesta. Painted flowers, fruit and still-life.
*exhib.* Madrid 1901–1906.

ARMFIELD, MAXWELL, R.W.S.                                  (*see* PLATE 2)
British School.
b. Ringwood 1882.
Studied at Birmingham School of Art and in Paris.
*repr.* *Flower Paintings*, M. Hardie.
*Floral Art*, H. Davis Richter.

ARMSTRONG, MISS EMILY S.
British School.
*op.* 1865–1872.
London address.
*exhib.* Various exhibitions (10), flowers.

ART, BERTHE
Flemish School.
b. Brussels 1857 (26th December).
Pupil of Alfred Stevens in Paris. Painted flowers, birds and portraits.
coll.   Antwerp; Brussels, Tournai.
exhib.  Salon; R.A. (2) 1897 and 1898 (from Brussels address), flowers.
auct.   Paris, 12.2.1937, still-life, pastel.

ASSELIN, MAURICE
French School.
b. Orleans 1882, d. 1947 (30th October).
Studied College Saint Croix, Orleans. Visited Italy and London. Painted flowers, still-life, portraits and landscapes.
coll.   Paris, Luxembourg, still-life.
exhib.  Salon des Tuileries 1909–1944; London; Lucerne; Munich; The Hague; Prague; Cologne, Abels Galerie 1963, vase of flowers.
auct.   Sotheby's, 5/6.7.1961, flowers; Paris, 2.3.1925, 13.12.1937, 27.1.1943, 2.7.1943, all flowers.

ASSELIN, PAUL MAURICE
French School.
19th century.
Working at Orleans. Visited Italy and Brittany.
exhib.  Salon d'Automne 1907; Salon des Independants 1910.

ASTON, JABEZ
British School.
19th century (see Vol. 3, Part I, p. 8).

ASTON, MISS LILIAS
British School.
op. 1865.
Birmingham address.
Painted flowers.

ATKINS, MISS EMMELINE
British School.
op. 1878–1885.
London address.
exhib.  R.A. (1); Suffolk Street (2); N.W.C.S. (1), still-life.

ATKINSON, JACOB
American School.
b. 1864, d. 1938.
A Philadelphian letter carrier. Painted trompe l'oeil still-life of letters, stamps, etc.
lit.    Frankenstein, 'After the Hunt', 1953.

ATKINSON, MAY
American School.
New Hope, Pa. address. 1892.
exhib.  Still-life 1892, awarded prize.

ATTENDU, ANTOINE FERDINAND
French School.
19th century.
Pupil of Mettling. Working in Paris.
exhib.  Salon 1870 and 1905.
auct.   Paris, 28.1.1925, still-life; 23.12.1942, 29/30.3.1943, fruit; 10.5.1944, still-life.

ATTLEE, MISS DELLA
British School.
op. 1886–1897.
London address, and later Dorking.
exhib.  R.A. (7); Suffolk Street (2); V.E. (6), flowers.

ATTLEE, KATHLEEN MABEL (or MARY)
British School.
op. 1886–1894
London address, and later Dorking.
exhib.  R.A. (7); Suffolk Street (2); V.E. (5).

ATWOOD, MISS CLARE
British School.
b. Richmond, Surrey, 1866; d. London 1962 (2nd August).
Daughter of Frederick Atwood, an architect. Pupil of L. C. Nightingale, and at Westminster and Slade Schools. Painted interiors, portraits, landscapes, still-life, and decorative flower compositions.
coll.   London, Imperial War Museum; New Zealand, National Gallery.
exhib.  R.A.

AUBERJONOIS, RENE VICTOR
Swiss School.
b. Yverdon 1872 (18th August).
Studied Kensington School of Art, and under J. P. Laurensen in Paris. Worked with Whistler.
exhib.  Vevey 1904, and Dusseldorf.
auct.   Paris 1902, still-life.

AUBLET, ALBERT
French School.
b. Paris 1851.
Pupil of Jacquand Gerome.
Legion of Honour 1890. Painted portraits, etc.
auct.   New York, 'Cueillant des Fleurs'.

AUMONIER, MISS LOUISA
British School.
*op.* 1868–1897.
London address.
*exhib.* R.A. (4); Suffolk Street (17); N.W.C.S. (13), flowers

AUSTIN, MISS EMILY
British School.
*op.* 1879–1887.
London address.
*exhib.* R.A. (1), flowers.

AUSTRIAN, BEN
American School.
b. Reading, Pennsylvania, 1870; d. Kempton, Pennsylvania 1921.
Painted still-life.
*repr.* The Old Print Shop Portfolio, Aug.-Sept. 1952.
*lit.* Frankenstein, 'After the Hunt', 1953.

AUTEROCHE, EUGENIE VENOT D'
French School.
19th century.
Pupil of Leon Cogniet. Painted flowers and portraits.
*exhib.* Salon 1876 and 1880.

AVANCON, ERNEST THIERION D'
French School.
19th century.
Pupil of E. Busson and de Comte
Painted still-life.
*exhib.* Salon 1868 and 1873.

AYRES, H. M. E.
British School.
*op.* 1873.
London address.
*exhib.* Suffolk Street (1), flowers.

AYRTON, MME ANNIE
British School.
*op.* 1878–1891, d. 1920.
Pupil of Chaplin in Paris.
Painted flowers and still-life and engraved.
*exhib.* R.A. (8), flowers; Salon 1889 and 1891.

AYRTON, WILLIAM
British School.
*op.* 1898.
Beccles, Suffolk, address.
*exhib.* R.A. (1), flowers.

AZAM, JEAN BAPTISTE
French School.
19th century.
Painted flowers and still-life.
*exhib.* Salon 1876–1879.

BAAS, MARIE
German School.
b. Hamburg 1844 (19th November).
Studied under Margarete Roosenboom. Second Prize Centenary Exhibition, Melbourne, 1889. Painted flowers and still-life.

BACH, EDWARD
British School.
*op.* 1874–1893.
Working in Ireland. Exhibited from a London address.
Painted genre, fruit and still-life.
*exhib.* R.A. (13); Suffolk Street (16). Graves says 'figures'. The exhibits at the R.A. in 1892 and 1893 were of fruit.

BACHTA, EVE
German School.
19th century (*see* Vol. 3, Part I, p. 9).

BACON, MISS H. M.
British School.
*op.* 1862.
London address.
*exhib.* B.I. (2), fruit.

BAES, FIRMIN
Flemish School.
b. Brussels 1874.
Son of Henri Baes. Studied under Leon Frederic at Brussels Academy. Painted still-life, genre, nudes and landscapes.
*exhib.* Brussels 1910.
*auct.* Brussels, 25.3.1938, flowers.

BAIL, JOSEPH
French School.
b. Limonest 1862 (22nd January), d. Paris 1921 (26th November).
Awarded Silver Medal, Universal Exhibition, Paris, 1900.
*auct.* Paris, 29.11.1900, fruit; 15.3.1902, still-life; 28.1.1907, flowers; 4/5.3.1920, 21.1.1928, 27.3.1931, 30.3.1942, all still-life.

**BAILLERGEAU**, YVES
French School.
b. Nantes 1881 (3rd October).
Pupil of Maxence, Sibatte, Baschet and Desiré Lucas.
Awarded Silver Medal Salon des Artistes Francais 1921.
*exhib.* Madrid, Acad. Roy.

**BAILLIE**, CAROLINE
British School.
*op.* 1872.
Brighton address. Painted flowers.

**BAINES**, B. COOPER
British School.
*op.* 1881.
London address. Painted flowers.

**BAKER**, ANNETTE (MRS. W. D. GLOAG)
British School.
*op.* 1890–1898.
*exhib.* R.A. (2); Suffolk Street (7); V.E. (5), flowers.

**BAKER**, HARRY H.
American School.
*op.* 1887.
From England. Studied art in England. Lived in St. Paul,
Minneapolis and California. Painted still-life.
*lit.* Frankenstein, 'After the Hunt', 1953.

**BAKER**, MISS M. K.
American School.
b. New Bedford, Mass.
Living in Boston, 1882. Painted flowers and still-life.
*exhib.* Boston Art Club and New York Academy.

**BAKER**, THOMAS
British School.
*op.* 1872–1882.
London address.
*exhib.* R.A. (1); Suffolk Street (2), fruit.

**BAKEWELL**, MISS H.
British School.
*op.* 1877–1893.
London address.
*exhib.* N.W.C.S. (1); V.E. (2), flowers.

**BALDWYN**, CHARLES H. C.
British School.
*op.* 1887–1893, d. Worcester.
Painted still-life, flowers, etc., in oil and water-colour.
*exhib.* R.A. (7); Suffolk Street (2); N.W.C.S. (3).

**BALE**, C. T.
British School.
*op.* 1868–1875.
London address.
*exhib.* R.A. (1); Suffolk Street (15), fruit.

**BALE**, GEORGE
British School.
19th century (*see* Vol. 3, Part I, p. 10).

**BANCROFT**, JOSEPH
British School.
19th century, d. 1857.
Apprenticed and worked at the Derby China factory early
19th century. After leaving Derby he worked at Minton's.
*lit.* Gilhespy, *Crown Derby Porcelain*, Lewis.

**BANKS**, MISS CATHERINE
British School.
*op.* 1869–1873.
*exhib.* Suffolk Street (2), flowers.

**BARAT-LEVRAUX**, GEORGES
French School.
19th and 20th centuries.
Chevalier Legion of Honour. Painted still-life, portraits, and
marines.
*exhib.* Independants 1907 and 1910; Salon 1921 and 1938.
*auct.* Paris, 4.6.26, still-life and flowers.

**BARBE**, JULES EDOUARD DESIRE
French School.
*op.* 1865–1876, d. Paris
Painted still-life.
*exhib.* Salon 1865 and 1876.

**BARBEY**, JEANNE MARIE
French School.
19th and 20th centuries.
Pupil of Ed. Cuyer and Desire Lucas in Paris. Painted still-life
and landscape.
*exhib.* Salon 1903; Salon Tuileries 1924 and 1925.

**BARBIER**, ANDRE
French School.
19th and 20th centuries.
*exhib.* Independants 1903; International Exhibition 1937,
flowers.

**BARBUT-DAVRAY**, LUC
French School.
b. Nimes 1863 (1st October).
Pupil of Roybet and Cabanel. Painted still-life and genre.
*auct.* Paris, 16.3.1925, still-life.

BARCLAY, A.
British School.
*op.* 1873.
London address.
*exhib.* Suffolk Street (1), flowers.

BARILLOT-BONVALET, LEONIE
French School.
b. Montigny-les-Metz, d. Paris 1901 (12th February).
Daughter and pupil of Leon Barillot-Bonvalet, Jules Lefebvre and Benjamin Constant.
*exhib.* Salon 1878.
*auct.* Paris, 21.1.1925, flowers.

BARKER, CLARISSA
British School.
*op.* 1885–1886.
Dolgelly address.
*exhib.* Suffolk Street (4), flowers.

BARKER, JOHN
British School.
19th century (*see* Vol. 3, Part I, p. 10).

BARLOFFA
French School.
19th century (*see* Vol. 3, Part I, p. 10).

BARNARD, GERTRUDE
British School.
*op.* 1892.
Putney address.
*exhib.* Suffolk Street (1); V.E. (1), flowers.

BARNARD, KATE L. (MRS.)
British School.
*op.* 1885–1888.
Chertsey address.
*exhib.* R.A. (1); N.W.C.S. (1), flowers.

BARNARD, MARY B.
British School.
*op.* 1894.
Norbiton address.
*exhib.* R.A. (1), flowers.

BARNES, MISS MARION L.
British School.
*op.* 1890–1895.
Lewisham address and New Cross.
*exhib.* R.A. (10); Suffolk Street (9); N.W.C.S. (4), flowers.
*auct.* London, 19.12.1908, flowers.

BARON, ANDRE EDGAR
French School.
19th century (*see* Vol. 3, Part I, p. 10).

BARRE, LOUIS DESIRE
French School.
*op.* 1881.
Painted flowers at the Sevres Porcelain Manufactory.

BARRIER, GUSTAVE
French School.
19th and 20th centuries.
Pupil of Gerome, Lefebvre and T. R. Fleury. Working in Paris. Painted flowers and fruit.
*exhib.* Salon 1911. Hon. Mention 1926.
*auct.* Paris, 4.6.1928, flowers and fruit.

BARRINGTON, W.
British School.
*op.* 1874.
Kingston Hill address.
*exhib.* Suffolk Street (1), still-life.

BARROW, LADY ANNA MARIA
South African School.
19th century (*see* Vol. 3, Part I, p. 10).

BARROW, EDITH ISABEL
British School.
*op.* 1894–1900.
Lee, London address and Dulwich.
*exhib.* R.A. (4), flowers.

BARTER, GERTRUDE MARY
British School.
*op.* 1889.
Watford address.
*exhib.* Suffolk Street (1), flowers.

BARTLETT, MISS ANNIE S.
British School.
*op.* 1864–1870.
London address.
*exhib.* R.A. (3); Suffolk Street (7), fruit.

BARTON, MISS C. A.
British School.
*op.* 1883.
Wincanton address.
*exhib.* G.G. (1), flowers.

BARTSCH, ELSE
German School.
19th and 20th century.
Studied Breslau and Vienna. Painted landscapes and flowers.
*exhib.* S.S. (1), 1891, landscape; Berlin 1906.
　　Graves gives 'E. Bartsch' exhib. at Suffolk Street, a landscape in 1891 from a London address.
*repr.* *Dekorative Vorbilder*, vol. xvi, pl. 43 (Stuttgart).

BARZAGHI, A.
Italian School.
*op.* 1889.

Painted flowers and still-life.
*exhib.* Independants 1906; Salon 1924.

BAYES, WALTER, R.W.S.
British School.
b. London 1868, d. there 1956 (21st January).
Son of A. W. Bayes, a painter and etcher; brother of Gilbert Bayes, the sculptor, and Miss Jessie Bayes, illuminator and

designer. Studied at Westminster School of Art. Head of Westminster School of Art 1918–1934. Director of Painting, Lancaster School of Art, 1944–1949.
*coll.* London, Tate Gallery, Imperial War Museum; Liverpool; Manchester; Oldham; Johannesburg.
*exhib.* R.A. 1895, flowers (water-colour) and 1895; Leger Galleries 1934.

BAYFIELD, MISS FANNY JANE
British School.
*op.* 1872–1897.
Norwich addresses and London.
*exhib.* R.A. (1); Suffolk Street (4), flowers.

BEARD, MISS ADA
British School.
*op.* 1885–1892.
London address.
*exhib.* R.A. (6), flowers.

BEARD, KATHERINE L.
British School.
*op.* 1885–1890.
London address.
*exhib.* Suffolk Street (3), flowers.

BECHERS, BEEKERS, BEKHER, BECKERS
Possibly one and the same artist.
(*See* Vol. 3, Part I, p. 12.)

BEECHEY, MISS AUGUSTA
British School.
*op.* 1870–1872.
London address.
*exhib.* Suffolk Street (3), still-life.

BEETHOLME, G. L. F. JUNR.
British School.
*op.* 1879–1880.
London address.
*exhib.* Suffolk Street (6), fruit.

BEHA-CASTAGNOLE, GIOVANNA
Belgian School.
b. Brussels 1871.
Studied at Hanau and Lugano.
Painted flowers and fruit.
*coll.* Lugano, Civic Palace.
*exhib.* Lugano 1891; Paris 1900; Stuttgart; Frankfort; Munich; Berlin.

BEHREND-CROISET, van der kop (mrs.)
Dutch School.
b. The Hague 1862, d. De Bilt 1943.
*coll.* The Hague, Mesdag Museum.

BEHRMANN, adolf
Russian School.
b. Riga 19th century
Painted still-life, figures and landscape.
*exhib.* Independants, Paris, 1910, still-life.

BEKHER
19th century (*see* Vol. 3, Part I, p. 12).

BELL, miss lucy hilda
British School.
*op.* 1889–1908.
London address.
*exhib.* R.A. (2); Suffolk Street (1); N.W.C.S. (2), fruit.

BELL, mrs. vanessa
British School.
b. London 1879, d. 1961.
Daughter of Sir Leslie Stephen and sister of Virginia Woolf, the novelist. Studied under Sir Arthur Cope, r.a., and at R.A. Schools. Contributed decorative work to Roger Fry's Omega Workshop and collaborated with Duncan Grant.
*coll.* Lincoln.
*repr.* *Bouquet*, pls. 31 and 32; *British Paintings* 1900–1930, Manchester Art Gallery 1954, No. 18.
*auct.* Sotheby's, 14.12.1960, 13.12.1961, 20.6.1962, flowers.

BELLAMY, a. s.
British School.
*op.* 1868–1874.
London address.
*exhib.* R.A. (1); Suffolk Street (13), fruit, etc.

BELSHAW, frank
British School.
*op.* 1881–1882.
Nottingham address.
*exhib.* R.A. (1); Suffolk Street (2), fish.

BENEDICTER *or* BENEDIKTER, alois josef
German School.
b. Disenhingen 1843 (4th June).
Studied Munich Academy. Visited Holland, Rome, Florence and Naples.
Painted still-life and architecture.

BENSON, miss h.
British School.
*op.* 1875.
London address.
*exhib.* Suffolk Street (1), flowers.

BENTLEY, edward
British School.
*op.* 1866–1883.
Bexley Heath address.
*exhib.* R.A. (1); Suffolk Street (38), fruit, etc.

BERGERET, denis pierre
French School.
b. Villeparisis 1846 (19th January).
Pupil of E. Isabey.
Silver Medal Universal Exhibition 1900. Chevalier of the Legion of Honour 1900. Painted still-life.
*coll.* Geneva; Nice; Rouen.
*exhib.* Salon 1905.
*auct.* Paris, 29.4.1921, fruit; 25.11.1942.

BERGHE, frits van den
Flemish School.
b. Ghent 1883, d. there 1939.
Pupil at Ghent Academy. Painted still-life and landscape.

BERNARD, emile
French School.
b. Lille 1868, d. Paris 1941 (16th April).
Painter, poet and critic. Painted portraits, flowers, still-life and landscapes. Visited Egypt.
*auct.* Paris, 30.6.1941, 30.11.1942, 5.6.1944, all still-life; Sotheby's, 5/6.7.1961, flowers.

BERNIER-HAPPE, mme jenny
Belgian School
19th century (*see* Vol. 3, Part I, p. 13).

BERTRAM, abel
French School.
b. St. Omer 1871 (9th September).
Pupil of Bonnat and Guillemet.
Painted flowers, marines and landscapes.
*exhib.* Berlin; Salon 1899; St. Louis; Liege; Pittsburg.
*auct.* Paris, 15.4.1924, 13.7.1942, 5.6.1944, flowers.

BERTRAND, georges jules
French School.
b. Paris 1849 (22nd November), d. there 1929 (11th August).
Pupil of Barrias and Bonnat. Chevalier of the Legion of Honour. Painted genre, portraits, flowers and fruit.
*exhib.* London, V.E., 1878–1881; Salon 1876.
*auct.* Paris 1898, fruit and flowers.

BEURDEN, ALFONS VAN                (*see* PLATE 2)
Flemish School.
b. Antwerp 1878, d. 1961.
Studied Antwerp Academy and taught there. Painted still-
life, figures and landscapes.
Known as BEURDON.
*coll.*    Antwerp, flowers.
Graves gives an Alphonse van Beurden as exhibiting sculptor
at the R.A. (1887–1892), from Antwerp, and Benezit refers
to him as a sculptor b. 1854.


BEVERS, MISS MAUD
British School.
*op.* 1899.
Oxford address.
*exhib.* R.A. (1), flowers.


BIBBS, LOUISA H.
British School.
*op.* 1864.
Worcester address.
*exhib.* Suffolk Street (1), fruit.


BICKNELL, C.
British School.
19th and 20th centuries.
Drew illustrations of plants.
*repr.*    *Flowering Plants of the Riviera*, by H. S. Thompson, 24
coloured plates, 1914.


BIDAU, EUGENE
French School.
19th century (*see* Vol. 3, Part I, p. 13).


BILLE, JACQUES
French School.
b. Paris 1880.
Painted flowers.
*exhib.* Salon Artistes Francais 1914 and 1939; R.A. 1926
and 1927 (4) flowers.
*auct.*    Paris, 29.6.1927, 23.12.1943, flowers.


BILOUL, LOUIS FRANCOIS
French School.
b. Paris 1874 (15th October), d. 1947.
Pupil of Benjamin Constant and Jean Paul Laurens. Chevalier
of the Legion of Honour 1926. Painted still-life and portraits.
*auct.*    Paris, 14.11.1921, still-life.


BINNS, MISS ELIZABETH J.
British School.
*op.* 1882–1893.
Worcester address.
*exhib.* R.A. (4); Suffolk Street (4), flowers.


BIRKBECK, GEOFFREY                (*see* PLATE 3)
British School.
*op.* 1875–c. 1940.
*coll.*    Durban, South Africa, Museum and Art Gallery,
flowers.


BISHOPP, GEORGE
British School.
*op.* 1880–1885.
Horsham address.
*exhib.* Suffolk Street (1), still-life.


BIVA, HENRI
French School.
b. Paris 1848 (21st January), d. 1928.
Pupil of A. Nozal and Leon Tanze. Bronze Medal 1900.
Chevalier of the Legion of Honour. Painted flowers and
landscapes in water-colour and pastel.
*exhib.* Salon Artistes Francais 1900–1905.
*auct.*    Paris, 12.12.1921, flowers; 22/26.11.1926, flowers.


BIVA, LUCIEN
French School.
19th century.
Pupil of Henri Biva. Painted flowers and landscapes.
Chevalier of the Legion of Honour.
*exhib.* Salon 1903 and 1914; Independants 1909.


BIVA, PAUL
French School.
b. Paris 1851, d. Avon 1900.
Painted flowers and fruit in water-colour.
*coll.*    Rouen; St. Brieuc.
*exhib.* Salon Artistes Francais 1900.
*auct.*    Paris, 30.5.1924, flowers; 1.2.1943.


BLACHE, CHARLES PHILIPPE
French School.
19th century (*see* Vol. 3, Part I, p. 13).


BLACKHALL, J.
British School.
*op.* 1862.
London address.
*exhib.* B.I. (1), still-life.

BLACK, MISS ANN SPENCE
British School.
19th and 20th century.
*exhib.* R.S.A. 1917, water-colour; R.S.A. Centenary
  Exhibition 1926, still-life.


BLACKBURNE, HELENA
British School.
*op.* 1894–1897.
London address.
*exhib.* R.A. (3), flowers.


BLACKALL, J.
British School.
*op.* 1862.
*exhib.* B.I. (1), still-life.


BLACKHAM, J.
British School.
*op.* 1867–1874.
Birmingham address.
*exhib.* R.A. (1); Suffolk Street (17), flowers.


BLAIKLEY, EDITH S.
British School.
*op.* 1880.
London address.
*exhib.* Suffolk Street (1), flowers.


BLANCHARD, MARIA
Spanish School.
b. Santander 1881, d. Paris 1932 (5th April).
Studied Madrid.
Painted still-life.
*coll.* Grenoble.
*auct.* Paris, 19.2.1921, 30.4.1921, 25.1.1923, 4.5.1923,
  23.12.1927, 21.11.1928, 8.3.1929, all still-life.


BLANCHE, JACQUES EMILE
French School.
b. Paris 1861 (1st February), d. 1942.
Pupil of Gervex and Humbert. Painted flowers and portraits.
*coll.* Luxembourg; Mulhouse; Paris.
*exhib.* London, Suffolk Street (5) from Paris 1882–1888.
*auct.* Sotheby's, 20.6.1962, still-life; Paris, 21.2.1920,
  26.5.1920, 12.5.1923, 29.6.1929, 15.12.33.


BLAND, MISS BEATRICE EMILY                    (*see* PLATE 3)
British School.
b. 1864, d. 1951.
Member New English Art Club. Painted flowers and landscapes.
*exhib.* R.A. and New English Art Club.
*repr.* *Bouquet*, pl. 46.
*auct.* London, 23.7.1931, flowers.


BLANDY, MISS L. V.
British School.
*op.* 1879–1881.
London address.
*exhib.* G.G. (5), flowers.


BLATHERWICK, MISS LILY (MRS A. S. HARTRICK, R.S.W.)
British School.
*op.* 1877–1897.
Helensburgh address. Painted flowers.
*coll.* London Victoria and Albert Museum, orchids.
*exhib.* R.A. (5); N.W.C.S. (5); G.G. (2); N.G. (2), flowers.


BLAU *or* BLAU-LANG, TINA
Austrian School.
b. Vienna 1845 (15th November), d. 1937.
Pupil of August Schaeffer and W. Lindenschmit in Munich.
Visited Holland, Italy and Hungary. Painted flowers and
landscapes.
*coll.* Vienna.
*exhib.* Salon, Hon. Men. 1883.


BLIGH, JABEZ
British School.
*op.* 1863–1889.
Worcester address.
*exhib.* R.A. (17); Suffolk Street (16); N.W.C.S. (6), fruit,
  etc.


BLOCK, L.
British School.
*op.* 1879–1893.
London address.
Painted still-life of books, etc. Several of his works are to be
found in U.S.A. collections.
*exhib.* R.A. (1); Suffolk Street (2); N.W.C.S. (5), fruit.
*lit.* Frankenstein, 'After the Hunt', 1953.


BLOOMFIELD, HARRY
British School.
19th century (*see* Vol. 3, Part I, p. 14).

BLOT, JACQUES EMILE
French School.
19th century.
Working in Paris. Painted flowers, portraits and genre.
*exhib.* Salon d'Automne 1909.
*auct.* Paris, 27.6.1941, flowers.

BLOXAM, MISS MARY A.
British School.
*op.* 1894.
Wimbledon address.
*exhib.* R.A. (1), flowers.

BOADAS, MARTIANA
Spanish School.
19th century (*see* Vol. 3, Part I, p. 14).

BOCH, ANNA
Flemish School.
b. La Louviere 1848, d. after 1914.
Pupil of J. Verheyden. Travelled in Holland and France.
Painted flowers, landscapes and marines.
*exhib.* Munich, 1909.

BOCH, EUGENE GUILLAUME
Flemish School.
19th century. b. La Louviere.
Painted flowers.
*exhib.* Salon d'Automne 1909 and 1910.

BOCQUET, LOUIS AUGUSTE HENRI
French School.
19th century.
Pupil of M. Adam. Working in Paris.
*exhib.* Salon 1878, flowers.

BODEN, HENRY
British School.
*op.* 19th century (*see* Vol. 3, Part I, p. 14).

BODKIN, FREDERIC E.
British School.
*op.* 1872–1893.
London address. Painted game.
*exhib.* R.A. (19); Suffolk Street (14); N.W.C.S. (2).

BODTKER, PETREA
Norwegian School.
b. Bergen 1850 (29th April), d. there 1945 (7th July).
Studied at the studio of Thurmann in Oslo in 1881 and
A. Uchermann in Bergen 1882–1884. Visited the studio of
Chr. Krohg in Oslo, later becoming a pupil of von Strechene
in Munich. Painted flowers and still-life.

BOGGIO, EMILE
French School.
b. Caracas (Venezuela), d. 1921.
Naturalized Frenchman. Pupil of J. P. Laurens and H. Martin.
Painted flowers, portraits, landscapes, etc.
*exhib.* Salon 1887; Universal Exhibition Bronze Medal
1889, Silver Medal 1900.
*auct.* Paris, 8.3.1943, flowers and fruit.

BOLLIGER, RODOLPHE
Swiss School.
b. Arbon 19th century.
Painted flowers, fruit, portraits, animals and views.
*exhib.* Salon des Independants 1909; Salon d'Automne
1922 and 1923.
*auct.* Paris, 27.2.1928, fruit and flowers.

BOMPARD, MAURICE
French School.
b. Rodez 1857, d. 1936.
Pupil of Boalanger and Jules Lefebvre. Painted flowers, fruit,
marine and genre. Officer of the Legion of Honour.
*exhib.* Salon 1878.
*auct.* Paris, 17.5.1944, flowers and fruit; 2.6.1943, flowers.

BOMPARD, PIERRE
French School.
19th century.
Working at Verdun. Painted still-life and landscape.
*coll.* Rennes Museum, still-life.
*exhib.* Salon des Independants 1911; Salon d'Automne
1924.
*auct.* Paris, 28.2.1930, still-life.

BONAMY, ARMAND JOSEPH
French School.
19th century.
Working in Nantes. Painted flowers, marines and portraits.
*exhib.* Salon Nationale 1910.

BONLIAN, MISS A.
British School.
*op.* 1873–1874.
*exhib.* Suffolk Street (2), fruit.

BONNARD, PIERRE                    (*see* PLATE 4)
French School.
b. Fontenay-aux-Roses 1867 (3rd October), d. Cannet 1947
(23rd January).
Pupil of Bouguereau. Painter and lithographer. Made
stained-glass windows, designed furniture, stage settings,
books and posters.
*coll.*   Glasgow; Grenoble.
*auct.*   Lucerne, 20.6.1935, fruit, flowers, still-life; 10.6.1937,
fruit; Paris, 18.2.1939, flowers; 4.12.1941, flowers;
15.12.1943, fruit.


BONNARDEL, ALEXANDRE FRANCOIS
French School.
b. Pajay 1867 (6th September).
Pupil of Zacharie and School of Art Lyon. Painted portraits
and still-life.


BONNEAU, MISS FLORENCE MARY (MRS. F. M. COCKBURN)
British School.
*op.* 1871–1884.
London address.
*exhib.* R.A. (1); Suffolk Street (14), flowers.


BONNEMAISON, GEORGES
French School.
d. 1885.
Painted flowers.
*auct.*   Paris, 25.6.1943, flowers.


BOOGAARD, WILLEM JACOBUS
Dutch School.
b. Haarlem 1842 (26th October), d. Antwerp 1887.
Pupil of P. F. Van Os. Visited Rotterdam.
Painted flowers.
*auct.*   London, 5.7.1935, flowers.


BOOTH, MISS ELIZABETH
British School.
*op.* 1879–1885.
Florence address.
*exhib.* R.A. (2), flowers.


BORDIGNON, NOE
Italian School.
b. Castelfranco 1842.
Working in Venice.
Painted flowers.
*exhib.* Paris 1878.


BOREL, ANNA JEANNE CHARLOTTE
French School.
b. Lille 1869 (3rd July).
Studied at Lille Academy.
Sister of Henriette Marie Evelina Borel.
Painted flowers.
*exhib.* Amiens 1890; Lille 1893.


BOREL, HENRIETTE MARIE EVELINA
French School.
b. Lille 1871.
Sister of Anna Borel. Studied at Lille Academy. Painted
flowers, still-life and portraits.
*exhib.* Amiens 1890; Lille 1893; Salon 1890.


BORGEK, LYDIE
Russian School.
19th century.
Painted still-life.
*exhib.* Salon des Independants 1907 and 1910.


BORIE, ADOLPHE
American School.
b. Philadelphia 1877 (5th January).
Studied Philadelphia Academy and Munich.
*exhib.* Salon National 1922 and 1924.
*repr.*   *Bouquet*, pl. 7.


BORROWS, HENRY
British School.
*op.* 1884–1889.
Huddersfield address.
*exhib.* R.A. (4), flowers.


BORSTONE, H.
British School.
*op.* 1868.
*exhib.* Suffolk Street (2), fruit.


BOSTOCK, MISS EDITH
British School.
*op.* 1863–1868.
London address.
*exhib.* R.A. (2), fruit.


BOUDOT-LAMOTTE, MAURICE
French School.
b. La Fère, 19th century.
Painted still-life, portraits and landscapes.
*exhib.* Salon des Independants 1902; Salon 1909 and 1924.

BOULARD, AUGUSTE THE YOUNGER
French School.
b. Paris 1852 (29th February), d. 1927.
Son of Auguste Boulard. Pupil of Bracquemond.
Painted flowers, fruit, landscapes, and engraved.
*exhib.* Salon 1874.
*auct.* Paris, 28.11.1904, fruit; 23/24.5.1927, flowers.

BOULOC, JACQUES E.
French School.
19th century.
Pupil of Gabriel Ferrier. Painted flowers and portraits.
*exhib.* Salon 1912.
*auct.* Paris, 11.4.1927, flowers.

BOURDELLE, MME STEPHANIE
French School.
19th century.
Painted flowers.
*exhib.* Salon des Independants 1907.

BOUVIER, ALFRED
French School.
19th century (*see* Vol. 3, Part I, p. 15).

BOWEN, OWEN
British School.
b. Leeds 1873 (28th April).
Painted landscapes and still-life.
*exhib.* R.A. (1), coast scene, 1892.

BOWSER, MISS ROSE MAUDE
British School.
*op.* 1886–1889.
London address.
*exhib.* R.A. (1); N.W.C.S. (2), flowers.

BRACQUEMONT, MME MARIE
French School.
19th century.
Painted flowers and genre.
*exhib.* Salon 1874; London 1881, V.E. (5), domestic.

BRADFORD, MISS HARRIETTE
British School.
*op.* 1862–1867.
London address.
*exhib.* R.A. (1); Suffolk Street (6), flowers.

BRADLEY, MRS. E.
British School.
*op.* 1865.
Putney address.
*exhib.* Suffolk Street (1), still-life.

BRADSTREET, MISS E.
British School.
*op.* 1868.
London address.
*exhib.* Suffolk Street (1), fruit.

BRAIN, MISS F.
British School.
*op.* 1864–1867.
London address.
*exhib.* B.I. (3); Suffolk Street (2), flowers.

BRAMBILLA, CARLOS
Spanish School.
19th century.
Working in Barcelona. Painted flowers.
*exhib.* Barcelona 1870.

BRANDON, MRS.
British School.
*op.* 1864.
London address.
*exhib.* Suffolk Street (1), flowers.

BRANGWYN, SIR FRANK, R.A.                    (*see* PLATE 5)
British School.
b. Bruges 1867 (13th May), d. Ditchling 1956 (11th June).
Studied at School of Art, South Kensington. Apprenticeship with William Morris 1882–1884. Chevalier of the Legion of Honour 1901, etc. Executed vast mural decorations; easel pictures, water-colours; lithographs and designs for textiles, pottery, furniture, stained glass, etc.
*coll.* Bruges, Des Moines, Dundee, Royal Academy, Southampton, Southport, Venice, Walthamstow, Wolverhampton, all flower and still-life subjects.
*exhib.* R.A. (16); Suffolk Street (26); N.W.C.S. (1); G.G. (3); N.G. (1); V.E. (5) from 1885 onwards. 184 Queen Gate, May–July 1924 (457); R.A. (Retrospective Exhibition) (470).
*repr.* 1924 Exhibition catalogue; Barbizon House Records; *The Water Colours of Sir Frank Brangwyn* (Bunt), 1958.
*The Oils and Murals of Sir Frank Brangwyn* (Galloway), 1962.
*Floral Art, Decoration and Design* (Richter), 1932.

BRAQUE, GEORGES
French School.
b. Argenteuil 1882 (13th May).
Apprenticed to a decorator. Studied School of Art, Le Havre, and in Paris. Executed lithographs, woodcuts, etchings and some sculpture. Painted still-life. Served in 1914–1918 War.

coll. Basle; Buffalo; Copenhagen; Detroit; Frankfurt; Glasgow; Le Havre; London, Tate Gallery; New York, Museum of Modern Art; Ottawa; Paris; Philadelphia; Washington.
exhib. Salon des Independants 1906.
repr. Braque, Douglas Cooper, pl. 16.
auct. Sotheby's, 6.12.1961, both illustrated in catalogue; Paris, 3.6.1937, fruit; 10.6.1937, still-life; 13.12.1940, still-life; 25.1.1943, fruit; Sotheby's, 5.7.1962, still-life.

BRECKENRIDGE, HUGH HENRY
American School.
b. Leesburg (Virginia) 1870, d. 1937.
Studied at Philadelphia Academy and in Paris under Bouguereau, Doucet and Ferrier. Member of New York Water-Colour Club.
exhib. Altana, Medal; Buffalo 1901, Medal; Philadelphia Art Club 1907.

BRIDGMAN, T. B. or D.
British School.
op. 1865.
London address.
exhib. Suffolk Street (1), still-life.

BROCK, FANNIE
British School.
op. 1883.
exhib. Suffolk Street (1), flowers.

BRODERICK, MARY
British School.
19th century (see Vol. 3, Part I, p. 16).

BROMLEY, C. SHAILOR
British School.
op. 1882–1886.
London address.
exhib. Suffolk Street (10), fruit.

BROOKS, NICHOLAS A.
American School.
op. 1880–1904.
Working in New York. Painted portraits and still-life.
repr. After the Hunt, Frankenstein, 1953, pl. 120.
lit. Frankenstein.

BROOME, G. J.
British School.
op. 1867–1873.
London address.
exhib. R.A. (3); Suffolk Street (3), fruit.
auct. Sotheby's, 8.3.1961, fruit.

BROOMFIELD, G. H.
British School.
op. 1877.
London address.
exhib. Suffolk Street (1), fruit.

BROS, MISS A.
British School.
op. 1868.
London address.
exhib. R.A. (1), flowers.

BROWN, G. A.
British School.
op. 1864.
exhib. R.A. (1), flowers.

BROWN, MISS HELEN
British School.
op. 1883–1887.
Forest Gate address.
exhib. R.A. (2); N.W.C.S. (4), flowers.

BROWN, MARGARET
British School.
op. 1881.
London address.
exhib. V.E. (1), flowers.

BROWNE, MRS. E.
British School.
op. 1871.
Horsham address.
exhib. R.A. (1), still-life.

BROWNE, MISS E.
British School.
op. 1877.
Horsham address.
exhib. Suffolk Street (1), flowers.

BROWNE, J. B.
British School.
op. 1861–1863.
exhib. R.A. (1); Suffolk Street (1), game.

BROWNE, MATILDA C. (MRS. FREDERICK VAN WYCK)
(*see* PLATE 6)
American School.
b. Newark, N.J., 1869 (8th May), d. Greenwich, Conn., 1947 (3rd November).
Daughter of Matilda Culver and Leonard P. Browne. Married Frederick Van Wyck, author of *Recollections of an Old New Yorker*, which she illustrated. Pupil of P. M. Dewey, H. S. Bisbing and Julien Dupre. Dodge Prize 1899; Halgarten Prize 1901. Painted animals, flowers and landscapes. Member National Academy of Women Painters and Sculptors.
*exhib.* National Academy of Design, New York, 1881 (aged 12); Chicago, Columbian Exposition 1893 (Hon. Mention; Paris Salon; New York, Anderson and Milch Galleries in 1920s, Berry-Hill Galleries.
*coll.* Bruce Museum, Greenwich, Conn., landscape with cows; Mrs. E. F. Lewis, Leigh-on-Sea, pink peonies; Mrs. G. W. Blunt White, Mystic, Conn., flower and still-life, several.
*lit.* *International Studio*, vol. 78 (Oct. 1923), p. 129. *Who's Who in American Art*, 1936–1947.

BROWNING, AMY KATHERINE (MRS. T. C. DUGDALE), R.P., R.O.I., A.R.C.A.
British School.
b. Belford 1882.
Pupil of Gerald Moira and Royal College of Art. Studied in Paris. Wife of T. C. Dugdale, R.A. Painted still-life and portraits.
*exhib.* R.A.; R.O.I.; New English Art Club; Salon des Artistes Francais, Silver Medal.
*repr.* *Bouquet*, pl. 45.

BRUCE, MRS. CARMICHAEL
British School.
*op.* 1883.
London address.
*exhib.* Suffolk Street (2), flowers.

BRUCE, MISS HELEN (*or* ELEANOR)
British School.
*op.* 1883.
London address.
*exhib.* N.W.C.S. (3); G.G. (4), flowers.

BRUNIN, *known as* LEON DE MEUTTER
Flemish School.
b. Antwerp 1861.
Began as a sculptor. Studied at Antwerp Academy. Later taught there. Visted Holland.
*exhib.* Salon.

BRUYN, CORNELIS JOHANNES DE
Dutch School.
19th century (*see* Vol. 3, Part I, p. 17).

BUCK, W.
British School.
*op.* 1864.
London address.
*exhib.* Suffolk Street (1), still-life.

BUDGETT, MISS S. E.
British School.
*op.* 1883–1884.
Painted flowers.

BUISSON, GEORGES
French School.
19th century.
Pupil of Garnier and Gros.
*exhib.* Salon 1879 and 1882, still-life.

BULLEID, GEORGE LAWRENCE, A.R.W.S.
British School.
b. London 1858, d. Bath 1933/34.
*coll.* Preston, H.M. and A.G., flowers (water-colour).
*exhib.* R.A. (3); O.W.C.S. (19); N.W.C.S. (3); V.E. (2). Graves says 'mythological'.

BULOT, EUGENE ALEXANDRE
French School.
b. Saint Cyr, 19th century.
Painted flowers and birds at the Sevres Porcelain Manufactory 1862–1883.
*exhib.* Salon 1868 and 1873, flowers and fruit.

BURDICK, HORACE R.
American School.
b. East Killingsly (Conn.) 1844.
Member of Boston Art Club. Painted still-life.

BURKHARDT, HEDWIG
Swiss School.
b. Zurich 1863 (13th November).
Worked in Munich and Paris. Painted flowers, still-life and portraits.
*exhib.* Salon 1893, flowers.

BURT, H. A. B.
British School.
*op.* 1878–1880.
Wokingham address.
*exhib.* V.E. (3), flowers.

BURY, MME LOUISE DE
French School.
19th century.
Pupil of Harpignies. Painted still-life.
*exhib.* Salon 1869.

BUTLER, MISS MARY E.                    (*see* PLATE 7)
British School.
*op.* 1867–1909.
London address. In 1909 living in Natal, South Africa.
*coll.*    London, Victoria and Albert Museum, flowers.
*exhib.* R.A. (12); Suffolk Street (1); N.W.C.S. (17).

BUTLER, MRS. THOMAS (NINA H.)
British School.
*op.* 1884.
London address.
*exhib.* Suffolk Street (1), flowers.

BUTTON, KATE
British School.
*op.* 1881.
Clevedon address.
*exhib.* Suffolk Street (1), flowers.

BUXTON, CATHERINE E.
British School.
19th century (*see* Vol. 3, Part I, p. 18).

BYWATER, MISS ELIZABETH
British School.
*op.* 1879–1891.
London address.
*exhib.* R.A. (22); Suffolk Street (8); N.W.C.S. (3); G.G. (4), flowers.

CABANZON, Y HERNANDEZ FRANCISCO
Spanish School.
19th century (*see* Vol. 3, Part I, p. 18).

CADELL, FRANCIS CAMPBELL BOLLEAU
British School.
b. Edinburgh 1883 (12th April).
*auct.*    London, 10.3.1930, flowers; Edinburgh, 31.10.1936.

CAIRATI, GEROLAMO
Italian School.
b. Trieste 1860.
Pupil of L. Conioni 1873–1885. Visited Munich. Painted still-life and landscape.
*exhib.* Munich 1909; Brussels 1910.

CALBET, ANTOINE
French School.
b. Engayrac 1860 (16th August), d. 1944.
Pupil of Michel, Cabanel and Marsai. Member of the Society des Artistes Francais. Painted figures, flowers, etc.
*auct.*    Paris, 16/17.5.1939, flowers.

CALTHROP, MRS. M. A.
British School.
*op.* 1877–1883.
Uppingham address.
Painted flowers.
*exhib.* R.A. (3); Suffolk Street (1), flowers.

CAMBIER, JULIETTE (*née* ZIANE)
Flemish School.
b. Brussels 1879.
Pupil of her husband, L. G. Cambier, and in Paris under Maurice Denis. Painted still-life, landscapes and figures.
*coll.*    Antwerp, flowers.

CAMERON, MISS JULIA
British School.
*op.* 1880–1891.
London address.
*exhib.* Suffolk Street (2); N.W.C.S. (1), flowers.

CAMOIN, CHARLES                    (*see* PLATE 7)
French School.
b. Marseilles 1879.
Painted flowers, fruit and still-life, marines, portraits and landscapes.
*coll.*    Cologne, flowers.
*repr.*    *Bouquet* (*Studio*), pl. 8.
*auct.*    Paris, 29.6.1928, still-life; 8.12.1928, fruit; 16.3.1929, fruit; 22.12.1941, flowers; 29/30.11.1943, still-life.

CAMPBELL, DUVAR
British School.
*op.* 1865–1873.
London address.
*exhib.* R.A. (1); B.I. (1); Suffolk Street (3), fruit.

CAMPBELL, J. A. D.
British School.
*op.* 1864.
London address.
*exhib.* Suffolk Street (1), fruit.
Possibly the same as DUVAR CAMPBELL.


CAMUS, HENRI LOUIS
French School.
19th and 20th century.
Painted still-life and landscape.
*exhib.* Salon des Independants 1908 and 1909.


CANCHOIS, HENRI
British School.
*op.* 1883–1890.
London address.
*exhib.* Suffolk Street (10), still-life.


CANZIANI, ENRICO FRANCESCO
British School.
b. Milan 1848 (21st November), d. Ditchling 1931 (9th March).
Friend of Sir Frank Brangwyn and was buried at Ditchling. Married Louisa Starr (1845–1909), a painter of portraits and figure subjects.
*coll.* Birmingham Art Gallery, study of blackberry fruit and foliage.
*lit.* Round about 3 Palace Green, E. Canziani (Methuen).


CAPEINICK, JEAN
Belgian School.
b. Ghent 1838, d. Brussels 1890.
Painted flowers.


CAPPIELLO, LEONETTO
French School.
b. Livourne 1875 (9th April), d. Paris 1942.
Naturalized Frenchman.
*auct.* Paris, 31.1.1929, Masque dans les fleurs.


CARLILL, STEPHEN BRIGGS
British School.
19th century.
Studied Hull School of Art. Examiner Department of Science and Art. Later farming in South Africa. Killed by Kaffirs in 1903.
*coll.* London, Victoria and Albert Museum, insects and animals.
*exhib.* R.A. (3); N.W.C.S. (1); N.G. (3); R.I. Graves says 'portraits'.


CARLINE, GEORGE F., R.B.A.
British School.
b. Lincoln 1855, d. Assisi 1920 (December).
Son of Richard Carline, a solicitor. Studied at Heatherley's, London, Antwerp and Paris. Lived at Lincoln, Repton, Oxford 1895, and then Hampstead. Painted flowers, gardens and rustic subjects.
*coll.* London, Victoria and Albert Museum, trees.
*exhib.* R.A. (9); Suffolk Street (3); N.W.C.S. (10); R.I.; Dowdeswell Galleries (59 works in 1896).


CARLSEN, SOREN EMIL
Danish School.
b. Copenhagen 1853, d. 1932.
Studied at Copenhagen Academy. In America 1872.
Painted still-life and was an architect.
*auct.* New York, 4.3.1904, still-life; 30/31.10.29, fruit; 2.3.1944, still-life.


CARLYLE, FLORENCE
Canadian School.
19th century (*see* Vol. 3, Part I, p. 19).


CARMAN, H. A.
British School.
*op.* 1867–1873.
Crayford address.
*exhib.* Suffolk Street (13), fruit, etc.


CARON, JULES
French School.
19th century.
Pupil of Remond. Working at Poissy and Paris. Painted still-life.
*coll.* Nantes Museum.
*exhib.* Salon 1861 and 1875.


CARPENTIER, EVARISTE
Flemish School.
b. Courtai 1845 (1st December).
Studied at Antwerp Academy and under Keyser.
*coll.* Namur, flowers of the Heath.


CARRINGTON, MRS. PATTY
British School.
*op.* 1883–1887.
Worcester address.
*exhib.* N.W.C.S. (3), flowers.

CARTER, CHARLES
British School.
*op.* 1868–1873.
London address.
*exhib.* Suffolk Street (2), fruit.

CARTER, MRS. E. S.
British School.
*op.* 1861–1874.
London address.
*exhib.* Suffolk Street (28), fruit.

CARTER, MISS M. AUSTEN
British School.
*op.* 1884–1893.
London address.
*exhib.* N.W.C.S. (3), flowers.

CARTER, MISS MARY E.
British School.
*op.* 1884.
London address.
*exhib.* Suffolk Street (1), flowers.

CASE, BERTHA L.
British School.
*op.* 1873–1913.
Maidstone address.
*exhib.* V.E. (2), flowers; Salon 1911 and 1913.

CASORATI, FELICE
Italian School.
b. Novara 1883 (4th December), d. Torino 1963 (1st March).
*coll.* Turin Museum.

CASTRO, CARLOS
Spanish School.
19th century.
Pupil of Tiger. Working at Madrid. Painted fruit.
*exhib.* Madrid, 1864.

CAUCHOIS, EUGENE HENRI                    (*see* PLATE 8)
French School.
b. Rouen 1850 (14th February), d. Paris 1911 (11th October).
Pupil of Duboc and Cabanel. Painted still-life, flowers and fruit.
*coll.* Aux Halles.
*exhib.* Salon 1874.
*repr.* *Connoisseur*, April 1963, Leggatt Brothers advert.

CAUDER, A.
British School.
19th century (*see* Vol. 3, Part I, p. 19).

CAUWER, LEOPOLD DE
German School.
19th century (*see* Vol. 3, Part I, p. 19).

CAVE, JULES CYRILLE
French School.
b. Paris 1859 (4th January).
Pupil of Bouguereau and Robert Fleury.
Painted flowers and genre.
*exhib.* Society Artistes Francais 1887. Bronze Medal 1889 and 1900.
*auct.* Paris, 9.2.1927, flowers.

CAZIN, JEAN CHARLES
French School.
b. Samer 1841, d. Lavandou 1901.
Director of the School of Art at Tours, and Curator of the Museum there. Visited England in 1871. Later in Holland, Italy and France. Painter, engraver and potter.
*auct.* Paris, 22.6.1927, flowers.

CENA, EDMOND
French School.
b. Evian-les-Bains 1884 (26th January).
*exhib.* Salon des Independants 1907.
*auct.* Paris, 17.12.1928, still-life; 14.6.1929, still-life; 23.3.1938, flowers and fruit; 9.6.1938, fruit; 27.11.1940, still-life.

CESBRON, ACHILLE THEODORE
French School.
b. Oran 1849 (5th November), d. 1915 (4th January).
Pupil of Bonnat and Cormon. Painted flowers.
Legion of Honour 1898.
*coll.* Paris, Mus. Decorative Arts; Angers; Mulhouse.
*exhib.* Society Artistes Francais 1883, Medal 1884 and 1886; Silver Medal Universal Exhibition Paris 1889 and 1900.
*auct.* Paris, 17.3.1904, 12.12.1921, 9.2.1942, flowers and fruit.

CHALFANT, JEFFERSON DAVID
American School.
b. Pennsylvania 1856 (6th November), d. Wilmington 1931 (3rd February).
Lived in Wilmington, Delaware. Began as a cabinet-maker. Self-taught painter. Sent to study in Paris under Bouguereau and Jules Lefebvre in 1890. Married Katherine Braunstein in 1903. Painted portraits and still-life.
*coll.* Brooklyn.
*repr.* *After the Hunt*, Frankenstein, 1953, pls. 67, 105 and 108.
*lit.* Frankenstein.

CHALLIE, MLLE ALPHONSINE DE
French School.
19th century.
Pupil of Chaplin. Painted flowers, portraits and genre.
*exhib.* Salon 1878 and 1891.

CHALLIE, JEAN LAURENT
French School.
19th and 20th century.
Painted flowers, interiors and figures.
*auct.* Paris, 30.5.1931, 27.4.1933, 2.3.1934, 5.5.1937, all
flowers.

CHAMBON, CHARLES MARIUS
French School.
19th century. b. Arpajon.
Pupil of G. Moreau and F. Flameng.
Painted flowers, fruit and still-life.
*exhib.* Society Artistes Francais 1920, Hon. Mention.
*auct.* Paris, 29.12.1927, fruit; 9.2.1929, flowers and still-
life.

CHANDLER, JOSEPH GOODHUE
American School
b. 1813, d. 1880(?)
Began his career as a cabinet maker, then an itinerant portrait
painter. Known to have painted still-life.

CHANTON, MME LOUISE (*née* BARONNE TRISTAN-LAMBERT)
French School.
19th century.
Pupil of M. M. Jeannin and Bergeret. Working in Paris.
Painted flowers and genre.
*exhib.* Salon 1878.

CHANTRE, C.
British School.
*op.* 1863.
Clapton address.
*exhib.* R.A. (1), fruit.

CHANTRON, ALEXANDRE JACQUES
French School.
b. Nantes 1842 (28th January), d. 1918.
Pupil of Pirot, Bouquereau and Robert Fleury. Painted
flowers, still-life, portraits and history.
*coll.* Calais; Nantes.
*exhib.* Salon 1877; Hon. Mention 1893; Medal 1899 and
1902.

CHANUT, PIERRE HENRI
French School.
b. Lyon 1857 (4th September).
Studied at School of Art, Lyon, 1874. Painted still-life and
portraits.

CHAPLIN, ARTHUR
French School.
b. Jouy-en-Josas 1869.
Son of Charles Chaplin. Pupil of Bonnat and Bernier.
Visited Holland 1898. Painted flowers.
*exhib.* Salon des Artistes Francais 1899.
*auct.* New York, 11.12.1930, flowers.

CHAPLIN, FRANK
British School.
*op.* 1879.
Worcester address.
*exhib.* Suffolk Street (1), fruit.

CHAPMAN, MRS. CATHERINE J.
British School.
*op.* 1894.
Cheshunt, Herts., address.
*exhib.* R.A. (1), flowers.

CHAPOTON, GREGOIRE
French School.
b. Saint Rambert-sur-Loire 1845 (21st December).
Studied at School of Art, Lyon, 1863. Pupil of Soulary and
Reynier. Painted flowers.
*coll.* Laval Museum; St. Etienne; Tours.

CHAPPEL, EDOUARD
Belgian School.
b. Antwerp 1859.
Studied at Antwerp Academy.
Painted still-life.
*coll.* Antwerp.
*exhib.* R.A. 1892, 1897 and 1903; Paris Salon 1907; Berlin
International Exhibition 1891.
Could be same artist as EDWARD CHAPPEL (*which see*).
Benezit says 'lived for some time in England and visited
Cornwall'.

CHAPPEL, EDWARD
British School (?)
19th and 20th century.
London and Cagnes (France) addresses.
Could be the same artist as EDOUARD CHAPPEL (*which see*).
The entry in the R.A. Catalogue for 1892 gives the name
'Edouard Chappel' and the address as 'Villa des Arts, 24
Gunter Grove, London, S.W.' This is the same address as for
'Edward' Chappel in 1907 catalogue onwards. His wife,
Alice, exhibited a flower picture at the R.A. in 1914.
*exhib.* R.A. 1907–1933 (23), landscapes and still-life; Salon
des Artistes Francais 1922, Hon. Mention.
*auct.* London, 17.3.1930, flowers.

CHARBONNEL, CHARLES
French School.
19th century (*see* Vol. 3, Part I, p. 20).


CHARCHOUNE, SERGE
Russian School.
19th century.
b. Bougourouslane.
Painted fruit.
*exhib.* Salon des Independants 1912.
*auct.* Paris, 3.3.1927, fruit.


CHARLES, JAMES
British School.
b. 1851, d. 1906.
Studied in London and Paris. Painted flowers, fruit, genre and landscapes.
*exhib.* R.A. (19); Suffolk Street (2); G.G. (8); N.G. (13). Graves says 'Domestic'.
*auct.* London, 22.4.1927, 13.7.1935, fruit, flowers and game.


CHARLOT, LOUIS
French School.
b. Cussy-en-Morvan 1878 (26th April).
Painted flowers, still-life and landscapes.
*exhib.* Salon des Artistes Francais 1901.
*auct.* Paris, 12.3.1941, still-life; 14.5.1943, flowers.


CHARLTON, LOUISA
British School.
*op.* 1897.
Shelton, Stoke-on-Trent, address.
*exhib.* R.A. (1), flowers.


CHARMY, MLLE EMILIE
French School.
19th and 20th century.
Working at St. Cloud. Chevalier of the Legion of Honour.
*exhib.* Salon des Independants 1904.
*auct.* Paris, 14.11.1921, 14.2.1922, 15.3.1923, 4.6.1923, 3.3.1924, 8.12.1928, 31.1.1929, 21.4.1943, 3.5.1944, flowers, fruit and still-life.


CHARPENTIER, MLLE H. P.
French School.
19th and 20th century.
Painted flowers.
*exhib.* Salon 1911 and 1912.


CHARRETON, VICTOR LEON JEAN PIERRE
French School.
b. Bourgoin 1864 (2nd March), d. 1937.
Pupil of Hareux and Japy. One of the founders of the Salon d'Automne. Officer of the Legion of Honour.
*coll.* Madrid, flowers.
*exhib.* Lyon, 1894.
*auct.* Paris, 16.5.1924, fruit and flowers.


CHASE, MISS JESSIE
British School.
*op.* 1885–1886.
Kilburn address.
Member of the Society of Lady Artists.
*exhib.* N.W.C.S. (3), flowers.


CHASE, MISS MARIAN EMMA, R.I.          (*see* PLATE 9)
British School.
b. London 1844 (18th April), d. there 1905 (15th March).
Daughter of John Chase and pupil of her father. Member of the New Water Colour Society. Painted flowers, gardens, interiors and landscapes. Royal Botanical Society Silver Medal 1888.
*coll.* London, Victoria and Albert Museum, wild flowers.
*exhib.* R.A. (8); Suffolk Street (9); N.W.C.S. (205).
*auct.* London, 2.12.1927.


CHASE, WILLIAM A.          (*see* PLATE 9)
British School.
b. Bristol 1878 (17th May).
Designed memorial windows and painted flowers.
Lived at Blewbury and in London.
*exhib.* R.A. 1910–1912.
*repr.* *Floral Art*, by H. D. Richter, 1932, pl. 11, 'Sunflowers and Dahlias', in colour.


CHASE, WILLIAM MERRITT          (*see* PLATE 10)
American School.
b. 1849, d. Franklin, Indiana, 1916.
Pupil of B. F. Hayes. Visited Europe 1872, Munich, Venice.
*coll.* Atlanta; Boston; Chicago; Cincinnati; Dallas; Kansas; St. Louis; Southampton; Tulsa and Washington. Also Universities of Indiana and Virginia. Mrs. Francis H. Markoe. All flower and still-life subjects.
*exhib.* Parrish Art Museum, Southampton, N.Y. (retrospective exhibition, June-July 1957). (124 exhibits, 23 flower and still-life).
*auct.* New York, 10.4.1930, flowers; 1.5.1930, still-life.

CHEMIAKIN, MICHEL THEODOROVISCH
Russian School.
19th and 20th century.
Painted flowers, genre and portraits.
*exhib.* St. Petersburg 1908 and 1909.

CHEYNEY, MISS EMMA S.
British School.
*op.* 1891–1894.
Redhill address.
Painted flowers.
*exhib.* R.A. (1); Suffolk Street (1); N.W.C.S. (1).

CHILTON, E.
British School.
*op.* 1869.
London address.
*exhib.* Suffolk Street (1), flowers.

CHOISY-CROT, MME JEANNE LOUISE
Swiss School.
b. Geneva 1843.
Studied at the School of Art, Geneva.
Painted flowers and portraits.
*exhib.* Berne 1890.

CHOWNE, GERALD
British School.
*op.* 1875–1917.
Painted flowers.
*auct.* Sotheby's, 17.1.1962, dated 1909.

CHRACTSKY
Russian School.
19th century (*see* Vol. 3, Part I, p. 21).

CHRETIEN, RENE LOUIS
French School.
b. Choisy-le-Roi 1867 (2nd October).
Pupil of Bonnat. Painted still-life and genre.
*coll.* La Rochelle.
*exhib.* Salon 1889; Brussels 1910; Universal Exhibition 1900, Silver Medal.
*auct.* London, 19.12.1934, flowers; Paris, 13.7.1942, 2.6.1943, 21.6.1943, all still-life.

CHRISTENSEN, ANTHONIE ELEONORE (ANIHONORE)
(*née* TSCHERNING)                    (*see* PLATE 11)
Danish School.
b. Copenhagen 1849 (5th July), d. Usserød 1926 (27th August).
Pupil of Emma Thomsen. Married Dr. Christensen 1871.
Painted flowers.
*coll.* Copenhagen Museum, signed and dated 1892.

CHRISTIAN, MISS CLARA L.
British School.
*op.* 1898–1900.
London address.
Painted flowers.
*exhib.* R.A. (2).

CHRISTIE, ROBERT
British School.
19th century.
Pupil of J. Lefebvre and T. Robert-Fleury. Painted flowers.
*exhib.* R.A. 1891 and Salon des Artistes Francais.

CHRUTZKIJ (*see* HRUTSKIJ)

CHURTON, EDOUARD
French School.
19th century.
Pupil of Justin Lequien and Bourgogne.
Painted still-life.
*coll.* Perigueux.
*exhib.* Salon 1881.

CLAES, PAUL
Flemish School.
b. Antwerp 1866, d. there 1940.
Painted still-life, figures, interiors, townscapes and portraits.
*coll.* Antwerp, still-life.

CLAPHAM, JAMES T.
British School.
*op.* 1862–1868.
Crayford address.
*exhib.* Suffolk Street (2), fruit.

CLARE, GEORGE                    (*see* PLATE 12)
British School.
*op.* 1864–1873.
Flower painter. Resident in Birmingham.
*coll.* Ian McInnes.
*exhib.* R.A. (3); B.I. (7); Suffolk Street (32), flowers.
*auct.* Sotheby's, 1.8.1962, fruit, etc.

CLARE, OLIVER
British School.
*op.* 1873–1883.
London address.
*exhib.* R.A. (1); Suffolk Street (2), fruit.
*auct.* Sotheby's, 8.3.1961, fruit; 9.5.1962, fruit; 1.8.1962, fruit.

CLARE, VINCENT
British School.
19th century (*see* Vol. 3, Part I, p. 22).

CLARKE, MISS KATE
British School.
*op.* 1863–1884.
London address.
*exhib.* B.I. (1); Suffolk Street (1); V.E. (4), flowers.

CLARKE, MISS POLLY
British School.
*op.* 1893.
Bushey address.
*exhib.* R.A. (1), flowers.

CLAUDE, EUGENE
French School.
b. Toulouse 1841 (16th July), d. 1923.
Painted flowers, still-life, fruit and animals.
*coll.*  Mulhouse; Pontoise; Reims; Saintes; Troyes.
*exhib.* Salon 1861.
*auct.*  Paris, 19.12.1923, 27.6.1941, 10.6.1942, 10.2.1943, 5.6.1944, all fruit and flowers.

CLAUSEN, MISS ELEANOR M.
British School.
*op.* 1886–1890.
London address.
*exhib.* Suffolk Street (1), flowers.

CLAUSEN, SIR GEORGE, R.A., R.W.S., R.I.        (*see* PLATE 12)
British School.
b. London 1852, d. 1912.
Studied at South Kensington for six years before going to Paris. Painted landscapes, pastorals, portraits, figure subjects and flower-pieces.
*coll.*  Cardiff, flowers and fruit; Walthamstow, carnations; Murals in St. Stephen's Hall, Westminster.
*exhib.* R.A.; Suffolk Street; O.W.C.S.; N.W.C.S.; G.G.; N.G.
*auct.*  London, 19.3.1937, flowers and fruit.

CLAVEY, PHILIP
British School.
19th century (*see* Vol. 3, Part I, p. 22).

CLAYTON, MISS MARY ANNA
British School.
*op.* 1884–1885.
Brighton address.
*exhib.* V.E. (3), flowers.

CLOUET, FELIX
French School.
d. 1882.
Pupil of Emile Lecomte-Vernet. Working at Puiset.
*coll.*    Bourges; Chartres.
*exhib.* Salon 1859.
*auct.*  28.6.1923, still-life; Paris, 23.12.1943, still-life.

CLOWES, MISS C.
British School.
*op.* 1878.
London address.
*exhib.* R.A. (1), flowers.

COCKX, PHILIBERT
Flemish School.
b. Ixelles 1879.
Studied Brussels Academy. Painted still-life, figures, religious, and landscape in oil and water-colour.

COHEN, MISS ELLEN G.
British School.
*op.* 1899.
London address.
*exhib.* R.A. (1), flowers.

COIGNET, MARIE
French School.
19th century (*see* Vol. 3, Part I, p. 23).

COLE, MISS H.
British School.
*op.* 1877.
London address.
*exhib.* Suffolk Street (1), still-life.

COLE, THOMAS W.
British School.
*op.* 1895.
London address.
*exhib.* R.A. (1), flowers.

COLEMAN, MRS. GERTRUDE
British School.
*op.* 1881.
London address.
*exhib.* Suffolk Street (1), flowers.

COLES, MISS MARY
British School.
*op.* 1873–1877.
Cheltenham address.
*exhib.* Suffolk Street (1), still-life.

COLLIER, MISS AMY
British School.
*op.* 1874.
Callington address.
*exhib.* Suffolk Street (1), still-life.

COLLIER, MRS. MARY J.
British School.
*op.* 1878–1881.
London address.
*exhib.* V.E. (5), flowers.

COLLIN, ANDRE
Belgian School.
b. Spa 1862.
Painted flowers and landscape.
*exhib.* Salon 1890, Hon. Mention.
*auct.* Paris, 15.2.1926, flowers.

COLLINGWOOD, LILLY
British School.
*op.* 1882.
London address.
*exhib.* V.E. (1), flowers.

COLLINGWOOD, W. GERSHAM
British School.
*op.* 1880–1894.
Windermere and Coniston addresses.
Painted landscapes and flowers.
*coll.* Preston, H.M. and A.G.
*exhib.* R.A. (6); Suffolk Street (3); N.W.C.S. (6); G.G. (1).

COLLINS, MISS ELIZABETH L.
British School.
*op.* 1866–1869.
London address.
*exhib.* Suffolk Street (4), still-life.

COLLINS, MISS MARY
British School.
*op.* 1895.
Epsom address.
*exhib.* R.A. (1), flowers.

COLLINS, T.
British School.
*op.* 1867–1873.
Birmingham address.
*exhib.* R.A. (1); Suffolk Street (5), flowers.

COLLINS, WILLIAM WIEHE
British School.
b. Kensington 1862 (4th August).
Studied Lambeth School of Art and Julian Academy in Paris.
Painted flowers, landscapes and marines.
*exhib.* R.A. (1); Suffolk Street (14); N.W.C.S. (10); N.G. (1); V.E. (3).

COLVILLE, MISS E.
British School.
*op.* 1880–1884.
London address.
*exhib.* Suffolk Street (1), flowers.

COMBE, MISS L. ELLA
British School.
*op.* 1887.
London address.
*exhib.* V.E. (1), flowers.

COMBES, MISS EMILY
British School.
*op.* 1879–1882.
*exhib.* Suffolk Street (6), flowers.

COMBES, MRS. G. E.
British School.
*op.* 1885–1887.
London address.
*exhib.* N.W.C.S. (3), flowers.
Probably the same as 'Grace Emily Coombes', who exhibited a flower picture at Suffolk Street 1879.

COMPTON, THEODORE
British School.
*op.* 1866–1874.
London address.
*exhib.* V.E. (2), flowers.

CONNARD, PHILIP, C.V.O., R.A., R.W.S.       (*see* PLATE 13)
British School.
b. Southport 1875, d. 1958 (8th December).
Studied in London and Paris. Taught for a time at the Lambeth School of Art. Member of the New English Art Club 1909. Keeper of the Royal Academy in 1945. Painted figures, landscapes and flowers.
*coll.* Durban, Museum and Art Gallery, South Africa, flowers; London, Tate Gallery.
*auct.* London, 17.12.1937, flowers.

CONRAD-KICKERT
Dutch School.
b. The Hague 1882 (23rd November).
In France 1906. Chevalier of the Legion of Honour and
Chevalier of the Order of Orange Nassau. Painted flowers,
fruit and still-life and engraved.
*coll.*   Alger; Belfort; Le Havre; Oran.
*exhib.*   Universal Exhibition 1937, Medal.
*auct.*   Paris, 22.3.1926, fruit; 11.4.1927, still-life; 27.2.1928,
        still-life; 23.3.1938, flowers.

COOK, NELLIE E.
British School.
*op.* 1887–1900.
London address.
*exhib.*   R.A. (2); Suffolk Street (1); N.W.C.S. (1), flowers.

COOK, MISS EMILY ANNIE
British School.
*op.* 1881–1889.
London address.
*exhib.*   R.A. (10); Suffolk Street (10), flowers.

COOK, GEORGE FREDERICK
British School.
*op.* 1879–1891.
London address.
*exhib.*   R.A. (4); Suffolk Street (14), still-life.

COOK, MISS L. S.
British School.
*op.* 1870–1881.
Rochdale address.
*exhib.*   G.G. 1880 (1); V.E. (1), flowers.

COOKE, MISS L.
British School.
*op.* 1884.
Bath address.
*exhib.*   N.W.C.S. (1), flowers.

COOMBES, GRACE EMILY
British School.
*op.* 1879.
London address.
*exhib.*   Suffolk Street (1), flowers.
Probably the same as 'Mrs. G. E. Combes'.

COOPER, A. D. M.
American School.
*op.* 1898.
Lived in San Jose, California. Painted still-life of jewels, etc.
*lit.*   Frankenstein, *After the Hunt*, 1953.

COPE, GEORGE
American School.
b. West Chester 1855, d. there 1929 (15th January).
Studied under H. Herzog in Philadelphia. Visited Far West
in 1876, painting landscapes. Returned to West Chester
1880. Painted still-life.
*repr.*   *After the Hunt*, Frankenstein, 1953, pls. 68, 107, 109
        and 110.
*lit.*   Frankenstein.

COPPENOLLE, JACQUES VAN
French School.
b. Montigny-sur-Loing       , d. 1915.
Painted flowers and landscapes.
*coll.*   Clamecy Museum, flowers.
*auct.*   Paris, 23.4.1943, flowers.

COPPIETERS, ALBERIE
Flemish School.
b. Ypres 1878, d. Paris 1902.
Painted still-life, figures and landscapes.
*coll.*   Antwerp, flowers and fruit; Brussels, still-life.

CORDEY, FREDERIC SAMUEL
French School.
b. Paris 1854 (9th July), d. there 1911 (18th February).
Painted still-life, portraits and landscapes.
*exhib.*   Salon des Independants 1887.
*auct.*   Paris, 18.3.1922, still-life; 3.5.1934, still-life;
        14.5.1943, fruit.

CORINTH, LOVIS                    (*see* PLATE 13)
German School.
b. Tapiau 1858 (21st July, Munich catalogue) (21st August,
Benezit).
Studied in Koenigsberg, Munich and Paris. Pupil of
Bouguereau and Bastien Lepage.
*coll.*   Munich State Gallery (2), still-life.
*exhib.*   Cologne, Galerie Abels.
*repr.*   Abels Exhibition Catalogue, No. 34, flowers, etc.

CORNUAUD, JEAN D.
British School.
*op.* 1875–1877.
Richmond address.
*exhib.*   V.E. (2), flowers.

CORNUEL, PAUL
French School.
19th and 20th century.
d. Paris 1934 (7th October).
Painted flowers and still-life.
*exhib.*   Salon des Independants 1927 and 1934.

CORRIE, MISS E. J.
British School.
*op.* 1877.
Exeter address.
*exhib.* R.A. (1), game.

CORTISSOS, CHARLES
British School.
*op.* 1872–1875.
London address.
*exhib.* Suffolk Street (1); V.E. (3), fruit.

COSTA, ORESTE
Italian School.
b. Florence 1851.
Painted still-life.

COTESWORTH, MISS LILLIAS E.
British School.
*op.* 1885–1888.
Winchester address.
*exhib.* R.A. (1); Suffolk Street (1), flowers.

COTTON, HENRY ROBERT
British School.
*op.* 1871.
London address.
*exhib.* Suffolk Street (1), fruit.

COUBINE, O.
Czech School.
b. Boskowitze 1883.
Studied at Prague and Antwerp. Visited France and Italy 1903. Painted flowers, still-life, engraved, and was a sculptor.
*exhib.* Salon des Independants; Salon d'Automne; International, Geneva.
*auct.* Paris, 12.12.1925, flowers; 2.6.1928, fruits; 6.6.1929, flowers; 12.4.1930, flowers; 14.10.1942, flowers; 3.5.1944, fruit.

COUDER, EMILE GUSTAVE
French School.
b. Paris      , d. there 1903.
Pupil of Wasselon. Painted flowers and fruit.
*coll.* Mulhouse.
*exhib.* Salon 1869.

COULTER, WILLIAM
British School.
*op.* 1869–1889.
London address.
*exhib.* R.A. (2); Suffolk Street (4), still-life.

COURTENS, HERMAN
Flemish School.
b. Brussels 1884 (23rd February).
Son and pupil of Franc Courtens and Verheyden. Visited Holland and Egypt. Professor at Antwerp Academy. Painted still-life.
*exhib.* Salon.
*auct.* Brussels, 17/18.3.1939, still-life.

COUSTURIER, LUCIE
French School.
b. Paris 1870 (19th December), d. there 1925 (16th June).
Visited Africa. Painted flowers and still-life.
*exhib.* Salon des Independants 1901.
*auct.* Paris, 16.5.1929, flowers and fruit; 5.6.1944, flowers.

COWPER, ANNA
British School.
*op.* 1871–1875.
London address.
*exhib.* V.E. (3), flowers.

COWPER, M. E.
British School.
*op.* 1875.
*exhib.* V.E. (1), flowers.

COX, MISS ADELA L.
British School.
*op.* 1899.
Dorking address.
*exhib.* R.A. (1), flowers.

CRAISTER, MRS. WALTER
British School.
*op.* 1870–1892.
Chester address.
*exhib.* Suffolk Street (3); N.W.C.S. (2), flowers.

CRAMER, HELENE
German School.
b. Hamburg 1844 (13th December).
Pupil of Oesterly and Margueretha Rosenboom at The Hague.
Painted flowers and genre.
*coll.* Breme, flowers.

CRESWELL, MISS HENRIETTA
British School.
*op.* 1875–1892.
London address.
*exhib.* R.A. (1); Suffolk Street (5), flowers.

CRESWICK, MRS.
British School.
*op.* 1865–1867.
*exhib.* R.A. (2), fruit.

CRISPE, MISS LEILA CONSTANCE
British School.
*op.* 1885–1887.
London address.
*exhib.* Suffolk Street (1), flowers.

CROMBIE, MISS E. E.
British School.
*op.* 1894.
London address.
*exhib.* R.A. (1), flowers.

CROME, VIVIAN
British School.
*op.* 1867.
London address.
*exhib.* R.A. (1); B.I. (2), flowers.

CROSSMAN, HON. MRS.
British School.
*op.* 1880.
Botanical artist.
*coll.* Eighty-seven water-colours of Cape Flowers in hands of a Preston dealer, 1962.

CROUGHTON, GEORGE
British School.
*op.* 1874.
London address.
*exhib.* Suffolk Street (1), flowers.

CRUIKSHANK, WILLIAM
British School.
b. 1844/8, d. 1922.
London address.
*coll.* Preston, H.M. and A.G., game.
*exhib.* R.A. (7); Suffolk Street (22), game.
*auct.* Sotheby's, 20.12.1961, flowers; 17.1.1962, dead game, birds and flowers; 9.5.1962, dead game.
Graves gives the name as 'CRUICKSHANK'.

CUMMING, MISS M.
British School.
*op.* 1874.
London address.
*exhib.* R.A. (1), flowers.

CUNDELL, NAOMI
British School.
*op.* 1883.
Reading address.
*exhib.* Suffolk Street (2), fruit.

CURREY, MISS FANNY
British School.
*op.* 1895–1897.
Lismore, Ireland, address.
*exhib.* R.A. (2), flowers.

CURRIE, ROBERT
British School.
*op.* 1880–1885.
Methven, N.B., address.
*exhib.* R.A. (1), birds.

CUSHING, HOWARD GARDINER
American School.
b. Boston 1869, d. New York 1916.
Studied at the University of Harvard and in Paris under B. Constant and J. P. Laurens. Painted portraits and still-life.

CZOBEL, BELA ADABERT
Hungarian School.
b. Budapest 1883 (4th September).
Studied in Munich and Paris. Resided in Montmorency and Paris. Painted still-life.
*exhib.* Cologne 1961, still-life.

CZYNCIEL, CELESTIN
Polish School.
b. Cracow 1858.
Painted flowers.

DAALHOFF, HENRI A. VAN
Dutch School.
b. Haarlem 1867, d. 1953.
Painter and engraver.
*exhib.* Dordrecht Museum 1955; Amsterdam 1939.

DABO, LEON
American School.
b. Detroit 1868 (9th July).
Pupil of Vierge and Galland at Academy Julian, Paris;
Member National Academy, New York, and National Art
Club. Chevalier of the Legion of Honour 1934. Painted
flowers, murals and landscapes.
*exhib.* Salon 1938, flowers.

DAINTREY, ALICE S.
British School.
*op.* 1879.
Petworth address.
Painted still-life.

DAMIS, J.
British School.
*op.* 1879.
*exhib.* R.A. (1), flowers.

DAM VAN ISSELT, LUCIE VAN
Dutch School.
b. Berg-op-Zoom 1871.
Studied at The Hague Academy and School of Art, Lyon.
Painted still-life, portraits and landscapes.
*coll.* Amsterdam; Arnheim. Eindhoven; Middelburg;

DARRU, LOUISE
French School.
19th century.
Pupil of Piette and A. Dore. Working at Neubourg.
*exhib.* Salon 1864.
*auct.* Paris, 1880, flowers; 24.5.1943, still-life.

DAUBIGNY, KARL PIERRE
French School.
b. Paris 1846 (9th June), d. Auvers-sur-Oise 1886 (25th May).
Son and pupil of Charles Francois Daubigny.
Painted flowers, fruit and landscapes.
*exhib.* Salon 1863–1874.
*auct.* Paris, 16.2.1928, fruit and flowers.

DAVEY, FLORENCE
British School.
*op.* 1881.
Horsham address.
*exhib.* Suffolk Street (2), flowers.

DAVIS, MISS F.
British School.
*op.* 1875–1876.
London address.
*exhib.* Suffolk Street (3), fruit.

DAVIS, MISS MIRIAM J.
British School.
*op.* 1884–1893.
London address.
*exhib.* R.A. (3); Suffolk Street (20); G.G. (1); N.G. (3);
V.E. (6), flowers.

DAVIS, VAL (J. VALENTINE)
British School.
b. Liverpool 1854.
Painted flowers and landscapes.
*exhib.* R.A. 1875–1900; Liverpool; Glasgow.

DAVISON, E. ELEANOR
British School.
*op.* 1880.
Painted flowers.

DAWSON, AMY
British School.
*op.* 1889–1891.
London address.
*exhib.* Suffolk Street (3), fruit.

DAWSON, MRS. B. (*née* ELIZABETH RUMLEY)
British School.
*op.* 1851–1876.
London address.
*exhib.* R.A. (9); B.I. (12); Suffolk Street (9), fruit, as
Rumley.
R.A. (10); B.I. (6); Suffolk Street (11), fruit, as
Dawson.

DAWSON, EDITH A.
British School.
*op.* 1895.
London address.
*exhib.* R.A. (1), flowers.

DAWSON, MABEL
British School.
*op.* 1880–1881.
Painted flowers.

DEACON, MISS VIRGINIA
British School.
*op.* 1885.
Eastbourne address.
*exhib.* N.W.C.S. (1), still-life.

DEANES, MISS MARY
British School.
*op.* 1870–1871.
London address.
*exhib.* Suffolk Street (2), fruit.

DEBRAUX, RENE CHARLES LOUIS
French School.
19th century (*see* Vol. 3, Part I, p. 27).

DECKER, JOSEPH
American School.
b. Wurtemburg 1853, d. Brooklyn 1920.
Went to U.S.A. in 1867. Studied in Munich and National
Academy of Design, New York. Painted landscapes, portraits and still-life.
May be two artists of the same name.
*exhib.* National Academy of Design 1880–1890.
*repr.* *After the Hunt*, Frankenstein, 1953, pl. 124.
*lit.* Frankenstein.

DEHOY, CHARLES
Flemish School.
b. Brussels 1872, d. 1940.
Painted still-life, figures and landscapes.

DEKAT, ANNE PIERRE
Belgian School.
19th and 20th century.
Came from Delft. Working in Belgium. Painted flowers
and still-life and portraits.
*exhib.* Salon des Independants; Salon d'Automne.

DELE, J. B.
Flemish School.
19th century (*see* Vol. 3, Part I, p. 27).

DELESTRE, EUGENE
French School.
b. Paris 1862 (8th September), d. 1919.
Pupil of Guadet. Painter and architect. Painted flowers and
landscapes.
*auct.* Paris, 17.6.1919, flowers.

DELORME, LUCIE
French School.
*op.* 1877–1896.
Working in Paris. Visited Geneva. Painted flowers and
painted porcelain.
*coll.* Alais Museum, flowers.
*exhib.* Salon.

DELORME, RENE
French School.
19th century (*see* Vol. 3, Part I, p. 27).

DELORME-CORNET, LOUISE
French School.
19th century (*see* Vol. 3, Part I, p. 27).

DELPY, HIPPOLYTE CAMILLE
French School.
b. Joigny 1842, d. Paris 1910 (4th June).
Pupil of Daubigny. Painted flowers, landscapes and engraved.
*exhib.* Salon 1869.
*auct.* 24.3.1947, flowers.

DEMARCAY, CAMILLE
French School.
19th century.
Pupil of Eugenie Hautier. Worked in Paris. Painted flowers
and portraits.
*exhib.* Salon 1869.
*auct.* Paris 1881, flowers.

DEMUTH, CHARLES
American School.
b. 1883, d. 1935.
Pupil at Pennsylvania Academy and studied in Paris. Painted
flowers and buildings.
*coll.* Mrs. E. G. Halpert, New York, Red Poppies, 1929.
Whitney Museum of American Art, New York,
August Lilies.
*exhib.* Philadelphia Museum, 'World of Flowers', 1963.

DENISE, ALEXANDRE
French School.
b. Lattaye-Descartes 19th century.
Pupil of Jeannin. Painted flowers.
*exhib.* Salon 1879.

DERAIN, ANDRE
French School.
b. Chatou 1880 (10th June).
Painter, engraver and sculptor.
*exhib.* Cologne.
*auct.* Paris, 2.12.1936, flowers; 11.5.1942, still-life;
19.12.1943, still-life; 25.3.1944, flowers; 26.4.1944,
still-life; 20.6.1944, still-life; 20.6.1947, fruit.
Sotheby's, 5/6.7.1961, fruit and flowers; 11.4.1962,
flowers.

DESBORDES-JONAS, LOUISE ALEXANDRA
French School.
19th century.
Pupil of Alfred Stevens. Painted flowers.
*exhib.* Salon 1876.
*auct.* Paris, 5/6.2.1920, flowers; 11/13.6.1923, flowers; 8/10.11.1926, flowers and butterflies.

D'ESPAGNAT, GEORGES
French School.
b. Paris 1870 (14th August).
Painter and engraver.
*coll.* Nantes Museum.
*auct.* Paris, 24.2.1947, still-life; 26.2.1947, flowers; 23.4.1947, flowers. Sotheby's, 5/6.7.1961, flowers.

DETMOLD, CHARLES MAURICE
British School.
b. London 1883 (21st December), d. 1908 (9th April).
Painted flowers and an illustrator.
*exhib.* R.A. (1), still-life.
*auct.* London, 1945, flowers.

DEVOLVE-CARRIERE, MME LISBETH
French School.
19th century.
Daughter of Eugene Carriere. Painted flowers.
*exhib.* Salon National 1899.
*auct.* Paris, 14.3.1931, flowers; 1919, flowers.

DEVOS, CHARLES
Flemish School.
19th century (*see* Vol. 3, Part I, p. 28).

DEZIRE, HENRI
French School.
b. Libourne 1878 (6th February).
Pupil of Bouguereau and G. Ferrier. Painted still-life, fruit and portraits.
*auct.* Paris, 30.4.1945, fruit; 25.6.1945, still-life; 7.11.1946, fruit.

DINKEL, JOSEPH
German School.
19th century (*see* Vol. 3, Part I, p. 28).

DIRANIAN, SERKIS
Turkish School.
19th century.
Working at Constantinople. Painted flowers.
*exhib.* Universal Exhibition 1892, Hon. Mention.
*auct.* New York, 18/19.2.1904, flowers.

DIXON, MISS EMILY
British School.
*op.* 1885–1886.
Hull address.
*exhib.* R.A. (2); Suffolk Street (2), flowers.

DOBELL, MISS ALICE
British School.
*op.* 1867.
Cheltenham address.
*exhib.* Suffolk Street (2), flowers.

DODDS, ANNIE
British School.
*op.* 1866.
Newcastle address.
*exhib.* Suffolk Street (2), flowers.

DODSLEY, ANNE M. J.
British School.
*op.* 1872.
London address. Painted fruit.

DOE, WILLIAM
British School.
19th century (*see* Vol. 3, Part I, p. 29).

DOLAN, PHILIP
British School.
*op.* 1867–1877.
London address.
*exhib.* R.A. (5); Suffolk Street (8), fruit.

DOLLAND, W. ANSTEY
British School.
*op.* 1879–1889.
Painted flowers and genre.
*exhib.* R.A. (5); Suffolk Street (4), Graves says 'figures'.
*auct.* London, 15.3.1925, 21.11.1927, 23.4.1928, 1.8.1935, all flowers.

DOMETT, A. N.
British School.
*op.* 1879.
London address.
*exhib.* R.A. (1), flowers.

DONALDSON, JAMES H.
British School.
*op.* 1883–1892.
Scarborough address.
*exhib.* R.A. (2); N.W.C.S. (1), still-life.

DONGEN, KEES VAN                    (*see* PLATE 14)
Dutch School.
b. Delfshaven 1877.
Pupil at the Academy, Rotterdam. Lived in Paris. Naturalized Frenchman. Painted flowers.
coll.    Amsterdam, Rijks. Mus., flowers.
auct.    15.12.1930, 19.6.1934, 1.7.1943, all flowers.


DOORMAEL, THEO VAN
Flemish School.
b. Standdaarbuiten 1871, d. Antwerp 1910.
Painted still-life, figures and landscapes.
coll.    Antwerp, flowers.


DRAKE, MISS
British School.
19th century (*see* Vol. 3, Part I, p. 29).


DRESSEL, CLARA
German School.
b. Stettin 1856 (26th October).
Painted still-life and landscapes.


DREW, S. J.
British School.
op. 1865-1867.
Bexley address.
exhib.    Suffolk Street (2), flowers.


DROUET, GILBERT
French School.
19th century (*see* Vol. 3, Part I, p. 29).


DRUMAUX, ANGELINA
Luxembourg School.
b. Bouillon 1881 (23rd January).
Painted flowers.
exhib.    Brussels.
auct.    Paris, 9.2.1927, flowers


DUBOIS, MARIA
French School.
b. Meaux 19th century.
Painted flowers and fruit.
coll.    Nice, flowers; La Rochelle, fruit.
exhib.    Salon 1869.


DUBOURG, MADAME VICTORIA
British School.
op. 1882-1893.
London address.
exhib.    R.A. (6); Suffolk Street (5); N.W.C.S. (24); G.G.
         (2), flowers.


DUBREUIL, V.
American School.
op. 1880-1890.
Painted still-life trompe l'oeil of bank notes.
repr.    *After the Hunt*, Frankenstein 1953, pl. 122
lit.    Frankenstein.


DUBRON, PAULINE
French School.
b. Arras 1852 (9th May).
Pupil of Rogier and J. Bail. Painted still-life.
exhib.    Society des Artistes Francais and Salon.


DUCHEMIN, VICTOIRE
French School.
19th century.
Pupil of Hugot in Paris. Painted still-life and portraits.
exhib.    Salon 1864-1879.


DUDGEON, MISS LOUISA
British School.
op. 1861-1868.
Painted still-life. Living at Leicester.
exhib.    Suffolk Street, (2).


DUDLEY, ARTHUR
British School.
op. 1894.
Painted fruit.
exhib.    R.A., (1).


DUFF, JOHN ROBERT KEITLEY
British School.
b. London 1862.
Living in 1899. Painted flowers and rustic subjects.
exhib.    R.A., (2); Suffolk Street, (6).


DUFFIELD, MISS C. M.
British School.
op. 1873-1874.
London address.
Painted fruit.
exhib.    Suffolk Street (2).

DUFRENOY, GEORGES LEON
French School.
b. Thiais 1870 (20th June), d. 1942.
Studied Julian Academy, Paris. Visited Italy. Chevalier of the Legion of Honour. Painted flowers, fruit, landscapes, figures, etc.
coll.  Paris, Museum of Modern Art.
exhib. Salon des Independants; Salon d'Automne; Brussels Universal Exhibition, 1910; Retrospective Exhibition La Musee Galliera, 1948.
auct.  Paris, 1.4.42, 21.12.42, 9.4.43, 2.7.43, 15.6.45, all flowers and fruit.


DUFRESNE, CHARLES GEORGES
French School.
b. Millement 1876 (23rd November), d. 1938 (8th August).
Painted flowers, fruit, still-life and birds.
coll.  Amsterdam; Grenoble; Limoges; Moscow; Stockholm.
auct.  Sotheby's 4.7.1962, flowers.


DUFY, RAOUL                          (see PLATE 15)
French School.
b. Havre 1877 (3rd June)
Studied National School of Art.
Painted racecourses, regattas, esplanades, still-life and fruit and flowers.
coll.  Cologne, flowers and still-life (3).
exhib. Salon des Artistes Francais 1901.
auct.  Paris, 31.1.1944, still-life; 18.5.1945, fruit; 28.5.1945, still-life; 1946, fruit.


DUKESELL, MRS. ELEANOR
British School.
op. 1862.
London address.
exhib. Suffolk Street (4), fruit.


DU MONCEAU DE BERGENDAL, COUNTESS MATHILDE
Flemish School.
b. Shaarbeek 1877.
Studied Liege Academy. Painted flowers, gardens and landscapes.


DUNCAN MISS EMILY
British School.
op. 1880–1890.
London address.
exhib. R.A. (5); Suffolk Street (3), flowers.


DUNDAS, MISS AGNES
British School.
op. 1863–1873.
London address.
exhib. R.A. (18); B.I. (17); Suffolk Street (10), still-life.


DUNN, MISS CONSTANCE
British School.
op. 1883–1884.
London address.
exhib. Suffolk Street (1), flowers.


DUNNING, R. S.
American School.
op. 1899.
Painted fruit and still-life. A signed and dated 1899 oil recently exhibited in New York.


DUNOYER DE SEGONZAC, ANDRE ALBERT MARIE
                                     (see PLATE 45)
French School.
b. Boussy St. Antoine 1884 (6th July).
Studied under L. O. Merson, J. P. Laurens and G. Guerin. Visited Italy, Spain and North Africa. Illustrated books. Painted figures, landscapes, flowers and still-life.
auct.  New York 21.10.1943, still-life, fruit—watercolour; Paris, 2.12.1936, still-life—watercolour; 15.12.1932, flowers, etc.


DURAN, A.                            (see PLATE 15)
American School.
op. 1895.
Painted still-life.


DURAN Y RIERA, JOSE
Spanish School.
19th century (see Vol. 3, Part I, p. 30).


DURELL, A. C.
British School.
op. 1882.
London address. Painted fruit.


DURENNE, EUGENE ANTOINE
French School.
b. Paris 1860 (11th December).
Painted still-life, fruit and flowers.
exhib. Salon de la Societe Nationale 1898; Salon des Independants; Salon d'Automne.
auct.  Paris, 24.2.1943, still-life; 1.7.1943, fruit; 23.12.46, flowers

DURHAM, MRS. C. B.
British School.
*op.* 1868–1870.
*exhib.* Suffolk Street (2), flowers.


DUROZE, FERNAND
French School.
19th century (*see* Vol. 3, Part I, p. 30).


DUTURCQ, MADAME T.
British School.
*op.* 1872.
London address.
*exhib.* Suffolk Street (1), flowers.


DUVAL, A.
British School.
*op.* 1873.
London address.
*exhib.* Suffolk Street (1), still-life.


DUVENECK, FRANK
American School.
b. Covington, Kentucky 1848 (9th October), d. 1919.
Painter, sculptor and engraver.
*exhib.* Paris 1895, Hon. mention.


EAST, MARY
British School.
*op.* 1873.
Newcastle address.
*exhib.* Suffolk Street (2), still-life.


EASTLAKE, CAROLINE H.          (*see* PLATE 16)
British School.
*op.* 1868–1873.
Plymouth address.
*coll.* London, Victoria and Albert Museum, wild flowers.
*exhib.* V.E. (28), flowers.


EATON, MARY EMILY
British School.
b. Coleford 1873, living 1950.
Spent much of her life in the U.S.A. Artist to the New York
Botanical Gardens.
*coll.*   M. E. Eaton
*exhib.* London, Nat. Book League, *Flower Books*, 1950,
     water-colour.
*repr.*   *Cactaceae*, Britton and Rose, 1919–1923.
*lit.*    Blunt.


EDELMANN, CHARLES AUGUSTE
French School.
b. Sulz, Alsace 1879 (16th August)
Pupil of Gerome and F. Humbert. Painted still-life.
*exhib.* Strasbourg and Mulhouse.
*auct.*  Paris, 2.3.1929, 26/27.4.1929, 5.2.1935, 20.12.1944,
     all still-life.


EDWARDS, ELLIN H.
British School.
*op.* 1879.
London address.
*exhib.* Suffolk Street (1), still-life.


EDWARDS, MISS LOUISA
British School.
*op.* 1884–1886.
London address.
*exhib.* Suffolk Street (4), flowers.


EILOART, MISS E. G.
British School.
*op.* 1859–1862.
London address.
*exhib.* R.A. (1); B.I. (4); Suffolk Street (5), flowers.


ELIAS, MISS ANNETTE
British School.
*op.* 1881–1897.
London address.
Member of Society of Lady Artists.
*exhib.* R.A. (6); Suffolk Street (12); N.W.C.S. (1);
     N.G. (5); V.E. (11), Graves says 'Landscape'. R.A.
     1897 exhibit was flowers.


ELIAS, MRS. EMILY
British School.
*op.* 1892–1893.
Tonbridge address
*exhib.* Suffolk Street (2), still-life.

ELLIOT, MISS REBECCA
British School.
*op.* 1878.
London address.
*exhib.* Suffolk Street (1), flowers.

ELLIS, PAUL H.
British School.
*op.* 1883–1891.
Handsworth address.
Painted thistles and wild flowers.
*exhib.* R.A. (1); Suffolk Street (7); N.W.C.S. (2).

ELLIS, MRS. T. H.
British School.
*op.* 1871.
Tulse Hill address.
*exhib.* Suffolk Street (2), flowers.

ELMER, EDWIN ROMANZE
American School.
b. Ashfield 1850, d. there 1923.
Studied at the National Academy of Design, New York.
Painted landscapes and still-life.
*repr.* *Magazine of Art*, Oct. 1952; *After the Hunt*, Frankenstein 1953, pl. 133.
*lit.* Frankenstein.

ELMORE, MISS EDITH
British School.
*op.* 1877–1887.
London address.
*exhib.* R.A. (11); Suffolk Street (4), flowers.

ELMORE, MISS FANNY
British School.
*op.* 1861.
Tunbridge Wells address.
*exhib.* Suffolk Street (1), fruit.

ELMORE, FRANCES MARY
British School.
*op.* 1872.
London address.
*exhib.* V.E. (1), fruit.

ELWES, CECILIA
British School.
b. 1874 (8th May).
Flower painter in oils and water-colour.
*lit.* *Flower Paintings in Water-colour*, Pitman, 1932.

ELWIN, MISS EMMA
British School.
*op.* 1873–1879.
Staines address.
*exhib.* R.A. (2), still-life; Dusseldorf.

EMERIC, JULES THEODORE
French School.
19th-century.
Studied at Aix. Painted fruit.
*exhib.* Salon 1867.
*auct.* Paris, 22.6.1942.

ENAULT, MME. ALIX LOUISE
French School.
19th century, d. Paris 1913.
Pupil of Tissier and Willems.
Painted flowers and genre.
*exhib.* Salon 1876; Universal Exhibition 1889, bronze
medal.
*auct.* Paris, 1883; 1884, flowers.

ENGELBACH, FLORENCE, R.O.I.
British School.
b. 1872, d. 1951.
*coll.* Leicester, tulips and irises; London, Tate Gallery, roses;
Newcastle, Laing Art Gallery, gladioli.

ENGELEN, PIET VAN
Flemish School.
b. Lierre 1863, d. Antwerp 1924.
Studied Antwerp Academy. Painted animals, genre and
still-life and taught painting.
*coll.* Liege, still-life.

ENGELHART, CATHERINE CAROLINE CATHINKA—MRS.
AMYOT
Danish School.
b. Copenhagen 1845 (6th February)
Pupil of Carl Bogh 1865. Visited Brussels and Dusseldorf.
In Christiana and Stockholm 1875. Married Dr. Thomas
H. Amyot in 1878 and was living at Diss in Norfolk from
1879. Painted portraits, scriptural subjects and flowers.
*exhib.* as Mrs. Amyot 1879–1890; R.A. (9); Suffolk Street
(2); V.E. (1).

ENSCHEDE, ADRIANA MARIA
Dutch School.
b. Haarlem 1864 (29th September).
Painted flowers.

ENSOR, MRS. HENRY (MARY)
British School.
*op.* 1871–1874.
Birkenhead address.
*exhib.* Suffolk Street (7), flowers.

ENSOR, JAMES                                    (*see* PLATE 16)
Belgian School.
b. Ostend 1860 (13th April), d. there 1949 (November).
Studied Brussels Academy 1877. Had an English father and
Flemish mother. Visited London in 1892. Painted still-life,
genre, portraits, marines and landscapes.
*coll.*    Antwerp; Brussels, Museum Modern Art; Liege;
           Ostend.
*exhib.*   Salon des Independants; London, Leicester Galleries
           1936; National Gallery, 1946.
*repr.*    *Benezit III,* 29, still-life, fish.
*auct.*    Paris, 8.2.1945, flowers.

EPSTEIN, SIR JACOB
British School.
b. New York 1880, d. 1959.
Went to Paris in 1902 and England in 1905.
World famous sculptor. Painted a number of flower pieces.
*auct.*    Sotheby's, 31.5.1961, eight flower pictures.

ERNST, RUDOLPH
Austrian School.
b. Vienna 1854 (14th February).
Studied at Vienna Academy. Visited Paris.
Painted portraits, genre and flowers.
*exhib.*   Munich; Paris; Universal Exhibition 1889, bronze
           medal; Vienna.
*auct.*    New York, 7.5.1909, flowers; Paris 14/15.12.1925,
           22.2.1936, flowers.

ESMEIN, MAURICE MARCEL MARIE
French School.
19th century, d. 1918 (4th February).
Medical auxiliary; died on field of battle 4th February 1918.
Painted still-life.
*exhib.*   Salon d'Automne

ESNAULT, MAURICE
French School.
19th century (*see* Vol. 3, Part I, p. 31).

ESPAGNAT, GEORGES D'
French School.
b. Paris 1870 (14th August).
Painted flowers, fruit and still-life.
*coll.*    Nantes.
*auct.*    Paris, 25.3.1944, flowers; 18.11.1946, still-life;
           24.2.47, still-life.

EULER, PIERRE NICOLAS
French School.
b. Lyon 1846 (12th January).
Pupil of Reignier. Painted flowers and fruit.
*coll.*    Angers; Clermont-Ferrand; Montpellier.
*exhib.*   Lyon; Paris; Salon 1904, medal.

EVANS, AMY
British School.
*op.* 1880.
Sydenham address.
*exhib.* Suffolk Street (1), flowers.

EVANS, DE SCOTT
American School.
b. Boston 1847, d. Bourgogne 1898 (4th July).
In Cleveland 1874. Paris 1877 pupil of Bouguereau. Professor
at Cleveland Academy. Painted portraits, genre and still-life.
*lit.*     Frankenstein, *After the Hunt,* 1953.

EVANS, MRS. F. M.
British School.
*op.* 1870–1881.
London address.
*exhib.* Suffolk Street (1); V.E. (7), fruit.

EVANS, HELENA M.
British School.
*op.* 1891–1893.
Carmarthen address.
*exhib.* Suffolk Street (1); N.W.C.S. (4), flowers.
Miss Lena M. Evans (London) *exhib.* Suffolk Street (1) 1890,
           flowers, probably the same person.

EVANS, HERBERT DAVIES
British School.
*op.* 1883–1894.
London address.
*exhib.* Suffolk Street (3), flowers.

EVANS, HERBERT E.
British School.
*op.* 1893.
London address.
*exhib.* R.A. (1), fruit.

EVANS, MISS KATE
British School.
*op.* 1884.
Norwood address.
*exhib.* R.A. (1), flowers.

EVANS, MISS MARJORIE, R.S.W.
British School.
*op.* 1892–1895.
Richmond and Aberdeen addresses. Painted flowers in water-colour.
*exhib.* R.A. (2); V.E. (1).


FACKERE, JEF VAN DER
Flemish School.
b. Bruges 1879.
Studied Bruges Academy and later became Professor, 1904. Painted flowers, still-life, figures and portraits.
*coll.* Bruges, flowers.

FAIRER, CHARLES G.
British School.
*op.* 1872–1876.
London address.
*exhib.* V.E. (3), flowers.

FAIVRE, JULES ABEL
French School.
b. Lyon 1867 (30th March), d. 1945.
Pupil of J. B. Poneet and in Paris under B. Constant and Lefebvre.
Painted, fruit, portraits, figures and caricatures.
*exhib.* Paris 1892; Universal Exhibition 1900, Hon. mention.
*auct.* Paris, 29.6.1945, still-life.

FALCHETTI, GUISEPPE                    (*see* PLATE 17)
Italian School.
b. Caluso Canavese 1843, d. Turin 1918.
Painted still-life.
*coll.* Turin Museum.

FANTY-LESCURE, EMMA
French School.
b. La Rochelle, d. 1935.
Pupil of Mmes Dumoulin and Pitolet and M. E. Claude.
Painted flowers.
*exhib.* Salon 1876.
*auct.* Paris 2/3.6.1926, flowers.

FAUNTHORPE, MRS.
British School.
*op.* 1874.
Painted flowers.


FAUNTLEROY, MISS C. S.
British School.
*op.* 1881.
Northcombe address.
*exhib.* Suffolk Street (1), flowers.


FAUCHE, LEON
French School.
b. Briey 1868.
Studied School of Art, Nancy and Paris. Painted still-life and landscape.
*exhib.* Salon des Independants and Salon Nationale.
*auct.* Paris, 14.5.1943, still-life.


FAUCHEUR, LEONIE EUGENIE
French School.
b. Paris 1873 (7th April)
Pupil of Rivoire.
Painted flowers.
*exhib.* Salon des Artistes Francais 1908.
*auct.* Paris, 14.12.1942.


FAUCON, JULES ANDRE
French School.
b. Lyon 1870 (30th November).
Studied at School of Art, Lyon. Painted still-life, interiors and figures.
*exhib.* Lyon 1896.


FAUX-FROIDURE, MME EUGENIE JULIETTE
French School.
b. Noyen-sur-Sarthe 1886 (Benezit—obviously incorrect).
Pupil of Albert Maignan. Painted flowers.
*coll.* Rouen, flowers.
*exhib.* Society des Artistes Francais 1893 (if born 1886 would be only 7 years of age), Hon. mention 1898; Universal Exhibition 1900.
*auct.* Paris, 2.6.1943, flowers—water-colour; 8.1.1945, 21.3.1947.

**FECHIN, NICOLAI**
American School.
b. Kazan, Russia 1881, d. California, U.S.A. 1955.
Son of a carver and gilder, he practiced in his father's shop as
a boy. In 1895 entered the newly opened Kazan Art School.
In 1900 entered the Imperial Art Academy, St. Petersburg.
Obtaining degree and travelling scholarship, visiting
Austria, Germany, Switzerland, Italy and France. 1909 won
The Prix d'Rome. Moved with his family from Russia to
New York in 1923, in 1926 settled in Taos, New Mexico.
Died in California. In much demand as a portrait painter,
but painted other things including flower-pieces. Represented in many Galleries and collections in the western
world.
*coll.*    Chicago; San Diego, The Albright Gallery.
*exhib.* Pittsburgh, 1910, etc.
*repr.*    *The Artist*, New York (illustrated article).


**FENNEL, THOMAS**
British School.
19th century (*see* Vol. 3, Part I, p. 32).


**FERAT, SERGE**
Russian School.
b. Moscow 1881 (28th March).
Studied Julian Academy in Paris. Painter, designer and
engraver. Painted still-life.
*auct.*    Paris, October 1945–46, still-life.


**FERGUSON, MRS. A.** (*see* MISS EDITH MARRABLE)


**FERGUSON, ELEANOR**
British School.
*op.* 1884.
London address.
*exhib.* Suffolk Street (1), fruit.


**FERGUSON, JOHN DUNCAN**
British School.
b. Edinburgh 1874.
Studied in Paris. Painted still-life and portraits.
*exhib.* Salon des Independants; Glasgow; R.B.A.
*auct.*    London, 2.6.1926, still-life.


**FERGUSON, T. R.**
British School.
*op.* 1867.
London address.
**Painted fruit.**


**FERNIER, GABRIELLE**
French School.
19th century.
Worked in Paris. Painted flowers in water-colour.
*exhib.* Salon 1868–1878.


**FERRER, CALATAYUD PEDRO**
Spanish School.
19th century.
Studied at Valencia School of Art. Painted flowers and
portraits.
*exhib.* National Exhibition 1878.


**FEURE, GEORGES DE**
French School.
19th century, d. 1928.
In Paris 1868. Painter and lithographer. Originally from
Holland.
*auct.*    Paris, 2.12.1946, fruit.


**FICKLIN, R.**
British School.
*op.* 1863.
London address.
*exhib.* B.I. (1), fruit.


**FICQUENET, CHARLES**
French School.
*op.* 1864–1881.
Painted flowers at the Sevres Porcelain Manufactory.


**FIELD, MISS FRANCES A.**
British School.
*op.* 1882–1889.
Oxford address.
*exhib.* R.A. (2); Suffolk Street (3); N.W.C.S. (6), flowers.


**FILDES, LADY,** *née* **FANNY WOODS**
British School.
*op.* 1875–1884.
Wife of Sir Luke Fildes, the well-known painter.
Painted flowers, fruit, genre and landscapes.
*exhib.* R.A. (3); V.E. (7), Graves says 'Domestic'.
*auct.*    London, 15.6.1923, flowers and fruit.


**FILLIARD, ERNEST**                     (*see* PLATE 18)
French School.
b. Chambery 1868, d. 1933.
Pupil of B. Molin. Chevalier of the Legion of Honour.
Painted flowers and fruit, some in water-colour.
*coll.*    Avignon; Chambery; Durban, S.A., Museum and
          Art Gallery.
*auct.*    Paris, 15.12.1944, 29.3.1945, 7.10.1946, 21.2.1947,
          9.6.1947.

FISHER, ALEXANDER
British School.
19th century.
Painted flowers and mythological subjects.
*coll.* London, Victoria and Albert Museum, flowers.
*exhib.* V.E. (1), 1886.

FISHER, MISS ELLEN
British School.
*op.* 1865–1866
London address.
Painted still-life.

FISHER, HORACE
British School.
*op.* 1882–1899.
London address.
Painted flowers and domestic subjects.
*exhib.* R.A. (17); Suffolk Street (7).

FISHER, MARK, R.A.
British School.
b. Boston, U.S.A. of Anglo-Irish parents 1841, d. 1923.
Painted landscapes.
A study of Roses sold at Sotheby's 19.12.1962. It had been
exhibited at R.A. Winter Exhibition 1928.

FITZGERALD, MISS K.
British School.
*op.* 1864–1866.
London address.
*exhib.* Suffolk Street (3), flowers.

FIX-MASSEAU, PIERRE FELIX
French School.
b. Lyon 1869 (17th March).
Pupil National School of Art. Director School of Art,
Limoges. Officer of the Legion of Honour.
Painter of flowers and fruit and a sculptor.
*auct.* Paris, October 1945–July 1946, flowers.

FLANDRIN, JULES LEON
French School.
b. Grenoble 1871 (9th July), d. 1947.
Pupil of Gustave Moreau. Painted flowers, fruit, still-life
portraits and landscapes.
*exhib.* Salon d'Automne; Salon des Independants.
*auct.* Paris, 2.7.1947, flowers.

FLEMING, W. B.
British School.
*op.* 1873–1874.
Croydon address.
*exhib.* Suffolk Street (3), still-life.

FLOCKTON, F.
British School.
*op.* 1866–1876.
Pangbourne address.
*exhib.* R.A. (2); Suffolk Street (4), still-life.

FLORENTIN
French School.
19th century (*see* Vol. 3, Part I, p. 33).

FLOURY, FRANCOIS LOUIS LUCIEN
French School.
19th century.
Pupil of d'Allonge. Working in Paris. Painted still-life.
*exhib.* Salon 1873–1882.

FLOWER, MRS. E. WICKHAM
British School.
*op.* 1872–1873.
Croydon address.
Painted flowers.

FORD, W. ONSLOW
British School.
b. London 1880.
Son of Edward Onslow Ford the sculptor. Studied at R.A.
Schools. Painted still-life and portraits.
*exhib.* R.A. (1), still-life, 1897.

FOSTER, MISS F. E.
British School.
*op.* 1871–1879.
Hitchin address.
*exhib.* Suffolk Street (21), fruit.

FOSTER, SARAH F.
British School.
*op.* 1876.
Burton Overy address.
Painted flowers.

FOWLER, MRS. E. MILLER
British School.
*op.* 1895.
Hereford address.
*exhib.* R.A. (1), flowers.

FOWLER, MISS R. J.
British School.
*op.* 1881.
Woodford address.
*exhib.* Suffolk Street (1), flowers.

FOWLER, REV. W. W.
British School.
19th century.
Drew illustrations for *The Coleoptera of the British Isles*, 6 vols. 1887–1913.

FOX, R.
British School.
*op.* 1867.
London address.
*exhib.* R.A. (1), fruit.

FRANCK, HELEN—MISS HELENE (Graves and Benezit)—MRS. A. FAIRLIE
British School.
*op.* 1883–1911.
London address.
Painted flowers, still-life and domestic.
*exhib.* R.A.(8); Suffolk Street(13); N.W.C.S.(1); V.E.(8).

FREEMAN, MISS PAULINE
British School.
*op.* 1869.
London address.
*exhib.* Suffolk Street (1), flowers.

FREER, MRS. JOHN (*see* MRS. JOHN C. STAPLES, *née* MISS MARY ELLIN EDWARDS)

FREEZOR, MRS.
British School.
*op.* 1866.
London address.
*exhib.* B.I. (1), fruit.

FRIEDLANDER, CAMILLA
Austrian School.
b. Vienna 1856 (10th December).
Daughter and pupil of Friedrich Friedlander. Painted flowers and fruit.
*auct.* Sotheby's 8.11.1961.

FRY, ROGER
British School.
b. Bristol 1866, d. 1934.
Educated Clifton and Kings College, Cambridge. After taking a degree in Science devoted himself to Art. Studied in London and Paris. Member of the New English Art Club. Art critic, historian and associated with the Burlington Magazine.
Painted landscapes, etc. (including flowers).

FURLONG, MARIANNE M.
British School.
*op.* 1891–1894.
Woolwich address.
*exhib.* R.A. (1), flowers; Suffolk Street (2); N.W.C.S. (3).

GABAIN, ETHEL LEONTINE, R.O.I., R.B.A.—MRS. COPLEY
British School.
b. Havre 1883, d. 1950 (30th January).
Studied Slade and Central School of Arts and Crafts and in Paris. Associate Salon des Artistes Francais. Painter and lithographer.
*repr.* Hardie, *Flower Paintings.*

GADSBY, JAMES
British School.
*op.* 1872–1874.
London address.
*exhib.* Suffolk Street (1), flowers.

GALANES, DEMETRIUS EMMANUEL
French School.
b. Athens 1882 (22nd May).
Naturalized Frenchman. Painter and engraver. Professor at Ecole des Beaux Arts, Paris.
*auct.* Paris, 20.6.1944, still-life; 15.6.1945.

GALBUSERA, GIOACHIMO
Italian School.
b. Milan 1871 (2nd April), d. 1944.
Working in Lugano. Painted flowers.
*repr.* Stehli Bros. Ltd., Zurich (in colour).

GALE, FRANCES
British School.
*op.* 1877–1885.
London address.
Painted wild flowers.
*exhib.* R.A. (1), thistles.

GALLAND, MME JOSEPHINE
French School.
b. Lyon 19th century.
Painted flowers, still-life and landscapes.
*exhib.* Lyon 1892.

GARDNER, G.
British School.
*op.* 1884–1885.
London address.
*exhib.* Suffolk Street (2), fruit.

GARDNER, MABEL
British School.
*op.* 1878–1879.
Cheltenham address.
Painted flowers.

GARRATT, ELIZA
British School.
*op.* 1872.
Putney address.
Painted still-life.

GARSTIN, NORMAN
British School.
19th century (*see* Vol. 3, Part I, p. 34).

GASKELL, GEORGE PERCIVAL
British School.
b. Shipley 1868 (1st January).
*exhib.* R.A. (1), flowers, 1900.

GASTEIGER, ANNA SOPHIE
German School.
b. 1878 (26th February).
Wife of the sculptor Mathias Gasteiger. Pupil of Dasio.
Working in Munich and Dresden. Painted flowers.
*repr.* Stehli Bros. Ltd., Zurich (colour facsimiles of her
        paintings).

GASTEL, FRANCOIS VAN
Flemish School.
19th century (*see* Vol. 3, Part I, p. 34).

GAUDISSARD, or GAUDISSART, EMILE
French School.
b. Algiers 1872.
Painted flowers, still-life and portraits.
*exhib.* Salon 1896, Hon. mention.
*auct.* Paris, 2.3.1929, 24.2.1934, flowers.

GAUGUIN, EUGENE HENRY PAUL
French School.
b. Paris 1848, (8th June) d. Atuana in the Marquesas (P. and F.
Murray), Dominica, Tahiti (Benezit), 1903 (6th or 9th May).
Spent some of childhood in Peru. Ran away to sea 1865–
1871. Stockbroker in Paris 1871. Began to collect Impression-
ists and to study painting under Camille Pissarro. Went to
Pont Aven in Brittany 1886–1890. Visited Panama and
Martinique in 1887. Returned to Paris and went with Van
Gogh to Arles in 1888. Went to Tahiti in 1891. Returned to
Paris in 1893 for an exhibition. Went back to South Seas in
1895 and died there.
*coll.* Boston Museum; Leningrad, Hermitage; Paris,
        Louvre; New York, Museum Modern Art; Stavros
        Niarchos Collection.
*exhib.* Paris, Gauguin Exhibition 1960; London, Tate
        Gallery, Gauguin Exhibition.
*repr.* Bazin, pl. 280; Estienne, pls. 34 and 81; Rewald
        pl. 17; Taralin, pls. I, II and 16; Taylor, pl. 57.
*lit.* J. Rewald; Charles Estienne; Jean Taralin; Germain
        Bazin; Basil Taylor, etc.
*auct.* Paris, 29.3.1962, still-life with oysters, signed and
        dated 1876; Sotheby's 14.6.1962, flowers, illustrated
        in catalogue.

GAY, MDLLE BERTHA
French School.
b. Paris 1852 (14th June), d. Geneva 1885.
Painted flowers.
*exhib.* Suffolk Street 1883, flowers.

GEBEL, F.
(*See* Vol. 3, Part I, p. 35.)

GELLER, MISS ANGELINA
British School.
*op.* 1865–1886.
London address.
*exhib.* Suffolk Street (2); N.W.C.S. (1), fruit.

GEMMELL, MISS MARY (R.?) MARION
British School.
*op.* 1876–1893.
Anerley address.
*exhib.* R.A. (4); Suffolk Street (3); V.E. (4), flowers.

GERARD, GASTON
French School.
b. St. Mande 1859 (11th March).
Studied under Julian and Jules Lefebvre.
Painted flowers.
*auct.* Paris 12/13.5.1919.

GERMAIN, LOUIS
French School.
b. Niort 19th century.
Painted history, still-life and lithographer. Chevalier of the
Legion of Honour.
*coll.* Niort Museum.
*exhib.* Salon 1868.


GEUDTNER, ANNA
German School.
b. Chemnitz 1844 (29th December).
Painted fruit.
*exhib.* Dresden 1881 and 1889.


GEUDTNER, ELISE
German School.
b. Dresden 1857 (31st December).
Sister of Anna Geudtner.
Painted flowers and fruit.
*exhib.* Dresden 1880, 1890.


GIANOLI, LOUIS
Swiss School.
b. Geneva 1868 (4th November).
Painted still-life, genre and landscapes.


GIBSON, CHARLES DANA                    (*see* PLATE 19)
American School.
b. Roxbury 1867 (14th September), d. 1944.
Black-and-White illustrator. Creator of the 'Gibson Girl'.
Painted places and people and massed flower compositions.
Pupil of St. Gaudens and Julian Academy.
*exhib.* New York, Berry Hill Galleries, October 1961, 35
        paintings including 5 flower-pieces.


GILARDELLI, AURORA
Italian School.
19th century (*see* Vol. 3, Part I, p. 35).


GILBERT, VICTOR GABRIEL
French School.
b. Paris 1847 (13th February).
Pupil of Adam and Busson. Painted genre and flowers.
*auct.* Paris, 22.6.1942, still-life; 1881, flowers.


GILLO, P.
Flemish School.
19th century (*see* Vol. 3, Part I, p. 35).


GILSOUL-HOPPE, MME KETTY
Flemish School.
b. Dusseldorf 1868.
Pupil of J. Portaels and Hendrick in Brussels. Daughter of
Ed. Hoppe and wife of Victor Gilsoul 1894.
Painted flowers and landscapes.


GINNER, CHARLES, C.B.E., A.R.A.
British School (Benezit says Spanish School).
b. 1878 (4th March), d. 1952 (6th January).
Studied in Paris. Settled in London 1910. Member of
London Group.
*auct.* London, 13.5.1938, flowers.


GIRARDOT DE
French School.
19th century (*see* Vol. 3, Part I, p. 35).


GIRAUD, JULES
French School.
19th century.
Working at Digne. Painted flowers.
*exhib.* Salon 1879; Salon des Artistes Francais 1890.


GIRAUD, MARTHE
French School.
19th century.
Painted flowers.
*exhib.* Society des Artistes Francais 1902.
*auct.* Sotheby's 28.2.1962, flowers.


GIRIEUD, PIERRE
French School.
b. Marseilles 1875, d. Paris 1940.
Painted frescoes and flowers.
*auct.* Paris, 12.12.1946, flowers; 20.6.1944, flowers.


GIRY, LILY
French School.
19th century.
Working at Havre in 1868. Painted flowers.


GLACKENS, WILLIAM J.
American School.
b. Philadelphia 1870, d. 1938.
Studied at Pennsylvania Academy. Visited Europe. Painter
and illustrator. Worked in New York with Robert Henri
and 'The Eight'. Elected Associate Member of the National
Academy of Design in 1906.
*coll.* Chicago; Detroit; New York, Metropolitan
        Museum, all landscapes; Whitney Museum of
        American Art, New York, still-life.

GLENDENING, ALFRED JUNIOR, R.B.A.
British School.
19th century, d. 1907.
Son of Alfred Glendening. Painted landscapes, domestic, markets.
*exhib.* R.A. (24); Suffolk Street (47); N.W.C.S. (2).
*auct.* 11.5.1925, flower market; fish market.

GLIZE,
French School.
19th century (*see* Vol. 3, Part I, p. 36).

GLOAG, ISOBEL LILIAN
British School.
b. London 1865 (1st August), d. there 1917 (5th January).
Member of the Ridley Art Club. Painted flowers.
*coll.* Paris Art Moderne.

GLORIA, GERMAINE
French School.
19th century.
Painted flowers in water-colour.
*exhib.* Salon 1910.

GOBEL, MARIE
German School.
b. 1863 (20th August), d. 1908 (17th July).
Daughter of Angelbert Gobel. Working in Frankfort.
Painted still-life.

GOBERT, AUGUSTE
French School.
19th century (*see* Vol. 3, Part I, p. 36).

GOBL, CAMILLA
Austrian School.
b. Vienna 1871 (27th January).
Studied Vienna School of Art. Painted flowers and still-life.

GODDARD, ELIZA
British School.
*op.* 1897.
Whitchurch address.
*exhib.* R.A. (1), flowers.

GODSELL, MARY E.
British School.
*op.* 1897.
Stroud address.
*exhib.* R.A. (1), fruit.

GOGH, VINCENT VAN
Dutch School.
b. Zundert 1853 (30th May), d. Auvers-sur-Oise 1890 (29th July).
Son of a Dutch pastor. First employed at The Hague, in London and Paris by picture dealers. Taught in two schools in England. In a bookshop in Holland and began studying for the Church. Went to coal mining district in Belgium and shared hardships of the miners. Dismissed from the Church in 1880. Lived in Brussels, The Hague, Antwerp and elsewhere learning to paint. In Paris 1886. In Arles 1888. Shot himself at Auvers in 1890.
*coll.* Amsterdam, Rijks. museum; Otterloo, Kroller-Muller Museum; Paris, Louvre; Tate Gallery.
*exhib.* R.A. Dutch Art 1929, nos. 448, 451-2, 464; Tate Gallery.
*repr.* Estienne, pl. 48, 56, 76, 111; Bazin pl. 304.
*lit.* Charles Estienne, *Van Gogh*; Germain Bazin, *Impressionist Paintings in the Louvre*.
*auct.* Sotheby's, 14.6.1962, fruit (illustrated in catalogue).

GONTCHAROVA, NATHALIE
Russian School.
b. Moscow 1881 (4th June).
Studied Moscow School of Art. In Paris 1914. Painter and sculptor.
*exhib.* Salon des Independants and Salon d'Automne.
*auct.* Paris, 18.5.1945, flowers and fruit.

GONTIER, L.
French School.
19th century.
Painted flowers.
*coll.* St. Omer Museum, signed and dated 'L. Gontier' 1879.

GONYN, LOUIS P.
French School.
19th century.
Working at Vaucressor and Nanterre. Pupil of Henner.
Painted still-life, genre and landscapes.
*exhib.* Salon des Artistes Francais 1907.

GONZALES, EVA, MME HENRI GUERARD
French School.
b. Paris 1849 (19th April), d. there 1883 (5th May).
Daughter of Emmanuel Gonzales. Painted flowers. Her full length portrait by Manet is in the Tate Gallery.

GORE, FREDERICK SPENCER
British School.
b. 1878, d. Richmond 1914.
First President of the Camden Town Group. Painted flowers and landscapes.
*auct.* Sotheby's 12.7.1961, flowers.

GOSLING, JESSIE W.
British School.
*op.* 1897.
Braintree address.
*exhib.* R.A. (1), fruit.

GOSSE, SYLVIA, R.B.A., R.E.          (*see* PLATE 20)
British School.
b. London 1881 (14th February).
Daughter of Sir Edmund Gosse. Pupil of W. R. Sickert.
Painted in oils and water-colours and etched—portraits,
still-life, and scenes from contemporary life. Living at
Hastings 1962.
*coll.*    British Museum.
*exhib.* London Group 1916, still-life.

GRACE, HARRIETTE EDITH
British School.
*op.* 1877–1900.
Brighton address.
Painted fruit and domestic.
*exhib.* R.A. (8); Suffolk Street (15); V.E. (3).

GRAEF, JAN DE
Flemish School.
b. Antwerp 1877.
Teacher at the Antwerp Academy. Painted still-life.
*coll.*    Antwerp.

GRAHAM, MRS. W. JOSEPHINE
British School.
*op.* 1883–1884.
London address.
*exhib.* N.W.C.S. (3), flowers.

GRANBERY, M. LEE—MOLLIE LEE GRANBERY—MRS.
WILLIAM CHAPMAN
American School.
*op.* 1880–1890.
Lived in Machias, Maine. Painted still-life.
*exhib.* National Academy of Design, New York.

GRANDVAL, GEORGES DE
French School.
19th century.
Painted flowers.
*exhib.* Salon 1897.

GRANT, DUNCAN
British School.
b. Rothiemurchus, Inverness 1885.
Studied Westminster Art School and in Paris 1906–7. In

1913–14 designing carpets, marquetry and needlework for
Roger Fry's Omego Workshop in Fitzroy Square, London.
Painted landscapes and still-life.
*auct.*    London, 31.10.1945, still-life; Sotheby's 14.12.1960,
13.12.1961.

GRATAMA, GERRIT DAVID          (*see* PLATE 20)
Dutch School.
b. Groningen 1874.
Studied at The Hague and Antwerp Academy. Painted
portraits and flowers.
*coll.*    Teylers Museum, Haarlem.

s'GRAVESANDE, CHARLES STORM VAN
(*see* STORM VAN 'S GRAVESANDE)

GRAY, J.
British School.
*op.* 1863–1872.
London address.
*exhib.* Suffolk Street (7), fruit.

GREEN, MISS ISABELLA
British School.
*op.* 1873–1875.
Kimbford address.
*exhib.* R.A. (1); V.E. (7), flowers.

GREEN, MISS M. HELEN
British School.
*op.* 1884–1887.
London address.
*exhib.* R.A. (3), flowers.

GREENBANK, ARTHUR
British School.
*op.* 1888–1899.
London address.
Painted figures and flowers.
*exhib.* R.A. (6); Suffolk Street (4); N.W.C.S. (8); V.E. (5).

GREENWOOD, MISS ISABELLA
British School.
*op.* 1864–1874.
Cheltenham address.
*exhib.* B.I. (1); Suffolk Street (1), still-life.

GREENWOOD, ORLANDO          (*see* PLATE 21)
British School.
19th and 20th century.
b. Nelson, Lancs.
*coll.*    Preston, Harris Museum and Art Gallery (2), flowers.

GREGORY, MISS J.
British School.
*op.* 1873.
London address.
Painted flowers.

GRENIER, J. B.
French School.
19th century.
Sotheby's sold a pair of still-life paintings (dated 1864), 9.5.1962.

GRIERSON, MISS C. G.
British School.
*op.* 1874.
Dublin address.
*exhib.* Suffok Street (1), game.

GRIEVE, WALTER G., A.R.S.A.
British School.
19th and 20th century.
*exhib.* R.S.A. Centenary Exhibition 1926 (2), still-life.
*repr.* R.S.A. Memorial Catalogue Centenary Exhibition, 1926, pl.99.

GRIFFITH, E. N.
American School.
*op.* 1894.
Painted still-life.
*repr.* *After the Hunt*, Frankenstein 1953, pl. 131.
*lit.* Frankenstein.

GRIFFITH, MISS KATE
British School.
*op.* 1879–1885.
Winchfield address.
*exhib.* R.A. (4); Suffolk Street (6), still-life.

GRIFFITH, WILLIAM
British School.
*op.* 1875–1883.
Brentford address.
*exhib.* R.A. (2); Suffolk Street (3), flowers.

GRIFFITHS, MISS GWENNY
British School.
19th century.
b. Swansea.
Pupil of A. Legros in London and Julian Academy in Paris.
Painted flowers and portraits.
*exhib.* Suffolk Street 1892, flowers.

GRIVEAU, GEORGES
French School.
b. Paris 1863 (26th January).
Pupil of Gerome. Chevalier of the Legion of Honour.
Painted fruit and landscape.
*coll.* Amiens Museum.
*exhib.* Universal Exhibition 1888, Hon. mention, bronze Medal 1900.
*auct.* Paris, 14.12.1944, 24.5.1945, fruit.

GROSE, MISS MILLICENT S.
British School.
*op.* 1870–1890.
Oxford address.
*exhib.* R.A.(1); Suffolk Street(14); N.W.C.S.(3), flowers

GRUN, JULES ALEXANDRE
French School.
b. Paris 1868 (26th May).
Pupil of Guillemet. Chevalier of the Legion of Honour.
Painted flowers.
*coll.* Pontoise
*auct.* Paris, 8.11.1946, 5.2.1947, flowers.

GUERIN, CHARLES FRANCOIS PROSPER
French School.
b. Sens 1875 (21st February), d. Paris 1939 (19th March).
Pupil of Gustave Moreau. Painted figures, portraits and still-life.
*exhib.* Salon 1897.
*auct.* 20.6.1947, still-life.

GUERIN, MRS. WILLIAM COLLINGS LUKIS (*née* ANNA MARIA EDMONDS)
British School.
*op.* 1867–1888.
Rome and London addresses.
Painted flowers and rustic subjects.
*exhib.* as Edmonds R.A. (1) from Rome; as Guerin R.A. (12); Suffolk Street (11); N.W.C.S. (1).
Benezit gives 'GUERIN, MARIE LOUISE ANNA' 19th century painter of still-life exhibiting at the Salon in 1877. Probably the same as above.

GUERMONT, EUGENE
French School.
b. St. Denis 1869.
Painted still-life.
*coll.* Rouen Museum.

GUGNON, LOUISE MME JOUSSERANDOT
French School.
19th century (*see* Vol. 3, Part I, p. 37).

GUHL, JOHANNA
Swiss School.
b. 1869.
Painted flowers.

GUILLAUMIN THE YOUNGER
French School.
19th century (*see* Vol. 3, Part I, p. 37).

GUILLOD, MISS BESSIE
British School.
*op.* 1876–1893.
London address.
*exhib.* R.A. (1); Suffolk Street (5); V.E. (5), flowers.

GUMMERY, H.
British School.
*op.* 1862–1878.
Worcester address.
*exhib.* Suffolk Street (5), flowers.

GUTHRIE, JOHN
British School.
*op.* 1882.
Glasgow address.
*exhib.* R.A. (1), flowers.

GUYOT, GEORGES LUCIEN
French School.
b. Paris 1885 (10th December).
Painted flowers and fruit and was a sculptor and engraver.
*auct.* Paris, 27.11.1942, fruit.

GYSIS *or* GYZIS, NICOLAS
Greek School.
b. l'ile de Tines 1842 (1st March), d. Munich 1901 (4th January).
Studied at School of Art at Athens and under Piloty at Munich 1865. Painted genre, etc.
*coll.* Munich, still-life.
*exhib.* Munich 1883 and 1892, medal.

HABERLE, JOHN
American School.
b. New Haven 1856, d. there 1933 (3rd Februuary).
Studied at National Academy of Design, New York.
Painted still-life.
*repr.* *After the Hunt*, Frankenstein, 1953, pls. 93–104.
*it.* Frankenstein; *Illustrated American*, 30.12.1898.

HABERT-DYS, JULES AUGUSTE
French School.
b. Fresnes 1850.
Pupil of Bernard, Gerome and Bracquemond. Painter, designer and engraver.
*coll.* Arras.
*repr.* *Dekorative Vorbilder*, Stuttgart.

HAGHE, MRS. L.
British School.
*op.* 1880.
London address. Wife of Louis Haghe, the artist.
*exhib.* R.A. (1), flowers.

HAHNEL, A.
British School (?)
*op.* 1870.
*exhib.* Suffolk Street (1), flowers.

HAIG, MISS M. C.
British School.
*op.* 1873.
London address.
*exhib.* Suffolk Street (1), fruit.

HAIN, MLLE H.
French School.
19th century (*see* Vol. 3, Part I, p. 38).

HAIN, MARGUERITE
French School.
b. Rouen 1876.
Painted flowers and landscapes.
*coll.* Rouen.
*auct.* Paris, 18.6.1945, flowers.

HAKING, HILDA B.
British School.
*op.* 1894.
London address.
*exhib.* R.A. (1), flowers.

HALE, LILIAN WESTCOTT
American School.
b. Connecticut 1881 (7th December).
Pupil of Chase and Tarbell. Wife of Philip Leslie Hale.
Painted still-life.
*exhib.* Buenos Aires 1910, Bronze Medal.
*auct.* New York, 1932.

HALE, MISS M. B.
British School.
*op.* 1878–1881.
Bath address.
*exhib.* R.A. (1); Suffolk Street (1), flowers.

HALEY, HERBERT
British School.
*op.* 1894.
Bradford address.
*exhib.* R.A. (1), flowers.

HALL, ARTHUR W.
British School.
*op.* 1872.
London address.
*exhib.* V.E. (1), fruit.

HALL, EDNA CLARKE
British School.
b. 1881.
*coll.* Newcastle, Laing Art Gallery (2).

HALLER, ANNA (*or* HANNA *or* HANNER) (*see* PLATE 22)
Swiss School.
b. Rupperswil 1872 (13th April), d. 1924.
Painted flowers.
*coll.* Berne Museum.
*exhib.* Munich, Geneva, Lausanne and Berne.

HALL THORPE, JOHN (*see* THORPE, JOHN HALL)

HAM, MISS ADA J.
British School.
*op.* 1885–1887.
London address.
*exhib.* R.A. (5), flowers.

HAMILTON, E. B.
British School.
*op.* 1874.
*exhib.* Suffolk Street (1), flowers.

HAMMOND, GERTRUDE DEMAIN, R.I.
British School.
*op.* 1886–1897.
London address.
Painted flowers and domestic.
*exhib.* R.A. (3); Suffolk Street (1); N.W.C.S. (10).

HANBURY, MISS ADA
British School.
*op.* 1875–1887.
London address.
Sister of Blanche Hanbury.
*exhib.* R.A. (5); Suffolk Street (1); N.W.C.S. (2), flowers.

HANBURY, MISS BLANCHE
British School.
*op.* 1876–1887.
London address.
Sister of Ada Hanbury.
*exhib.* R.A. (2); Suffolk Street (11); N.W.C.S. (2), flowers.

HANCOCK, MISS E. J.
British School.
*op.* 1876.
London address.
*exhib.* Suffolk Street (1), flowers.

HANLEY, EDGAR
British School.
*op.* 1878–1883.
London address.
*exhib.* R.A. (22); Suffolk Street (5); V.E. (6), still-life.

HANNON, THEODORE
Flemish School.
b. Brussels 1851, d. Etterbeck 1917.
Painted flowers, still-life, genre and landscapes.

HARDESS, MISS MARIA A.
British School.
*op.* 1867–1869.
London address.
*exhib.* Suffolk Street (3), flowers.

HARDING, MISS MARY E.
British School.
*op.* 1880–1893.
Blackheath address.
*exhib.* R.A. (12); Suffolk Street (1); V.E. (6), flowers.

HARDMAN, MRS. EMMA L.
British School.
*op.* 1888–1895.
Potter's Bar address. Wife of Thomas Hardman.
Painted flowers.
*exhib.* R.A. (2); Suffolk Street (7); N.W.C.S. (3).

HARNETT, WILLIAM MICHAEL                    (*see* PLATE 23)
American School.

b. Clonakilty, Co. Cork, Ireland, 1848 (10th August), d. New York 1892 (29th October).

Taken to Philadelphia, U.S.A., when one year old. Commenced as engraver on silver. Studied Pennsylvania Academy, National Academy of Design, and Cooper Union in New York. Began career as a painter in 1875 with a studio in Philadelphia till 1878. Went to Europe 1880–1886. Spent some time in Munich and Frankfort. Lived in New York 1886–1892. Painted trompe l'oeil, still-life.

*coll.*   Boston; Brooklyn; Buffalo; Chicago; Connecticut; Detroit; St. Louis; San Francisco; Mr. and Mrs. Paul Peralta-Ramos, N.Y.C.

*exhib.* R.A.; Salon; Munich; Frankfurt; Downtown Gallery 1939.

*repr.*   *After the Hunt*, Frankenstein, 1953, pls. 1–4, 6, 17, 23–29, 31–39, 46, 49–60, 62–66, 76–78, 82.
*Encyclopaedia of Painting*, Myers, 1956, pl. 93, colour.

*lit.*   Frankenstein.

HARPER, F. G.
British School.
*op.* 1884.
London address.
*exhib.* Suffolk Street (1), flowers.

HARRIS, GEORGE WALTER
British School.
*op.* 1864–1893.
London address.
*exhib.* R.A. (20); Suffolk Street (14), fruit.

HARRIS, MAUDE E.
British School.
*op.* 1883–1892.
*exhib.* Suffolk Street (2); N.W.C.S. (1), flowers.

HARRISON, MISS EMILY H.
British School.
*op.* 1892–1893.
London address.
*exhib.* V.E. (2), flowers.

HARRISON, MISS FANNY
British School.
*op.* 1870–1871.
*exhib.* Suffolk Street (1), fruit.

HARRISON, F. E.
British School.
*op.* 1862–1867.
London address.
*exhib.* R.A. (3), flowers.

HARRISON, M. E.
British School.
*op.* 1875.
London address.
*exhib.* V.E. (1), flowers.

HARTLEY, MISS E. A.
British School.
*op.* 1871.
Boston, Lincs., address.
*exhib.* R.A. (1), fruit.

HARTLEY, MARSDEN
American School.
b. 1878, d. 1943.
Pupil of Dumond, Mora and Chase. Painted still-life, portraits and landscapes.

HARVEY, HERBERT JOHNSON, R.B.S.A.
British School.
b. London 1884, d. there 1928.
Son of John R. Harvey, artist. Travelled in Italy as a young man. Known principally for his paintings and etchings of figure subjects.
*coll.*   Birmingham, carnations and gladioli.
*exhib.* R.A.; R.B.S.A.

HASSELL, HILDA CLEMENTS
British School.
19th century.
Painted flowers.
*exhib.* Salon des Independents 1911.

HASTIE, GRACE H.
British School.
*op.* 1874–1897.
Member of the Society of Lady Artists.
Painted flowers and fruit.
*exhib.* R.A. (14); Suffolk Street (18); N.W.C.S. (18); G.G. (2); N.G. (2); V.E. (6).

HAVILAND, MISS HARRIET M.
British School.
*op.* 1864.
Bridgwater address.
*exhib.* B.I. (2), flowers.

HAY, PETER ALEXANDER, R.S.W.
British School.
b. Edinburgh.
op. 1892–1897.
London address.
Studied R.S.A. and under Bouguereau.
Painted portraits, domestic, and fruit.
exhib. R.A. (3); Suffolk Street (2); N.W.C.S. (1); N.G.
(1); V.E. (1).
Paris, Hon. Mention 1908.

HAYCOCK, G. B.
British School.
op. 1862–1868.
London address.
exhib. R.A. (11); B.I. (12); Suffolk Street (9), still-life.

HAYDEN, HENRI
French School.
b. Varsovie 1883 (24th December). Naturalised Frenchman.
Painted still-life.
coll. Barcelona; Bucharest; Copenhagen; Dusseldorf;
Grenoble; Luxembourg; Mannheim; Nantes;
Paris; Philadelphia.
auct. Copenhagen, 27.4.1949; Paris, 1951.

HAYLLAR, JESSICA
British School.
op. 1898–1899.
Wallingford and Bournemouth addresses.
exhib. R.A. (2), flowers.

HAYLLAR, KATE
British School.
op. 1898.
Wallingford address.
exhib. R.A. (1), flowers.

HAYNES, ADELINE
British School.
op. 1879.
exhib. Suffolk Street (1), flowers.

HAYWARD, A. F. W., R.O.I.
British School.
b. Port Hope, Canada, 1856.
Pupil of Frederick Brown. Lived in London, Winchester,
Norwood, and St. Ives, Hunts. Painted portraits and flowers.
exhib. R.A. (18); Suffolk Street (1); G.G. (1); N.G. (9);
V.E. (14).

HAYWARD, MISS MARY
British School.
op. 1867–1874.
London address.
exhib. Suffolk Street (8), flowers.

HEINE, E.
British School.
op. 1863.
exhib. R.A. (1), flowers.

HELBERGER, ALFRED HERMANN
German School.
b. Frankfurt 1871 (23rd May).
Painted flowers and engraved.

HELLEU, PAUL CESAR
French School.
b. Vannes 1859 (17th December), d. Paris 1927 (23rd **March**).
Pupil of Gerome. Painter and engraver.
auct. Paris, 24.2.1943, fruit; October 1945, flowers.

HEMSLEY, WALTER HOWARD
British School.
op. 1868–1870.
London address.
exhib. Suffolk Street (2), fruit.

HENNEQUIN, VICTOR
French School.
19th century (see Vol. 3, Part I, p. 41).

HENSLEY, MRS. MARIE
British School.
op. 1897.
London address.
exhib. R.A. (1), flowers.

HER, CHARLES VAN
Flemish School.
b. Brussels 1884.
Painted marines, portraits and still-life.
Known as HERBRUGGEN.
coll. Antwerp, still-life.

HERBIN, AUGUSTE
French School.
b. Quevy 1882 (29th April).
Painted flowers, fruit, still-life and abstract.
coll. Cologne.
auct. Paris, 24.3.1947, still-life.

HERING
Flemish School.
19th century (*see* Vol. 3, Part I, p. 41).

HERMANSEN, OLAF AUGUST
Danish School.
b. Copenhagen 1849 (30th July), d. there 1897 (25th November).
Painted flowers.

HERRINGTON, FRED W.
British School.
*op.* 1882–1890.
London address.
*exhib.* Suffolk Street (1), still-life.

HESS, JULIUS
German School.
b. Stuttgart 1878 (16th April).
Working in Munich. Painted still-life.
*coll.* Munich.

HEUZE, EDMOND AMEDEE
French School.
b. Paris 1884 (26th September).
Painted flowers, portraits and figures.
*auct.* Paris, 1945, flowers.

HICKSON, MISS MARGARET
British School.
*op.* 1879–1892.
London address.
Painted still-life.
*exhib.* R.A. (7); Suffolk Street (7); N.W.C.S. (4); N.G. (1); V.E. (6).

HIGGINSON, MAY
British School.
*op.* 1894.
Torquay address.
*exhib.* R.A., flowers.

HILBERTH, IREN
Hungarian School.
b. Budapest 1872.
Painted still-life and portraits.

HILL, FANNY
British School.
*op.* 1879.
Leamington address.
*exhib.* Suffolk Street (1), flowers.

HILL, JAMES STEVENS, R.B.A., R.O.I., R.I.
British School.
b. Exeter 1854, d. 1921.
Pupil at R.A. Schools.
Painted flowers and landscapes.
*exhib.* R.A. (8); Suffolk Street (31); N.W.C.S. (1); G.G. (1); V.E. (18).

HILLIARD, CONSTANCE
British School.
*op.* 1877.
Uxbridge address.
Painted flowers.

HILLIARD, LAWRENCE
British School.
*op.* 1876–1887.
Uxbridge address.
*exhib.* N.W.C.S. (7); V.E. (15), still-life.

HINDLEY, GODFREY C., R.O.I.
British School.
*op.* 1876–1893.
London address.
Painted flowers and genre.
*exhib.* R.A. (28); Suffolk Street (9); N.W.C.S. (1); V.E. (20).

HIPSLEY, JOHN HENRY
British School.
*op.* 1882–1892.
London address.
*exhib.* Suffolk Street (2); N.W.C.S. (1), flowers.

HIPWOOD, MISS SARAH
British School.
*op.* 1868–1869.
London address.
*exhib.* Suffolk Street (2), fruit.

HIRD, W.
British School.
*op.* 1867.
London address.
*exhib.* B.I. (1), flowers.

HIRST, CLAUDE RAGUET (MRS. W. C. FITLER)   (*see* PLATE 23)
American School.
b. 1855, d. New York 1942 (2nd May), aged 87.
Lived in New York. Married the artist William C. Fitler.
Painted flowers, fruit and still-life of pipes and books.
*exhib.* National Academy of Design 1884–1890.
*repr.* *After the Hunt*, Frankenstein, 1953, pl. 126.
       *Antiques* Magazine, New York, February 1962, p.
       175 (ad.).
*lit.* Frankenstein, p. 153–4.

HIRTH, EDOUARD
French School.
b. Reichweiller 1885 (14th September).
Studied Strasburg.
Painted still-life and portraits.

HODDER, MRS. CHARLOTTE
British School.
*op.* 1883.
Worcester address.
*exhib.* R.A. (1), flowers.

HODGKINS, FRANCIS
British School.
b. New Zealand 1871 (Victoria and Albert Museum catalogue), b. 1869 (Tate Gallery catalogue), b. 1870 (Benezit),
d. 1947.
Came to Europe 1900 and travelled Holland, Italy, France,
Palestine and North Africa. Taught at Academie Colarossi,
Paris. Designed textiles. Painted flowers, etc.
*coll.* Bedford, Cecil Higgins Museum, flowers and still-
       life; London, Victoria and Albert Museum; Tate
       Gallery.
*exhib.* R.A.

HODGSON, MRS. DORA
British School.
*op.* 1885.
London address.
Painted fruit.

HOFER, KARL
German School.
b. 1878, d. 1955.
Studied at Karlsruhe Academy.
Painted still-life and figures.
*repr.* *Encyclopedia of Painting*, Myers, pl. 96 (colour).

HOFFMAN, FRANZ XAVER
Austrian School.
19th century (*see* Vol. 3, Part I, p. 42).

HOFFMANN-CANSTEIN, BARONNE OLGA
Polish School.
b. Lwow 1872 (4th November).
Pupil of Karl Karger and Alfred Zoff.
Painted flowers and landscapes.
*exhib.* Vienna.

HOLL, MRS. FRANK
British School.
*op.* 1881–1882.
London address.
*exhib.* Suffolk Street (6), flowers.

HOLLIDAY, EDWARD
British School.
*op.* 1874–1884.
Croydon address.
*exhib.* R.A. (5); Suffolk Street (33), fruit.

HOLLIDAY, LILY
British School.
*op.* 1879–1884.
Croydon address.
*exhib.* Suffolk Street (14), flowers.

HOLM, HARALD MARTIN HANSEN        (*see* PLATE 24)
Danish School.
b. Horne (Faaborg) 1866 (26th August), d. Genua 1920 (20th
February).
Painted flowers.
*coll.* Copenhagen, Royal Museum, orchids. Signed and
       dated 1900.
*exhib.* Universal Exhibition 1900, Hon. Mention.

HOLT, MISS A. H. (*see* MRS. JACKSON, Vol. 3, Part I, p. 44)

HOLT, MISS MARY ANN
British School.
*op.* 1863–1868.
London address.
*exhib.* Suffolk Street (2), flowers.

HOOTON, MARY T.
British School
*op.* 1874.
Croydon address.
Painted flowers.

HOPKINS, MISS
British School.
*op.* 1862–1864.
Worcester address.
*exhib.* Suffolk Street (5), flowers.

HOPKINSON, MISS ANNE E.
British School.
op. 1877–1887.
Forest Hill address.
exhib. R.A. (2); Suffolk Street (5); N.W.C.S. (2), fruit.

HOPPE, C. A. W.
German School.
19th century (see Vol. 3, Part I, p. 43).

HOPPE, HEDWIG
German School.
19th century.
In Berlin 1886. Painted still-life and portraits.

HORNCASTLE, MISS JANE A.
British School.
op. 1863–1869.
London address.
exhib. R.A. (1); Suffolk Street (5), flowers.

HORNEL, EDWARD ATKINSON
British School.
b. Baccus Marsh, Victoria, Australia, 1864, d. Kirkcudbright 1933.
Studied under Verlat in Antwerp. Went to Japan in 1893, Ceylon and Australia in 1907. Member of the International Society of Painters, Gravers and Sculptors. Close friend of George Henry (1858–      ), with whom he painted several pictures in collaboration. Painted children and flowers in a landscape setting.
exhib. Glasgow Institute, 1890.
auct. Glasgow, 26.10.1945.
lit. Scottish Art Review, Vol. 7, No. 4, 1960 (illus.).

HOSKYN, MARY G.
British School.
op. 1879.
Kilburn address.
exhib. Suffolk Street (1), still-life.

HOUTEN, VAN (see VAN HOUTEN)

HOWELL, MISS CONSTANCE E.
British School.
op. 1878–1882.
London address.
exhib. Suffolk Street (3); V.E. (3), flowers.

HRUTSKIJ, IVAN
Finnish School.
19th century. d. 1900.
Painted fruit and still-life.
Known as CHRUTZKIJ.
coll. Helsingfors Museum.

HUBBARD, G. A.
British School.
op. 1865.
Bexley Heath address.
exhib. Suffolk Street (4), fruit.

HUBBARD, W.
British School.
op. 1867.
Crayford address.
exhib. B.I. (1); Suffolk Street (4), flowers.

HUBER, LEON CHARLES
French School.
b. Paris 1858 (11th January), d. there 1928 (25th August).
Studied under Dawant and Jules Grun. Painted flowers, fruit and animals.
auct. Paris, 23.12.1943, flowers; October 1945–July 1946, flowers.

HUDSON, HENRY
British School.
op. 1898.
Sherborne, Dorset, address.
exhib. R.A. (1), still-life.

HUGHES, WILLIAM
British School.
b. Lanarkshire 1842, d. Brighton 1901 (18th December).
London address.
Painted still-life, flowers and fruit.
Pupil of Lance and William Hunt.
coll. South Africa, Cape Town Museum, fruit.
exhib. R.A. (30); B.I. (8); Suffolk Street (71); G.G. (31); V.E. (21).
auct. Sotheby's, 17.1.1962, fruit.

HULBERT, KATHERINE ALLMOND (MRS. CHARLES ALLEN)
American School.
b. Sacramento, California.
op. 1907–1934.
Studied at School of Design, San Francisco, and National Academy of Design, New York. Working in Massachusetts in 1934. Painted flowers and still-life.

HULL, MISS MARY A.
British School.
*op.* 1877–1887.
Leicester address.
*exhib.* R.A. (1); N.W.C.S. (3), fruit.

HULME, MISS ALICE L.
British School.
*op.* 1877–1890.
London address.
*exhib.* R.A. (3); Suffolk Street (2), still-life.

HULME, ROBERT C.
British School.
*op.* 1862–1876.
London address.
*exhib.* R.A. (1); Suffolk Street (2), fruit.

HUMMEL, THEODOR
German School.
b. Schliersee 1864 (15th November).
Painted still-life.
*coll.* Munich.
*exhib.* Berlin; Munich; Paris, Universal Exhibition 1900, Hon. Mention.

HUNT, CECIL ARTHUR
British School.
b. Torquay 1873.
Painted landscapes and some flower pictures in water-colour.
*exhib.* R.A.; R.W.S.
*repr.* *Bouquet*, pl. 21.

HUNT, MRS. EMMA C. W.
British School.
*op.* 1884.
London address.
*exhib.* R.A. (4), flowers.

HUNT, MISS EVA E.
British School.
*op.* 1885–1897.
Greenwich and London addresses.
*exhib.* R.A. (6); Suffolk Street (16); G.G. (3), flowers.

HUNTER, G. LESLIE
British School.
b. Rothesay 1877, d. Glasgow 1931.
Went to Canada and to study in San Francisco, Paris, and London. Settled in Glasgow. Painted still-life and landscapes.
*coll.* Glasgow; Luxembourg; Paris.
*exhib.* New York; Paris; San Francisco; Toronto.
*auct.* Glasgow, 25.1.1946, still-life.

HUNZIKER, ELISE
Swiss School.
b. Kulm 1860 (15th March).
Painted still-life.

HURTON, C. F.
British School.
*op.* 1865.
Stoke address.
Painted flowers.

HUSSARD, LOUIS CHARLES
French School.
b. Paris 1857 (15th December).
Painted flowers and fruit.
*exhib.* Salon 1837–1852.

HUSSEY, MISS AGNES
British School.
*op.* 1877–1887.
Salisbury address.
*exhib.* Suffolk Street (1); N.W.C.S. (4); V.E. (3), flowers.

HUTCHISON, ROBERT GEMMELL
British School.
19th century (*see* Vol. 3, Part I, p. 44).

HYNER, AREND
Dutch School.
b. Arnheim 1866 (18th September), d. 1916 (July).
Pupil of Schulmann. Painted still-life, genre and portraits.

HYTCHE, MISS KEZIA
British School.
*op.* 1869–1870.
London address.
*exhib.* Suffolk Street (2), flowers.

IAVLENSKI, ALEXEI VON (*see* JAWLENSKI)

IMAO, KEINEN
Japanese School.
19th century.
Painted flowers and genre.
*exhib.* Universal Exhibition 1900, Bronze Medal.

IMGRABEN, CACILIE
German School.
b. Karlsruhe 1879 (29th June).
Painted flowers and landscapes.
*exhib.* Karlsruhe.

INNES, MISS ALICE
British School.
*op.* 1869–1870.
London address.
*exhib.* Suffolk Street (2), flowers.

IRWIN, MISS ANNIE L.
British School.
*op.* 1886–1890.
Sunderland address.
*exhib.* R.A. (1); V.E. (2), flowers.

IZARD, MISS GERTRUDE M.
British School.
*op.* 1890–1891.
London address.
*exhib.* Suffolk Street (2), flowers.

JAARSMA, E. H.
Dutch School.
b. Sneek 1879.
Pupil of E. van Biever and H. Krabbe.
Painted flowers.

JACKSON, MISS EMILY F.
British School.
*op.* 1875–1887.
Carshalton address.
Painted flowers.
*exhib.* R.A. (16); Suffolk Street (19); N.W.C.S. (6); G.G. (2); V.E. (17).

JACOBS, J. F.
British School.
*op.* 1884.
London address.
*exhib.* Suffolk Street (1), flowers.

JACOBSON, MISS S. H.
British School.
*op.* 1875.
London address.
*exhib.* Suffolk Street (1), flowers.

JACOMB-HOOD, GEORGE PERCY, R.B.A., R.E.
British School.
b. London 1877.
Painted flowers, domestic and interiors.
*exhib.* R.A. (22); Suffolk Street (27); G.G. (13); N.G. (11); V.E. (11).

JACQUE, EMILE
French School.
b. Epervans 1848, d. Paris 1912.
Son of Charles Jacque. Pupil of Gerome. Painted still-life and animals.
*exhib.* Universal Exhibition 1889, Hon. Mention.
*auct.* Paris, 4.11.1924, still-life.

JACQUELIN, MARGUERITE
French School.
19th century.
b. Bordeaux.
Pupil of Auguin, Lalanne, R. Henry and Bonnat. Painted flowers.
*exhib.* Salon 1879.

JACQUET, EDMOND
French School.
19th century (*see* Vol. 3, Part I, p. 45).

JACQUET, MME HENRIETTE
French School.
19th century (*see* Vol. 3, Part I, p. 45).

JACQUET, MARIE EUPHROSINE
French School.
19th century (*see* Vol. 3, Part I, p. 45).

JAGGER, WILSON
British School.
*op.* 1900.
Cardiff address.
*exhib.* R.A. (1), still-life.

JAMES, EDITH AUGUSTA
British School.
b. Eton 1857, d. Tunbridge Wells 1898.
Pupil of Chaplin and Luminaes in Paris. Painted flowers, portraits and studies of St. Paul's Cathedral.
*coll.* London, Victoria and Albert Museum.
*exhib.* Paris; R.A. (3); Suffolk Street (2); G.G. (1).

JAMES, FRANCIS EDWARD, R.W.S., R.B.A.     (*see* PLATE 24)
British School.
b. Willingdon, Sussex, 1849, d. Great Torrington, Devon, 1920 (26th August).
Son of Rev. H. James. Member of New English Art Club. Noted for his paintings of white flowers against a white background. Confined for many years to house by ill health. Painted flowers and landscapes.
*coll.*     Birmingham; Durban, South Africa; London, British Museum and Victoria and Albert Museum.

JAMES, MISS M.
British School.
*op.* 1873–1878.
London address.
*exhib.* Suffolk Street (4), flowers.

JAMISON, MRS. ARCHER *or* ARTHUR (ISABEL)
British School.
*op.* 1877–1889.
St. Helen's address.
*exhib.* R.A. (4); Suffolk Street (1); N.W.C.S. (1); V.E. (5), flowers.
    At R.A. 1887 'Mrs. Jamison, St. Helens, Lancashire'. 1889, 'Miss I. Jamison, London'.

JANNOCK, VERA
British School.
*op.* 1898–1900.
King's Lynn address.
*exhib.* R.A. (2), flowers.

JAWLENSKI, ALEXEJ VON     (*see* PLATE 25)
Russian School.
b. Wiesbaden 1864 (13th March), d. Switzerland 1941.
Studied at St. Petersburg Academy.
*coll.*     Cologne; Elberfeld, flowers; Essen.
*exhib.* Berlin, 1920.
*auct.* Sotheby's, 6.12.1961, still-life; 4.7.1962, still-life.

JEANNIN, GEORGES
French School.
b. Paris 1841, d. there 1925.
Pupil of Vincelet. Chevalier of the Legion of Honour 1903. President, Society of Flower Painters. Painted flowers and still-life.
*coll.*     Beziers; Epinal; The Hague, Mesdag Museum; Mulhouse; Nancy; Paris, Ville de Paris; Rochefort; Rouen; Valenciennes.
*exhib.* Salon; Salon des Artistes Francais; Universal Exhibition 1889, Bronze Medal.
*auct.* Paris, 12.5.1944, 16.7.1947, flowers.

JEFFERY, MISS ANNIE
British School.
*op.* 1884–1890.
Haywards Heath address.
*exhib.* R.A. (1); Suffolk Street (2), flowers.

JEFFERYS, MARCEL     (*see* PLATE 25)
Flemish School.
b. Milan 1872 (9th August), d. Brussels 1924 (14th May).
Pupil of Mme Henriette Ronner and Alfred Ronner.
Visited Paris, London and Venice. Painted flowers.
*coll.*     Antwerp; Brussels.
*exhib.* Brussels, Ghent, Berlin, Glasgow, Prague.

JEHIN, HENRI
Flemish School.
b. Spa 1880 (14th June).
Painted flowers.
*exhib.* Paris and London.

JENKINS, MISS ANNE
British School.
*op.* 1876–1885.
London address.
*exhib.* R.A. (10); Suffolk Street (12); V.E. (11), flowers.

JENKINS, BLANCHE
British School.
*op.* 1872–1894.
London address.
Member of the Society of Lady Artists.
Painted flowers and domestic.
*coll.*     Leeds.
*exhib.* R.A. (32); Suffolk Street (18); G.G. (4); N.G. (9); V.E. (26).

JENSEN, OLGA WILHELMINE (*née* MEISSNER)
Danish School.
b. 1877 (12th February).
Studied in Paris. Painted flowers.

JENSEN, OLUF CARL CHRISTIAN
Danish School.
b. 1871 (17th February).
Painted flowers and porcelain at Copenhagen.

JESSOP, J.
British School.
*op.* 1867–1868.
Croydon address.
*exhib.* Suffolk Street (2), fruit.

JOBSON, HENRY
British School.
*op.* 1873–1877.
Tottenham address.
*exhib.* Suffolk Street (1); V.E. (6), flowers.

JOETS, JULES ARTHUR
French School.
b. St. Omer 1884 (1st September).
Studied in Paris. Visited Belgium and England.
Painted still-life.
*coll.* Arras; Paris, Art Moderne.
*auct.* Paris, 24.2.1936.

JOHN, AUGUSTUS EDWIN, O.M., R.A.
British School.
b. Tenby 1878 (4th January), d. Fordingbridge, Hants, 1961 (31st October).
Studied Slade School, London. Was teaching in Liverpool 1901–1902. Travelled much in England and France in the gipsy fashion. Painted portraits, landscapes, genre, flowers and still life.

JOHNSON, MISS ADELINE
British School.
*op.* 1867–1872.
London address.
*exhib.* Suffolk Street (1); V.E. (2), flowers.

JOHNSON, LOUISA
British School.
*op.* 1865.
London address.
*exhib.* Suffolk Street (1), fruit.

JOHNSON, MISS LOUISA H. K.
British School.
*op.* 1894.
Carrington, Notts., address.
*exhib.* R.A. (1), flowers.

JOIGNY, G. DE
French School.
19th century (*see* Vol. 3, Part I, p. 45).

JOLDEN, FRIEDA BLANCA VON
German School.
b. Darmstadt 1878 (23rd April).
Working in Frankfort. Painted flowers.

JONGE, EVA MARIA ALIDA DE
Dutch School.
b. Amersfoort 1872 (24th December).
Studied Amsterdam Academy. Painted still-life.

JONGE, JOHAN ANTONIO DE
Dutch School.
b. Rotterdam 1864 (7th November).
Painted still-life, interiors and landscapes.
*exhib.* Berlin and Munich.

JOORS, EUGENE
Flemish School.
b. Borgerhout 1850, d. Antwerp 1910.
Pupil of C. Verlat. Painted still-life, animals and landscapes.
*coll.* Antwerp.

JOUBERT, ANDREE
French School.
19th century (*see* Vol. 3, Part I, p. 46).

JOUENNE, MDM (*née* BOSSEY)
Flemish School.
19th century (*see* Vol. 3, Part I, p. 46).

JOULIN, LUCIEN
French School.
b. Paris 1842 (20th September).
Painted still-life and genre.

JOWETT, PERCY HAGUE, C.B.E., A.R.C.A., R.W.S.
British School.
b. Halifax 1882 (1st June), d. 1955 (4th March).
Head of the Royal College of Art.
*coll.* Birmingham, flowers; Preston H.M. and A.G., flowers.

JUILLERAT, MARIE
Swiss School.
b. Rolle 1843.
Pupil of Mme Hegg de Landerset and B. Menn in Geneva.
Painted flowers and landscapes in water-colour.

JUILLIARD
French School.
19th century (*see* Vol. 3, Part I, p. 46).

JULYAN, MISS MARY E.
British School.
*op.* 1863–1866.
Dublin address.
*exhib.* R.A. (2); Suffolk Street (2), flowers.


KAERCHER, AMALIE
German School.
19th century (*see* Vol. 3, Part I, p. 46).

KAMMERER, CHRETIEN
French School.
d. 1903.
Painted flowers.
*coll.*    Mulhouse Museum, flowers, water-colour.

KANOLDT, ALEXANDER
German School.
b. Karlsruhe 1881 (29th September).
Painted still-life. Lithographer.
*coll.*    Munich.

KARLOVSZKY, BERTALAN
Hungarian School.
b. Munkacs 1858 (24th October).
Pupil of Munkacsy. Painted still-life and portraits.
*exhib.* Universal Exhibition 1900, Silver Medal.

KAYSER, ELBA
Swedish School.
b. Stockholm 1846 (15th February).
Painted flowers and landscapes.

KEANE, WILLIAM
American School.
*op.* 1880–1890.
Lived in Camden. Painted still-life.
*repr.*    *After the Hunt*, Frankenstein, 1953, pl. 134.
*lit.*    Frankenstein.

KEELHOL, A.
19th century (*see* Vol. 3, Part I, p. 46).

KEELING, MISS AGNES
British School.
*op.* 1878.
Sydenham address.
*exhib.* R.A. (1), flowers.

KEHR, KARL
German School.
b. Nuremberg 1866 (16th March), d. Neuenstein 1919 (9th December).
Painted still-life and landscapes.

KEMPF, ANNA
German School.
19th century.
Painted flowers and still-life.
*exhib.* Berlin 1888.

KENNELL, W. H.
British School.
*op.* 1872–1880.
London address.
*exhib.* Suffolk Street (5), still-life.

KENWORTHY, MISS ESTHER
British School.
*op.* 1881–1882.
Ealing address.
*exhib.* R.A. (2); Suffolk Street (1), flowers.

KERNKAMP, ANNA *or* ANNY
Flemish School.
b. Antwerp 1868 (19th June).
Pupil of Blanc-Garin and H. Rul. Painted still-life, landscapes, marines and interiors.

KETTLEWELL, JOHN WILLIAM
British School.
*op.* 1866.
Leeds address.
*exhib.* Suffolk Street (1), flowers.

KIERDORF, CELINE
French School.
19th century (*see* Vol. 3, Part I, p. 47).

KILLICK, T.
British School.
*op.* 1864.
Petworth address.
*exhib.* R.A. (2), still-life.

KIND, AUGUSTE
French School.
b. Forbach 1863 (1st April).
Pupil of P. Thomas and P. Bourgogne and Jules Lefebvre.
Painted flowers.
*coll.* Nancy Museum.
*auct.* Paris, 26.1.1945, flowers.

KING, F. H.
British School.
*op.* 1873.
London address.
*exhib.* Suffolk Street (1), still-life.

KING, MISS KATHERINE
British School.
*op.* 1869.
London address.
Painted game.

KINGSLEY, LYDIA
British School.
*op.* 1890–1895.
London address.
*exhib.* R.A. (1); Suffolk Street (1); N.W.C.S. (3), fruit
    and still-life.

KIRKPATRICK, ETHEL
British School.
*op.* 1891–1893.
Harrow address.
Painted flowers, landscapes and marines.
*exhib.* Suffolk Street (2); N.W.C.S. (2).

KIRKPATRICK, IDA
British School.
*op.* 1888–1918.
London address.
Painted flowers and marines.
*exhib.* Suffolk Street (11); N.W.C.S. (1).
*repr.* *Colour Magazine,* July 1919.

KIRKSTEIN, MAX
German School.
d. Munich 1871.
Painted still-life.

KIRSCHNER, MARIE LOUISE
Austrian School.
b. Prague 1852 (7th January), d. after 1900.
Pupil of Ad. Lier at Munich and J. Dupre and Alfred Stevens
in Paris. Went to Prague again and visited Berlin and Rome
*exhib.* Vienna Salon 1873 and Paris Universal Exhibition
    1900.

KLEIN, CATHARINA                    (*see* PLATE 26)
German School.
b. Preussisch Eylau 1861 (4th November), d. Berlin 1929 (1st
December).
Prolific painter of flowers and fruits in water-colour.
*exhib.* Berlin 1890.
*repr.* Stehli Freres of Zurich reproduced approximately
    200 different studies in facsimile colours.
    *Dekorative Vorbilder,* vols. 8, 10, 12, 13, 15 (in colour).

KLEY, HEINRICH
German School.
b. Karlsruhe 1863 (15th April).
Pupil of F. Keller in Karlsruhe and C. Smith in Munich.
Painted still-life and genre.

KLINGSOR, LEON LECLERE (TRISTAN)
French School.
b. La Chapelle-aux-Pots 1874 (8th August).
Painted still-life. Artist and poet.

KLONNE, HUGO
German School.
19th century (*see* Vol. 3, Part I, p. 47).

KNAPPING, MISS M. HELEN
British School.
*op.* 1876–1890.
Blackheath address.
*exhib.* R.A. (2); Suffolk Street (13); N.W.C.S. (3); G.G.
    (1), flowers.

KNIGHT, ALFRED E.
British School.
*op.* 1879.
Hackney address.
*exhib.* Suffolk Street (1), fruit.

KNITTEL, ANNA
Austrian School.
b. Untergibeln 1841 (28th July), d. Wallens 1915 (28th
February).
Painted flowers and portraits.

KOENIG, JEANNE
Alsatian School.
19th century.
Pupil of Mme Regnard. Working at Thann.
*exhib.* Salon 1877.

KOMLOSY, IRMA
Hungarian School.
b. Prague 1850 (30th August).
Pupil of Sturn. Working in Vienna. Painted flowers in water-colour.

KONCHALOVSKY, PYOTR. P.
Russian School.
b. 1876.
Studied in the Academie Julien, Paris, and the Academy of Fine Arts, St. Petersburg, from which he graduated in 1907. Painter of flowers and still-life. Represented in many Russian museums.

KONIG-LORINSER, MINNA
Austrian School.
b. Vienna 1849 (2nd July), d. there 1893 (1st May).
Pupil of Sturn. Painted flowers and still-life.

KRATKE, MARTHE
French School.
b. Paris 1884 (13th October).
Painted flowers.

KRESS, MICHAEL
German School.
b. Wurzburg 1845 (3rd June), d. there 1915 (1st September).
Pupil of F. Keller at Karlsruhe.
Painted still-life.

KRICHELDORF, HERMAN GOTTLIEB
German School.
b. Celle 1867 (1st October).
Painted still-life.
*exhib*. Munich 1901, Medal.

KROLL, LEON
American School.
b. New York 1884.
Pupil of J. P. Laurens in Paris. Painted still-life, portraits and landscape.

KRONER, MAGDA (*née* HELMCKE)
German School.
b. Rendsburg 1854 (24th January).
Painted still-life, genre and landscapes.
*exhib*. Berlin Academy 1884.

KRUCHEN, MEDARD
German School.
b. Dusseldorf 1877 (8th June).
Painted flowers and still-life.
*exhib*. Berlin 1909.

KUHN, WALTER
American School.
b. Brooklyn, New York, 1877 (27th October), d. 1949.
Studied in Paris, Munich, Holland and Italy. Painter and lithographer.
*coll*.   Brooklyn Museum; Des Moines Art Center; Detroit Institute of Arts; William Averell Harriman ; Kuhn Estate Collection; Museum of Modern Art, New York; Metropolitan Museum, New York; University of Nebraska, Lincoln.
*exhib*. Munich 1905, Silver Medal.

KUITHAN, ERICH
German School.
b. Bielefeld 1875 (24th October), d. Jena 1917 (30th December).
Pupil of Carl Raupp in Munich. Painted flowers and landscapes.

KUNZ, LUDWIG ADAM
Austrian School.
b. Vienna 1857 (5th June).
Painted still-life.
*coll*.   Munich.
*exhib*. Munich 1895 and 1897, Medals;  Universal Exhbition, Berlin, 1891, Hon. Mention.
*auct*.   New York, 11.12.1946, still-life.

KVAPIL, CHARLES
Flemish School.
b. Antwerp 1884 (1st November).
Painted still-life, landscapes and portraits.
*auct*.   Paris, October 1945–July 1946, flowers.

LABARRE, ANATOLE
French School.
d. 1906.
Pupil of Sillas Labarre. Working in Paris. Painted flowers and still-life.
*exhib*. Salon 1874.

LABBE, EMILE CHARLES
French School.
b. Missy-sur-Seine, d. Alger 1885 (6th July).
Painted flowers and landscapes.
*exhib*. Salon 1836–1876.

LACHENAL-CHEVALET, GEORGES
French School.
19th century.
Pupil of Pils. Painted fruit and still-life. Working in Paris.
*exhib.* Salon 1872.

LACHEVRE, HENRY
French School.
19th century.
Pupil of J. Dupre. Painted still-life. Working in Rouen.
*exhib.* Salon 1864–1866.

LA FOREST, PAULINE DE
French School.
b. Paris 1849 (5th July).
Painted flowers.
*exhib.* Salon 1869–1873.

LAGE, JULIE VON DER
German School.
b. Charlottenburg 1841 (30th January).
Pupil of H. Stilke, T. Gromland and Eschk in Berlin. Visited Italy. Painted flowers, still-life, portraits, working in water-colour and pastel.

LAHOGUE, LEON
French School.
19th century (*see* Vol. 3, Part I, p. 49).

LAING, MISS ISABELLA
British School.
*op.* 1868–1872.
Twickenham address.
*exhib.* R.A. (1); Suffolk Street (5), fruit.

LAIR, ALBERT EUGENE
French School.
19th century (*see* Vol. 3, Part I, p. 49).

LAMANIERE, GUSTAVE
French School.
19th century (*see* Vol. 3, Part I, p. 49).

LAMBERT-TRISTAN, BARONNE LOUISE DE (*née* CHANTON)
French School.
b. 1847, d. Neuilly 1899 (2nd August).
*exhib.* Salon des Artistes Francais.

LA MORNAY
French School.
19th century (*see* Vol. 3, Part I, p. 49).

LANCBQUIN, BERTHE
French School.
19th century.
Working in Paris. Painted flowers in water-colours.
*exhib.* Salon 1877.

LANDI, ARISTODEMO
Italian School.
19th century (*see* Vol. 3, Part I, p. 49).

LANE, MISS E.
British School.
*op.* 1865–1868.
London address.
*exhib.* V.E. (6), flowers.

LANE, H.
British School.
*op.* 1868–1870.
Bexley Heath address.
*exhib.* Suffolk Street (4), flowers.

LANG, FRITZ
German School.
19th century (*see* Vol. 3, Part I, p. 49).

LANG-KURZ, PAUL
German School.
b. 1877 (28th July).
Studied at Stuttgart, Dresden and Munich. Professor at School of Art at Metiers, Magdeburg and Krefeld. Painted flowers, landscapes, still-life, and designed textiles.
*coll.* Metiers; Stuttgart.
*repr.* *Dekorative Vorbilder*, Stuttgart.

LANGLOIS, M. E. W.
British School.
*op.* 1867–1872.
London address.
*exhib.* R.A. (3), still-life.

LANSDOWN, BEATRICE
British School.
*op.* 1897.
Wimbledon address.
*exhib.* R.A. (1), fruit.

LAPRADE, PIERRE                    (*see* PLATE 27)
French School.
b. Narbonne 1875 (25th July), d. Fontenay-aux-Roses 1931 (23rd December).
Painter and engraver. Painted flowers.
*coll.* Paris, Museum of Modern Art.
*repr.* Benezit, v. 9.

LARIS, F. G.
British School.
*op.* 1883.
*exhib.* Suffolk Street (1), flowers.

LARROGUE, MATHILDE
French School.
19th century.
Pupil of Lesourd de Beauregard. Working at Grenoble.
Painted flowers in water-colours.
*exhib.* Salon 1864–1868.

LARUE, MME LISE
French School.
19th century (*see* Vol. 3, Part I, p. 49).

LATHROP, MRS. IDA P.
American School.
b. New York 1859.
Painted still-life, portraits and landscapes.

LAUBER, ADOLPH
British School.
*op.* 1870–1879.
London address.
*exhib.* R.A. (4); Suffolk Street (1), flowers.

LAUREAUX, PAUL
French School.
b. Dijon 1847 (29th June), d. there 1901 (24th April).
Studied School of Art, Dijon.
Painted still-life.
*coll.* Dijon Museum, still-life.

LAURENT, ERNEST JOSEPH
French School.
b. Paris 1859 (8th June), d. there 1929.
Pupil of Herbert, Lehmann and L. O. Merson.
Chevalier of the Legion of Honour 1903.
Painted flowers, fruit, still-life, portraits and religious subjects.
*exhib.* Salon 1889, Bronze Medal.
*auct.* Paris, 24.2.1943, 17.3.1944.

LAURON, ALBERT (*or* ALBIN) FREDERIC
French School.
b. Weserling (Alsace) 1841.
Pupil of Regnier and Lyon School of Art.
Painted flowers and genre.
*coll.* Mulhouse Museum (who give Husseren as birthplace).
*exhib.* Salon 1865–1873.

LAURY, PIERRE
French School.
19th century (*see* Vol. 3, Part I, p. 50).

LAUVERNAY-PETITJEAN, JEANNE
French School.
b. Amiens 1875 (26th January).
Painted still-life and flowers.
*exhib.* Salon 1914, Silver Medal; Salon des Artistes Francais

LAUX, MARIE
German School.
b. Wiesbaden 1852 (15th August).
Pupil of B. Adam. Visited Munich and Prague.
Painted flowers and animals.
*exhib.* Paris, 1887.

LAVERTY, A. *or* G. SOREL
British School.
*op.* 1881–1886.
Ryde address.
*exhib.* Suffolk Street (6); V.E. (2), flowers.

LAWFORD, MRS. ROWLAND
British School.
*op.* 1866–1882.
London address.
*exhib.* Suffolk Street (2); V.E. (17), flowers.

LAWRENCE, MISS EDITH M.
British School.
*op.* 1884–1886.
London address.
*exhib.* Suffolk Street (9), flowers.

LAWSON, MRS. CECIL (*née* CONSTANCE B. PHILIP)
British School.
*op.* 1874–1892.
Haslemere address.
Wife of Cecil Lawson, the well-known landscape painter.
*exhib.* as Philip, 1874–1879, R.A. (10); Suffolk Street (11);
    V.E. (7);
    as Lawson, R.A. (14); Suffolk Street (3); N.W.C.S.
    (13); G.G. (12); N.G. (7); V.E. (7), flowers.

LAWSON, E.
British School.
*op.* 1877.
*exhib.* Suffolk Street (1), flowers.

LAYTON, f. w.
British School.
*op.* 1873.
London address.
*exhib.* Suffolk Street (3), game.

LEADER, mrs. b. w. (mary)
British School.
*op.* 1878–1885.
Worcester address.
Wife of Benjamin Williams Leader, r.a. (1831–1923).
*exhib.* R.A. (4), flowers.

LEATHER, walter e.
British School.
*op.* 1867–1868.
London address.
*exhib.* R.A. (1), flowers.

LEBASQUE, henri                    (*see* PLATE 27)
French School.
b. Champigne 1865 (25th September), d. Cannet 1937.
Studied School of Art, Angers and in Paris under Bonnat.
Painted flowers, landscapes and portraits.
*exhib.* Cologne, Abels Galerie, 1963, anemones.
*auct.* 25.2.1930, flowers.

LECHARLES, henri
French School.
19th century.
Painted still-life, portraits and landscapes.
*exhib.* Salon des Independants 1895.

LECHNER, odon
Hungarian School.
b. Budapest 1874 (2nd January), d. there 1910 (30th October).
Working in Bayreuth and Berlin.
*exhib.* Universal Exhibition Paris 1900.

LECLUSE, henriette anne
French School.
19th century (*see* Vol. 3, Part I, p. 51).

LECOMTE, leonidas
French School.
b. Bavay 1841.
Pupil of Pils. Painted still-life and genre.
*exhib.* Salon 1868.

LECOMTE, victor
French School.
b. Paris 1856 (4th November), d. there 1920.
Pupil of Pignot and A. Gilbert.
Painted still-life and portraits.
*exhib.* Salon 1877–1892, Hon. Mention; Universal Exhibition 1900, Bronze Medal.

LE COSTY, t.
19th century.
*auct.* Sotheby's, 9.5.1962, flowers and fruit, signed and dated 1865.

LECREUX, gaston alfred
French School.
b. Paris 1846, d. there 1914 (9th January).
Pupil of Boucher and Noel. Painted flowers and landscapes.
*exhib.* Salon 1877–1889, Hon. Mention.
*auct.* Paris, 5/7.11.1941, flowers.

LECUYER, leon louis
French School.
19th century.
Pupil of Dupuis and Baudry. Painted flowers and still-life.
Working in Paris.
*exhib.* Salon 1864–1868.

LEDBROOK, emily
British Sahool.
*op.* 1897.
Leamington address.
*exhib.* R.A. (1), flowers.

LEDOUX, eugene
French School.
b. Paris 1841 (29th March).
Painted flowers.
*exhib.* Salon 1869–1870.

LEDUC, ozias
Canadian School.
b. 1864, d. 1955.
Lived near Montreal. Painted landscapes and fruit. Had as a pupil Paul Emile Borduas.
*coll.* Mme Paul Emile Borduas.
*exhib.* Memorial exhibition 1955.
*repr.* R.S.A. Journal No. 5076, vol. CX, f. 11, p. 936.
*lit.* Dr. R. H. Hubbard, R.S.A. Journal.

LEE, RACHAEL
British School.
*op.* 1882.
Putney address.
*exhib.* Suffolk Street (1), flowers.

LE FAUCONNIER, HENRI VICTOR GABRIEL
French School.
b. Hesdin 1881, d. Paris 1946.
Painted flowers and portraits.
*auct.* Paris, 2.3.1929, flowers.

LEFEBVRE, ERNEST EUGENE
French School.
b. Havre 1850, d. there 1889 (30th November).
Pupil of G. Morin. Painted still-life.
*coll.* Rouen Museum, 3 still-life.
*exhib.* Salon 1879.

LEFEBVRE, LUCIEN
French School.
19th century.
Painted portraits and flowers.
*exhib.* Salon 1872–1873.

LEGER, FERNAND
French School.
b. Argentan 1881 (4th February), d. 1955.
Painted still-life, etc. Designed for the Swedish Ballet.
*coll.* London, Tate Gallery; New York; Paris, Art Moderne.
*auct.* Sotheby's, 6.7.1961, still-life.

LEGRAND, RENE
French School.
b. Paris 1847 (22nd March).
Pupil of Pies. Painted flowers and genre.

LEHNERT, HILDEGARD
German School.
b. Berlin 1857 (6th January).
Painted still-life, fruit and birds.
*exhib.* Berlin; Munich; Vienna.

LEICESTER, R. NEVILLE
British School.
*op.* 1883.
London address.
*exhib.* Suffolk Street (2), fruit.

LEIGHTON, MISS SARAH
British School.
*op.* 1883.
London address.
*exhib.* N.W.C.S. (1), flowers.

LELONG, LUCIEN
French School.
19th century (*see* Vol. 3, Part I, p. 51).

LELONG, RENE
French School.
19th century (*see* Vol. 3, Part I, p. 51).

LEMARCHAND, MME ANNE (*née* BENARD)
French School.
19th century (*see* Vol. 3, Part I, p. 51).

LEMAIRE, MME MADELEINE JEANNE (*née* COLL)
French School.
b. Ares 1845, d. Paris 1928 (8th April). Born Saint-Rostoline (Var) according to Mulhouse Museum.
Pupil of Mme Herbelin. Painted flowers, genre and portraits. Legion of Honour 1906.
*coll.* Mulhouse; Rheims; Toulouse.
*exhib.* Salon 1864.
*auct.* Paris, 30.1.1947, 13.6.1947, flowers.

LEMMEN, GEORGES
Flemish School.
b. Brussels 1865, d. there 1916 (5th June).
Painted still-life, interiors, portraits and landscapes. Went to Paris.

LENKEI-HOFFMANN, ILONA
Hungarian School.
b. Budapest 1869 (27th February), d. there 1914 (3rd October).
Painted still-life and portraits.

LEPELLE, MME MARIE
French School.
19th century (*see* Vol. 3, Part I, p. 51).

LERE, JULES BERTRAND
French School.
19th century.
Pupil of E. Villain. Painted still-life.
*exhib.* 1864–1865.

LEROY, CLAIRE
French School.
19th century.
Pupil of Rivoire. Painted flowers.
*exhib.* Salon 1879.

LEROY, HENRI
French School.
b. Paris 1851 (26th June).
Pupil of Oudry and Defaux. Painted still-life.
*exhib.* Salon 1875.

LESCA, MME LOUISA (*née* ESTEVENOT)
French School.
19th century (*see* Vol. 3, Part I, p. 52).

LE SIDANER, HENRI EUGENE AUGUSTIN         (*see* PLATE 28)
French School.
b. l'Ile Maurice 1862 (7th August), d. 1939.
Painted landscapes and flowers.
*exhib.* Universal Exhibition 1900, Bronze Medal; Cologne.
*auct.* London, 27.6.1947, still-life; Paris, 20.6.1947, flowers.

LESSER-URY (*see* URY)

LE SOUEF, MISS JESSIE
British School.
*op.* 1866.
Wanstead address.
*exhib.* R.A. (1), flowers.

LETSCH, LOUIS
Austrian School.
b. Wolfurt 1856 (19th August).
Painted flowers.
*coll.* Mulhouse Museum.

LEVASSEUR, LEON
French School.
19th century.
Pupil of Durand and Palisch. Working in Paris.
Painted flowers.
*exhib.* Salon 1876.

LEVIER, ADOLF
Italian School.
b. Trieste 1873 (3rd January).
Visited Paris and Vienna. Painted still-life and game.

LEVREAU, GEORGES
French School.
b. Nantes 1867 (11th July).
Pupil of Bonnat and Jules Lefebvre.
Painted still-life and interiors.
*coll.* Vannes Museum.

LEVY, FANNY
German School.
b. Konigsberg 1854 (10th August).
Pupil of A. Volkmar, Eschke and Gussord in Berlin and Duran and Henner in Paris. Painted flowers, still-life and landscapes.

LEVY, MARGUERITE
French School.
19th century.
Pupil of Mme B. Matignon. Painted fruit.
*exhib.* Salon 1880.

LEWIN, JOHN WILLIAM
British School.
19th century (*see* Vol. 3, Part I, p. 52).

LEWIS, MISS ANNE MADELAINE
British School.
*op.* 1880–1893.
Sevenoaks address.
*exhib.* R.A. (2); Suffolk Street (8); V.E. (4), flowers.

LEWIS, MISS FLORENCE E.
British School.
*op.* 1881.
London address.
*exhib.* R.A. (1), flowers.

LEY, SOPHIE
German School.
b. Bodman-am-Bodensee 1859 (20th May), d. Karlsruhe 1918 (16th August).
Studied School of Art, Stuttgart. Painted flowers and landscapes and engraved.
*exhib.* Berlin; Munich.

LHOTE, ANDRE
French School.
b. Bordeaux 1885 (5th July), d. Paris 1962 (24th January).
At 21 years of age went to Paris. Visited London 1927 and 1946. Inaugurated Anglo-French Art Circle in London 1946. Painter and critic.
*exhib.* Salon des Independants; London, Claridge Gallery 1927, Grafton Galleries 1912.
*repr.* *Escales*, by Jean Coiteau.
*auct.* Paris, 22.10.1943, flowers.
Sotheby's, 6.12.1961, flowers.

LIBERTY, MISS OCTAVIA
British School.
*op.* 1881–1882.
Nottingham address.
*exhib.* G.G. (2), flowers.

LIE, JONAS
American School.
b. New York 1880 (29th April).
Painted still-life and landscapes.

LILLIE, CHARLES T.
British School.
*op.* 1882.
London address.
*exhib.* Suffolk Street (2), flowers.

LIN, CLIFTON
British School.
*op.* 1884–1887.
*exhib.* Suffolk Street (10); G.G. (3), flowers.

LINDSAY, LADY CAROLINE BLANCHE ELIZABETH
(*née* FITZROY)
British School.
d. London 1912 (10th August).
Wife of Sir Coutts Lindsay, Bart, R.I. Painted flowers and
still-life.

LINDSAY, MRS. RUTH
British School.
*op.* 1882.
Rugeley address.
*exhib.* V.E. (1), fruit.

LINGE, JULES DOMINIQUE
French School.
b. Paris 1884 (31st May).
Painted flowers and landscapes.

LISCHKE, EMMY
German School.
b. Elberfeld 1860 (13th November), d. Munich 1919 (14th
May).
Painted still-life and landscapes.

LISTER, HON. BEATRIX
British School.
*op.* 1881.
*exhib.* G.G. (1), flowers.

LISTER, E. M.
British School.
*op.* 1882.
Leyton address.
*exhib.* Suffolk Street (1), flowers.

LISTER, GEORGE
British School.
*op.* 1881–1882.
London address.
*exhib.* Suffolk Street (2), flowers.

LLEWELYN, MISS E.
British School.
*op.* 1877.
London address.
*exhib.* R.A. (1), flowers.

LLEWELYN, J. D.
British School.
*op.* 1874.
London address.
*exhib.* Suffolk Street (1), flowers.

LLOYD, MISS M.
British School.
*op.* 1865.
London address.
*exhib.* R.A. (1); B.I. (2), flowers.

LOCKWOOD, WILTON
American School.
b. Wilton, Connecticut, 1862 (12th September), d. Brooklyn
1914 (20th March).
Pupil of John La Farge. Studied in Paris. Associate of
National Academy.
Painted genre and still-life.
*exhib.* Pittsburg 1897, Hon. Mention; Paris, Universal
Exhibition, Silver Medal, 1900.

LOESCHER, PAUL
German School.
19th century.
Working in Berlin. Painted still-life and landscapes.
*exhib.* 1887–1893.

LOGEROT, MME LOUISE (*née* LENOT)
French School.
19th century (*see* Vol. 3, Part I, p. 52).

LOHR, ANNA
German School.
b. Brunswick 1870 (10th February), d. there 1955 (May).
Painted still-life and landscapes.
*coll.* Brunswick Museum.

LOISEAU, GUSTAVE                    (*see* PLATE 28)
French School.
b. Paris 1865 (3rd October), d. 1935.
Painted landscapes and flowers.
*exhib.* Cologne, Galerie Abels.

LONGCHAMP, HENRIETTE DE
French School.
19th century (*see* Vol. 3, Part I, p. 53).

LONGMAN, ELEANOR D.
British School.
*op.* 1879–1880.
London address.
*exhib.* Suffolk Street (1), flowers.

LONGPRE, PAUL DE
French School.
b. Lyon 1855 (18th April), d. Hollywood 1911 (29th June).
Working in Paris, New York and Los Angeles.
Painted flowers.

LOUGUININE-WOLKONSKY, MARIE
French School.
b. Paris 1875 (9th May).
Studied Moscow Academy and Paris.
Painted flowers and portraits.
*auct.* Paris, 7.5.1943, flowers; 2.6.1943, flowers.

LOUPPE, LEO
French School.
b. Rheims 1869 (18th September).
Painted flowers.

LOVELL, MISS ELIZABETH M.
British School.
*op.* 1883–1884.
London address.
*exhib.* Suffolk Street (1); N.W.C.S. (1), flowers.

LOW, CHARLOTTE E.
British School.
*op.* 1880.
London address.
*exhib.* Suffolk Street (1), flowers.

LOWENTHAL, BERTHA
British School.
*op.* 1888–1919.
London address.
*exhib.* R.A. (2); Suffolk Street (2); N.W.C.S. (2); V.E. (1), flowers.

LUBEN, A.
German School.
*op.* 1875.
Berlin address.
*exhib.* R.A. (1), fish.

LUCAS, C.
British School.
*op.* 1875.
Croydon address.
*exhib.* Suffolk Street (3), flowers.

LUCAS, MRS. JEANIE
British School.
*op.* 1873.
London address.
*exhib.* Suffolk Street (2), fruit.

LUCAS, MISS MARY
British School.
*op.* 1877.
London address.
*exhib.* Suffolk Street (1), fruit.

LUCAS, MRS.
British School.
*op.* 1867.
London address.
*exhib.* B.I. (1), fruit.

LUCHIAN, STEFAN                    (*see* PLATE 29)
Roumania School.
b. Stenefanesti 1868, d. Bucharest 1916.
Studied at the Julian Academy in Paris from 1891–1893.
Painted genre, portraits and flowers.
*coll.* Bucharest, Muziel de Arta al Republicii Populare Romine, five flower paintings.

LUCKIE, A. D.
British School.
*op.* 1874.
London address.
*exhib.* Suffolk Street (1), flowers.

LUDKE, ALFRED
German School.
b. Madebourg 1874 (9th January).
Painted flowers and landscapes.

LUDOVICI, MISS MARGUERITE
(MRS. E. CATHELINE LUDOVICI)
British School.
op. 1876–1895.
London address. Painted flowers.
R.A. Catalogue 1895 gives name as 'Marguerite' and in address list as 'Madame E. Cathelin Ludovici'. Graves gives 'Miss Marguerite'.
exhib. R.A. (4); Suffolk Street (62); V.E. (10).

LUHRIG, GEORG
German School.
b. Goettingen 1868 (26th January).
Working in Dresden. Painted flowers, landscapes and portraits, and produced lithographs.

LUKER, MISS
British School.
op. 1868.
London address.
exhib. Suffolk Street (1), game.

LUNDAHL, FANNY
Finnish School.
b. Helsingfors 1853 (16th May), d. Abo 1918 (1st April).
Painted flowers on porcelain.

LUPTON, MISS EDITH
British School.
op. 1871–1893.
London address.
exhib. R.A. (2); Suffolk Street (8); V.E. (4), flowers.

LYONS, THOMAS
British School.
op. 1867.
Painted fruit.

MACFARLANE, J. L. (or JOHN R.)
British School.
op. 1863–1868.
London address.
exhib. R.A. (4); B.I. (2); Suffolk Street (5), flowers.

MACGREGOR, W. Y., R.S.A., R.S.W.
British School.
b. 1855 (14th October), d. Oban 1923.
Visited South Africa, France and Spain.
exhib. R.A. (2), 1883–1885, fruit, from Glasgow address.
R.S.A. Centenary Exhibition 1926, still-life, etc.

MACHENRI
French School.
19th century (see Vol. 3, Part I, p. 53).

MACNAB, MME MARIE (née D'ANGLARS)
French School.
b. Bonny-sur-Loire, d. Paris 1911.
Pupil of Rudder. Painted flowers, portraits and genre.
exhib. Salon 1866.

MACPHERSON, MARGARET CAMPBELL
British School.
19th century.
Pupil of G. Courtois in Paris.
Painted still-life.
exhib. Salon 1898–1914; New English Art Club 1917.

MAGAUD, ADOLPHE
French School.
19th century (see Vol. 3, Part I, p. 54).

MAHIEU, MATHILDE
French School
19th century (see Vol. 3, Part I, p. 54).

MAHLER, EMMA
Swiss School.
19th century (see Vol. 3, Part I, p. 54).

MAJOR, H. L.
British School.
op. 1868.
London address.
exhib. Suffolk Street (1), fruit.

MALBET, AURELIE LEONTINE
French School.
b. Vienna of French parents, 19th century.
Pupil of Vidal and Gleyre.
Painted still-life.
exhib. Salon 1868.

MALCOLM, MISS L.
British School.
*op.* 1870.
London address.
*exhib.* Suffolk Street (2), fruit.

MALHERBE, WILLIAM
French School.
19th century.
Pupil of Bonnard and Renoir.
Painted still-life, genre and portraits.

MALLET, HARRIETTE
British School.
*op.* 1882.
Painted flowers.

MALOISEL, EMILE FRANCOIS
French School.
19th century (*see* Vol. 3, Part I, p. 54).

MANGIAPAN, FELIX PIERRE
French School.
b. Villefranche 1884 (3rd June).
Painted still-life.

MANGUIN, HENRI CHARLES                    (*see* PLATE 30)
French School.
b. Paris 1874 (23rd March), d. St. Tropez 1943 (25th December).
Pupil of Gustave Moreau. Painted flowers, fruit and landscapes.
*coll.*    Cologne; Luxembourg.
*exhib.*  Salon des Independants 1902.
*auct.*    Paris, 21.6.1950, flowers; 10.5.1950, flowers and fruit.

MANLEY, H. B.
British School.
*op.* 1863–1868.
London address.
*exhib.* R.A. (1); Suffolk Street (2), fruit.

MANN, MABEL M.
British School.
*op.* 1885.
London address.
*exhib.* Suffolk Street (1), flowers.

MANSON, JAMES BOLIVAR
British School.
b. 1879 (26th June), d. 1945 (3rd July).
Studied Heatherley's Art School 1890, Academie Julian, Paris, under Jean-Paul Laurens. Member and Secretary

Camden Town Group 1910; London Group 1914; New England Art Club 1927; Monarro Group with the Pissarros 1920; Assistant Tate Gallery 1912; Assistant Keeper 1917–1930; Director 1930–1938. Author of books on Rembrandt, Degas, Cezanne, etc. Painted flowers, portraits and landscapes.
*coll.*    London, Tate Gallery, self portrait and two flowerpieces.
*exhib.*  R.A. from 1939; N.E.A.C. from 1915; Leicester Galleries 1923; Wildenstein's 1946, Memorial Exhibition.
*repr.*    *Modern Masterpieces of British Art*, Part I, colour plate of flowers.

MARC-BONNEMEE, LOUIS MATHILDE (*née* MARQUET)
French School.
(*See* Vol. 3, Part I, p. 55.)

MARCERON-MAILLE, MME JEANNE
French School.
b. Brive 1871 (12th February).
Pupil of A. Baschet. Painted still-life.
*exhib.* Salon des Artistes Francais 1894, Hon. Mention 1896.

MARCHAND, JEAN HIPPOLYTE
French School.
b. Paris 1883 (21st November), d. 1941; d. 1940 (Benezit).
Pupil of Merson, Bonnat and H. Martin. Visited Syria.
Painted still-life. Lithographer and engraver.
*coll.*    Brussels; Chicago; Havre; London, Tate Gallery; Nantes; Paris; Vienna.
*exhib.*  Barcelona; Berlin; Chicago; Liverpool, W.A.G. 'personal choice' No. 48; London; New York.
*auct.*    Paris, 1946, 1943.

MARCOTTE, MARIE ANTOINETTE
French School.
b. Troyes 1869 (31st May).
Studied Brussels Academy and pupil of Jules Lefebvre in Paris. Painted flowers.
*coll.*    Brussels.
*exhib.*  Berlin; Brussels; Munich; Paris and St. Petersburg.

MARCOUSSIS, LOUIS CASIMIR LADISLAS MARKOUS
French School.
b. 1883 Varsovie (14th November), d. Cusset 1941 (22nd October). Naturalised Frenchman.
Painted fruit and still-life.
*auct.*    Sotheby's, 6.12.1961; Paris, 3/4.5.1949.

MARGETTA, MARY
British School.
d. 1886.
Painted flowers.

MARGETTS, MISS ADA
British School.
*op.* 1861–1863.
Oxford address.
*exhib.* R.A. (3); B.I. (3); Suffolk Street (2), flowers.

MARIE LOUISE, ALEXANDRINE CAROLINE, COMTESSE DE
FLANDRE (*née* PRINCESS DE HOHENZOLLERN)
German School.
b. Inzigkofen 1845 (17th November), d. Brussels 1905 (17th
November).
Painted still-life, genre and landscapes.

MARITAIN, GENEVIEVE (*née* FAVRE)
French School.
19th century.
Pupil of Legrand. Working in Paris.
Painted still-life.
*exhib.* Salon 1878–1880.

MARKS, GEORGE
British School.
*op.* 1876–1900.
Penge and Guildford addresses.
Painted flowers and landscapes.
*exhib.* R.A. (46); Suffolk Street (29); N.W.C.S. (16);
V.E. (32).

MARQUET, PIERRE ALBERT
French School.
b. Bordeaux 1875 (27th March), d. Paris 1947 (13th June).
Pupil of Matisse.
Painted history, landscapes, etc., and produced lithographs.
*exhib.* Liverpool, W.A.G. 'Personal Choice', No. 50.

MARRABLE, MISS EDITH (MRS. A. FERGUSON)
British School.
*op.* 1878–1882.
London and Kircaldy addresses.
*exhib.* V.E. (4), flowers, as Miss Marrable; at G.G. (1),
portrait, as Mrs. A. Ferguson.

MARRS, MRS.
British School.
*op.* 1871.
London address.
*exhib.* Suffolk Street (2), flowers.

MARSH, MISS J.
British School.
*op.* 1875.
London address.
*exhib.* Suffolk Street (1), flowers.

MARSHALL, F.
British School.
*op.* 1876.
Croydon address.
*exhib.* Suffolk Street (1), still-life.

MARSHALL, JOHN
British School.
*op.* 1881–1893.
Croydon address.
*exhib.* R.A. (10); N.G. (1); V.E. (10), fruit.
A 'John Marshall' exhibited 'Sporting' 1840–1879. R.A. (8);
Suffolk Street (17).

MARSHALL, J. FITZ
British School.
*op.* 1876–1893.
Croydon address.
*exhib.* R.A. (16); Suffolk Street (13); G.G. (6); N.G. (17);
V.E. (20), still-life.
Could be the same as F. Marshall above.

MARSHALL, MRS. PHILIPPA
British School.
*op.* 1868–1880.
Exeter address.
*exhib.* Suffolk Street (2); V.E. (3), flowers.

MARSHALL, R.
British School.
*op.* 1877.
Oxford address.
*exhib.* Suffolk Street (1), game.

MARSHALL, MRS. ROSE
British School.
*op.* 1879–1890.
Leeds address.
*exhib.* R.A. (10); Suffolk Street (16); G.G. (2); V.E. (6);
flowers.

MARTIN, DOROTHY
British School.
b. 1882, d. 1949.
Art Mistress at Roedean School 1916–1946. Made 450
studies of wild flowers, plants, etc., at Keswick during War.
*coll.* Miss N. H. Horobin.
*exhib.* National Book League, Flower Books, 1950.
*lit.* Blunt.

MARTIN, EMILE ELISABETH PAULINE
French School.
19th century.
Pupil of Koller and Trebuchet in Paris.
Painted flowers in water-colour.
*exhib.* Salon 1878.

MARTIN, JACQUES
French School.
b. Villeurbanne 1844, d. Lyon 1919 (13th November).
Painted flowers, still-life and genre.
*coll.*　　Digne; Narbonne; Luxembourg; Paris.

MARTIN, SILAS
American School.
b. Columbus 1841 (20th November), d. there 1906 (2nd September).
Professor of Art at Ohio State University. Had as pupil George Bellows. Painted landscapes, portraits and still-life.
*lit.*　　Frankenstein, *After the Hunt*, 1953.

MARTINE, ADRIANE MARIE TOULON
French School.
19th century (*see* Vol. 3, Part I, p. 55).

MARTINEAU, MRS. BASIL (CLARA)
British School.
*op.* 1873–1890.
London address.
*exhib.* R.A. (3); Suffolk Street (4); V.E. (3), flowers.

MARSTON, MISS MABEL G.
British School.
*op.* 1885–1893.
London address.
*exhib.* R.A. (4); Suffolk Street (10); G.G. (1); V.E. (4), flowers.

MASELLI, PIETRO
Italian School.
b. Figgino 1848, d. there 1892.
Painted still-life and genre.
*exhib.* Turin and Milan.

MASHKOV, ILYA IVANOVICH
Russian School.
b. 1881, d. 1944.
*coll.* Tretyakov Gallery.
*exhib.* R.A. (Russian Art) 1959, 'Moscow loaves'.

MASON, BLOSSOM
British School.
*op.* 1881–1885.
London address.
*exhib.* Suffolk Street (2), flowers.

MASON, MRS. EVELYN
British School.
*op.* 1884–1887.
London address.
*exhib.* R.A. (2); Suffolk Street (2), flowers.

MASON, MAUD M.
American School.
b. Russellville, Kentucky, 1867 (18th March).
Pupil of Chase, Dow and Snell in New York and Brangwyn in London. Member of the Federation of American Arts.
Painted flowers.

MASZ, HELENE
German School.
b. Schonlanke 1871 (1st April).
Pupil of Flickel and Dettmann.
Painted flowers and landscapes.

MATHIEU, ALEXIS
French School.
19th century.
Pupil of Billon. Working in Paris.
Painted still-life.

MATHIEU, PAUL
Flemish School.
b. St. Josse-ten-Noode, Brussels, 1872.
Pupil of Marie Josephine Meyer. Teacher in Brussels Academy. Painted still-life, interiors and landscapes.

MATISSE, CAMILLE
French School.
19th century.
*auct.* Sotheby's, 25.10.1961, flowers.

MATISSE, HENRI　　　　　　　　　　　(*see* PLATE 30)
French School.
b. Le Cateau 1869 (31st December), d. 1954.
*coll.*　　Glasgow; Leningrad, Hermitage; Manchester, Whitworth; Munich; Paris, Modern Art.
*repr.*　　*Bouquet*, pl. 27; Moscow Museum of Modern Art Portfolio 1938.
*auct.*　　Paris, 1947, flowers; 1946, still-life.

MAUCHERAT DE LONGPRE, RAOUL VICTOR MAURICE
French School.
19th century.
Painted flowers.
*exhib.* Salon 1876.

MAUDUIT, LEONIE
French School.
19th century (*see* Vol. 3, Part I, p. 56).

MAUFRA, MAXIME EMILE LOUIS                    (*see* PLATE 31)
French School.
b. Nantes 1861 (17th May), d. Ponce 1918 (23rd May).
Painted flowers, landscapes and marines.
*exhib.* Cologne, Abels Galerie, 1963, vase of flowers.
*auct.* Sotheby's, 5/6.7.1961, flowers.

MAURER, ALFRED HENRY
American School.
b. New York 1868 (21st April).
Studied National Academy, New York, and Paris.
Painted still-life and landscapes.
*exhib.* Munich 1905, Medal.
*auct.* Paris, 12.12.1949, flowers.

MAUS, EUGENE
Flemish School.
b. Brussels 1847, d. there 1881 (27th May).
Pupil of P. F. Van Os and W. Verschur. At The Hague 1870.
Painted still-life and landscapes.
*coll.* The Hague; Rotterdam.

MAWSON, MISS ELIZABETH CAMERON
British School.
*op.* 1877–1892.
Gateshead address.
*exhib.* R.A. (2); Suffolk Street (4); N.W.C.S. (7); V.E.
(2), flowers.

MAX-EHRLER, LUISE
Italian School.
b. Florence 1850 (10th August).
Visited Prague and Munich.
Painted still-life, genre and history.
*exhib.* Vienna; Munich; Berlin.

MAY, BRUNO
German School.
b. Berlin 1880 (3rd September).
Pupil of Hackl and Diez at Munich and Holzelat at Stuttgart.
Painted still-life and figures. Married Valerie Hulsmann, a
painter.

MAY-HULSMANN, VALERIE
German School.
b. Rogatz 1883 (7th May).
Pupil of Knirr, Groeber Weinhold. Married the painter
Bruno May.
Painted still-life and portraits.

MAZZETTI, EMO
Italian School.
b. Treviso 1870 (24th October), d. Venice 1955.
Studied Venice Academy.
Painted still-life and landscapes.
*coll.* Venice, Gallery of Modern Art; Udine.

MAZZONI, A.
British School.
*op.* 1875.
London address.
*exhib.* V.E. (1), flowers.

McGREGOR, MISS SARAH
British School.
*op.* 1869–1885.
London address.
*exhib.* Suffolk Street (7), flowers.

McLACHLAN, MISS H.
British School.
*op.* 1881–1882.
London address.
*exhib.* Suffolk Street (2), still-life.

McWHIRTER, MISS AGNES ELIZA
British School.
*op.* 1867–1879.
Edinburgh address.
*exhib.* R.A. (3); V.E. (19), still-life.

MEDLAND, J. G.
British School.
*op.* 1875–1877.
London address.
*exhib.* Suffolk Street (6), flowers.

MELLERY, XAVIER
Flemish School.
b. Brussels 1845 (9th August), d. there 1921 (4th February).
Painted still-life, genre and landscapes.
*auct.* Brussels, 14.5.1937, fruit.

MELLOR, GEORGE
British School.
19th century (*see* Vol. 3, Part I, p. 56).

MENASSADE, DONA EMILIA
Spanish School.
19th century (*see* Vol. 3, Part I, p. 56).

MERRE, JOHANNA H. (*née* WIRTHMILLER)
German School.
b. Munich 1867 (7th December).
Pupil of J. Seyler. Married the painter Franz Hienl Merre.
Painted flowers and landscapes.
*coll.* Munich.

MERTEN, ELISE (*née* FISCHER)
German School.
b. 1847 in Moscow.
Pupil of Th. Grosse at Dresden and K. Gussow in Berlin.
Painted flowers, still-life and portraits.

MERTIN *or* MARTIN, F. CHR.
German School.
19th century (*see* Vol. 3, Part I, p. 57).

MESDAG-VAN CALGAR, GESINE
Dutch School.
b. Hoogezand 1851, d. The Hague 1936.
Was the wife of Taco Mesdag (1829-1902). Pupil of Gabriel.
*coll.* The Hague, Mesdag Museum, pansies.

MESTROVIC, MATHILDE VON
Austrian School.
b. Gospie 1843 (14th March).
Pupil of Jos. Schuster in Vienna. Painted still-life.

MEUCCI, M.
19th century (*see* Vol. 3, Part I, p. 57).

MEULEN, EDMOND VAN DER
Flemish School.
b. Brussels 1841 (14th June), d. there 1905.
Pupil of Duyck. Painted still-life and animals.
*coll.* Bruges; Brussels; The Hague; Louvain; Munich;
Prague; Tournai, mostly animals.

MEURER, CHARLES
American School.
b. Germany of American parents 1865.
Grew up in Clarksville, Tennessee. Studied with Duveneck
in Cincinnati and in Paris and Lyon. Painted landscapes,
garden scenes, portraits, flowers and still-life.
*repr.* *After the Hunt*, Frankenstein, 1953, pls. 74 and 128.
*lit.* Frankenstein.

MEUTTER, LEON DE (*see* BRUNIN)

MEYER, MISS CONSTANCE
British School.
*op.* 1866-1882.
London address.
*exhib.* V.E. (23), flowers.

MEYER, LINA
Swiss School.
b. Mannedorf 1842 (11th December).
Pupil of J. Stadler. Painted flowers and landscapes.

MEYER, MISS MARGARET
British School.
*op.* 1872-1886.
London address.
*exhib.* R.A. (1); Suffolk Street (2); V.E. (5), flowers.

MEYER, MARY H.
British School.
*op.* 1868-1885.
London address.
*exhib.* V.E. (16), flowers.

MICHAELIS, ALICE (*née* PRIESTER)
German School.
b. Berlin 1875 (5th April).
Pupil of Uth, Corinth and Baluschek. Painted still-life,
landscapes and interiors.

MICHAILOFF, M.
Russian School.
19th century (*see* Vol. 3, Part I, p. 57).

MICHAUX, JOHN
Flemish School.
b. Antwerp 1876.
Pupil of F. Hens. Painted still-life, figures and landscapes.

MICHEL, CHARLES
Flemish School.
b. Liege 1874 (26th February).
Pupil of Benjamin Constant and Gerome. Painted still-life,
portraits, figures and landscapes.

MICHEL, MARIUS
French School.
19th century.
Pupil of Carolus Duvan. Painted still-life, genre an landscapes.
*exhib.* Salon 1879, Hon. Mention 1885; Universal Exhibition 1889, Silver Medal.

MIESLER, ERNST
German School.
b. Dusseldorf 1879 (30th September).
Pupil of G. Hacker. Painted flowers, landscapes and marines.

MIGNON, JULES ALBERT
French School.
b. Angers 1875 (3rd May).
Pupil of Gustave Moreau. Painter and lithographer.
*exhib.* Salon des Artistes Francais 1922, Silver Medal.
*auct.* Paris, 1946, fruit.

MIGNON, LUCIEN
French School.
b. Chateau-Gontier 1865 (13th September), d. Paris 1944 (13th March).
Pupil of Gerome. Painted still-life.
*coll.* Paris; Luxembourg.
*auct.* Paris, 1.6.1950; Sotheby's, 5/6.7.1961.

MIKESCH, FRITZE
Austrian School.
b. Vienna 1853 (23rd February), d. Hielzing 1891 (12th March).
Painted still-life.
*coll.* Prague.

MILES, ANNIE STEWART
British School.
*op.* 1888–1894.
London address.
*exhib.* R.A. (4); Suffolk Street (3), flowers.

MILLER, MISS HENRIETTA
British School.
*op.* 1884–1889.
London address.
*exhib.* R.A. (2); Suffolk Street (5); N.W.C.S. (2); G.G. (1), flowers.

MILLER, JOHN DOUGLAS
British School.
*op.* 1869–1877.
London address.
*exhib.* R.A. (3); Suffolk Street (8), fruit.

MILLER, KONRAD VON
German School.
b. Munich 1878 (26th February).
Studied in Munich, Dresden and Dusseldorf.
Painted flowers and portraits.

MILLER, MRS. SOPHIA
British School.
*op.* 1892–1894.
London address.
*exhib.* R.A. (2), N.W.C.S. (2), flowers.

MILLET, FRANCOIS
French School.
b. 1851, d. Barbizon 1917, aged 66.
Son and pupil of Jean Francois Millet.
Painted still-life, portraits and genre.
*exhib.* Salon 1870.

MILNE, H. D.
British School.
*op.* 1875–1881.
Crayford address.
*exhib.* Suffolk Street (4), still-life.

MINCHIN, HAMILTON
British School.
*op.* 1882.
London address.
*exhib.* Suffolk Street (1), still-life.

MINOT, EDWIN *or* EDWARD
British School.
*op.* 1864–1875.
London address.
*exhib.* B.I. (3); Suffolk Street (5); V.E. (2), still-life.

MITCHELL, MRS. JAMES B.
British School.
*op.* 1879–1887.
London address. Wife of James B. Mitchell, a portrait painter.
*exhib.* R.A. (2); G.G. (7); V.E. (4), flowers.

MITCHELL, MISS M. D.
British School.
*op.* 1876–1882.
London address.
*exhib.* Suffolk Street (2); G.G. (2); V.E. (2), flowers.

MITTEY, JOSEPH
French School.
b. Vix 1853 (1st April).
Pupil of Jeannin, Llequien and Hugot. Painted flowers and figures.
*exhib.* Salon 1877.

MOBERLEY, ALFRED
British School.
*op.* 1882.
Hythe address.
Painted flowers.

MOLINEUX, E.
British School.
*op.* 1874.
London address.
*exhib.* Suffolk Street (1), flowers.

MOLL, CARL
Austrian School.
b. Vienna 1861 (23rd April).
Studied Vienna Academy. Painted still-life and landscape.
*exhib.* Salon; Universal Exhibition 1900, Silver Medal.

MOLLBACK, CHRISTIAN JUEL FRIJS
Danish School.
b. Copenhagen 1853 (27th November), d. 1921 (6th July).
Painted flowers.

MOLS, ROBERT CHARLES GUSTAVE LAURENS    (*see* PLATE 31)
Flemish School.
b. Antwerp 1848 (22nd June), d. there 1903 (8th August).
Son of Florent Mols. Studied Antwerp Academy and in Paris under J. F. Millet and J. Dupre. Worked at Fontainebleau. Painted still-life, marines and landscapes.
*coll.* Antwerp, flowers.
*exhib.* R.A. 1879.
*auct.* Paris, 25.3.1942, flowers.

MONBLOND, CHARLES
French School.
19th century.
Pupil of M. Ch. Polisch.
Painted flowers and still-life.
*exhib.* Salon 1866–1870.

MONLUCON *or* MOLUCON, ALPHONSE
French School.
*op.* 1882–1903.
Painted flowers and engraved.

MONNICKENDAM, MARTIN
Dutch School.
b. Amsterdam 1874 (25th February).
Studied Amsterdam Academy. Went to Paris 1895 and returned to Amsterdam.
*coll.* Amsterdam, Rijks. Mus., fruit-seller.

MONNOT, MAURICE LOUIS
French School.
b. Paris 1869 (22nd October).
Pupil of Joseph Bail. Painted still-life, interiors and rustic.
*exhib.* Salon des Artistes Francais 1906; Salon des Independants 1913.
*auct.* Paris, 7.5.1951, still-life.

MONTAGUE, ALICE L.
British School.
*op.* 1869.
Dover address.
Painted flowers.

MONTAGUE, MRS.
British School.
*op.* 1871.
London address.
Painted still-life.

MONTALD, CONSTANT
Flemish School.
b. Ghent 1862 (4th December).
Pupil of T. Canneel. In Italy 1886. Later Professor at Brussels Academy. Painted still-life, landscapes and portraits.

MONTEVERDE, LUIGI                    (*see* PLATE 31)
Swiss School.
b. Lugano 1843 (10th September), 1841 (Berner Kunstmuseum), d. 1923.
Studied Milan Academy. Painted still-life, portraits and genre.
*coll.* Bale; Berne; Lausanne; Prague.
*exhib.* Universal Exhibition 1878, Bronze Medal.

MOODY, MISS MARY
British School.
*op.* 1877–1878.
London address.
*exhib.* Suffolk Street (2), fruit.

MOONEY, JOHN
American School.
b. New York State 1843, d. Richmond 1918.
Served in the Confederate Army during Civil War. Worked in Washington and Richmond. Painted still-life.
*lit.* Frankenstein, *After the Hunt*, 1953.

MOOR, PIETER CORNELIS DE
Dutch School.
b. Rotterdam 1866 (28th May).
Studied Antwerp and Amsterdam. Painted flowers, figures, landscapes, and engraved.

MOORE, MISS AGNES E. C.
British School.
op. 1881–1885.
London address.
exhib. N.W.C.S. (1); G.G. (1); V.E. (4), flowers.

MOORE, ALBERT JOSEPH, A.R.W.S.
British School.
b. York 1841, d. London 1893.
Fourteenth child of William Moore, a portrait painter.
Brother of Henry and J. C. Moore. Studied School of
Design, York, and R.A. Schools, 1855. Visited Rome and
settled in London. In addition to painting figures designed
for stained glass, wallpapers, tiles, etc.
coll.  London, Tate Gallery.
exhib. R.A. (42); Suffolk Street (2); O.W.C.S. (16);
   N.W.C.S. (1); G.G. (31); N.G. (2).
auct.  London, 23.4.1937, fruit.

MORAND, E. E.
French School.
op. 1881.
Paris address.
exhib. G.G. (3), flowers.

MORBY, KATE
British School.
op. 1871.
London address.
Painted flowers.

MORGAN, ALFRED
British School.
op. 1862–1902.
London address. Painted flowers, animals, genre and landscapes.
coll.  London, Victoria and Albert Museum.
exhib. R.A. (22); B.I. (7); Suffolk Street (35); G.G. (22);
   V.E. (6).

MORGAN, MRS. MARY VERNON
British School.
op. 1880–1895.
Birmingham address.
exhib. R.A. (6); Suffolk Street (16); V.E. (3), flowers.

MORGAND, MME CECILE
French School.
19th century.
exhib. Society des Artistes Francais 1901 and 1902, Hon.
   Mention.

MORITZ, C.
German School.
19th century (see Vol. 3, Part I, p. 59).

MORREN, GEORGES
Flemish School.
b. Eeckeren 1868 (28th July), d. Brussels 1941.
Pupil of E. Claus and of A. Roll and Carriere in Paris.
Painted still-life, landscapes and figures.

MORRIS, J.
British School.
op. 1873–1877.
London address.
exhib. Suffolk Street (2), fruit.

MORRIS, R.
British School.
op. 1863.
London address.
exhib. Suffolk Street (1), game.

MORTELMANS, FRANS                    (see PLATE 32)
Flemish School.
b. Antwerp 1865, d. there 1936.
Painted flowers, fruit and still-life.
coll.   Antwerp; Courtrai.

MORTIER, ROBERT
French School.
b. Nice 1878 (20th July), d. Paris 1940.
Pupil of T. Robert Fleury and Carriere.
Painted still-life, landscapes and portraits.

MOUSSET, PIERRE JOSEPH
French School.
b. Paris, d. there 1894 (30th May).
Pupil of Villar.
Painted flowers and genre.
exhib. Salon 1880.

MULLER, ANTON
Austrian School.
b. Vienna 1853 (29th June), d. there 1897 (19th October).
Pupil of Eisenmenger at Vienna Academy.
Painted still-life and genre.
exhib. Berlin 1886, Silver Medal.

MULLER-HEYDENREICH, MARTHA
German School.
19th century.
In Dresden 1882. Painted flowers and still-life.

MULLER-WISCHIN, ANTON
German School.
b. Weissenhorn 1865 (30th August).
Painted flowers, still-life and portraits.
*coll.*    Munich, New Pinakothek.
*repr.*    Catalogue New Pinakothek, Munich.


MULREADY, AUGUSTUS E.
British School.
*op.* 1863–1886. d. 1886.
London address.
*exhib.* R.A. (12). Graves says 'Domestic'.
*auct.*   Sotheby's, 7.6.1961, flowers.


MUNCH, CONSTANCE (COUNTESS HOHENWART)
MUNCH-BELLINGHAUSEN (Benezit)
German School.
b. Frankfurt 1859.
*coll.*    Strasbourg.
*exhib.* R.A. (1), flowers, 1894, as Countess Hohenwart from
         Trieste address.


MUNKÁCSY, MICHAEL (MIHÁLY) LEIB          (*see* PLATE 32)
(MICHEL LIEB—Benezit)
Hungarian School.
b. Munkacs 1844 (20th February), d. Endenich (Bonn) 1909
(1st May).
Studied in Vienna under Carl Rahl, later in Munich and
finally in Paris, where he was greatly influenced by Theodule
Ribot.
Painted still-life, flowers, portraits, history and genre.
*coll.*    Moscow, flowers.
*exhib.* Cologne, Galerie Abels.


MUNN, GEORGE FREDERIK
American School (British—Benezit).
b. Utica 1852, d. New York 1907 (10th February).
Member of Society of British Artists.
Painted flowers, figures and landscapes, and was a sculptor.
*exhib.* R.A. (13); Suffolk Street (19); G.G. (5); V.E. (12).
         (Graves says 'figures'.)


MUNTHE-NORSTEDT, ANNA KATARINA FREDRIKA
                                      (*see* PLATE 33)
Swedish School.
b. Doderhult 1845 (28th July), d. 1936.
Wife of Reinhold Norstedt. Painted still-life, figures,
interiors, etc.
*coll.*    Stockholm, National Museum; Goteborg.


MURATON, MADAME
French School.
*op.* 1873.
Paris address.
*exhib.* R.A. (1), flowers.


MURET, ALBERT
Swiss School.
b. Morges 1874 (1st June).
Pupil of B. Constant, J. P. Laurens and Merson.
Painted still-life, figures and landscapes.
*coll.*    Chaux-de-Fonds; Vevey.


MURPHY, HERMANN DUDLEY
American School.
b. Marlborough, Mass., 1867 (25th August), d. Lexington,
Mass., 1945.
Studied Boston and Paris.
Painted still-life, portraits and landscapes.
*coll.*    Buffalo; Dallas; Nashville.


MUSSILL
Austrian School.
19th century (*see* Vol. 3, Part I, p. 59).


NAFTEL, MISS MAUD, A.R.W.S.
British School.
b. 1856, d. London 1890.
Daughter of Paul Jacob Naftel. Studied Slade School and
under Carolus Duran in Paris. Painted flowers and landscapes.
*exhib.* R.A. (9); O.W.C.S. (16); N.W.C.S. (5); G.G. (11);
         N.G. (2); V.E. (10).


NAGY, IGNAC
Hungarian School.
b. Szatmar-Nemeti 1866
Studied Budapest. Painted still-life.


NANCY, ANATOLE
French School.
19th century (*see* Vol. 3, Part I, p. 59).


NARBONA BELTRAN, FRANCISCO
Spanish School.
b. Seville 1860 (14th April), d. there 1926 (24th March).
Pupil of E. Cano and J. Villegas. Painted flowers and figures.
*coll.*    Seville Museum.


NARDI, HEDWIG AUGUSTA PAULINA
German School.
b. Stettin 1885.
Painted still-life.
*coll.*    Bucharest Museum.

NAVEZ, ARTHUR
Flemish School.
b. Antwerp 1881, d. Brussels 1931.
Studied Antwerp and in Paris under J. L. Gerome.
Painted still-life.

NEES VON ESENBECK, ELISE
German School.
b. Schloss-Grabow 1842 (3rd February), d. Jannowitz 1921
(11 November).
Pupil of Mme Anna Storch at Breslau, Margareth Hormuth-
kallmorgen at Karlsruhe and Margueretha Roosenboom in
Holland. Visited Italy and Tyrol.
Painted flowers.
*coll.* Breslau Museum.

NEGRO, TERESA
Italian School.
19th century (*see* Vol. 3, Part I, p. 59).

NEILSON, E.
British School.
*op.* 1883.
London address.
*exhib.* Suffolk Street (1), still-life.

NEPPEL, KARL
German School.
b. Munich 1883 (3rd November).
Studied Munich Academy. Painted still-life.

NESTE, ALFRED VAN JOSEPH AUGUSTE DE
Flemish School.
b. Bruges 1874 (4th May).
Studied Bruges and Antwerp Academies. Teacher at
Antwerp Academy. Visited Venice.
Painted still-life, figures and landscapes.

NEWMAN, MISS E.
British School.
*op.* 1862–1863.
London address.
*exhib.* R.A. (2), fruit.

NEWMAN, E. E.
British School.
*op.* 1871.
London address.
Painted flowers.

NEWNHAM, MISS MARGARET
British School.
*op.* 1864–1865.
London address.
*exhib.* R.A. (1); B.I. (1), fruit.

NICHOLSON, MISS ALICE M.
British School.
*op.* 1884–1888.
Newcastle address.
*exhib.* R.A. (2); Suffolk Street (1); N.W.C.S. (1), still-life.

NICHOLSON, SIR WILLIAM                    (*see* PLATE 33)
British School.
b. Newark-on-Trent 1872, d. 1949.
With his brother-in-law, James Pryde known as the Beggar-
staff Brothers, famous poster designers and for woodcuts of
Victorian characters. Painted still-life and portraits. Studied
under Bouguereau in Paris.
*coll.* Birmingham; Cambridge, Fitzwilliam; Glasgow;
London, Tate Gallery; Nottingham.
*exhib.* R.A., etc.
*auct.* Sotheby's 14.12.1960, flowers etc.; 28.3.1962, fruit—
chalks.

NICZKY, EDUARD
German School.
b. Cassel 1850 (17th July).
Pupil of Ramberg at Munich. Painted flowers and genre.

NIEKERK, MAURITS
Dutch School.
b. Amsterdam 1871 (11th September).
Visited Brussels, Paris and Rotterdam. Painted still-life and
engraved.

NIGHTINGALE, LEONARD CHARLES
British School.
*op.* 1877–1895.
London address.
Painted domestic and flowers.
*exhib.* R.A. (10); Suffolk Street (8); N.W.C.S. (1); V.E. (4).

NILL, MARTHA
German School.
b. Stuttgart 1859 (3rd August).
Pupil of G. Igler and J. Kerschen Steiner. Painted still-life
and landscapes.

NISBETT, MISS ETHEL C.
British School.
*op.* 1884–1897.
London address.
*exhib.* R.A. (4); Suffolk Street (5); N.W.C.S. (6), flowers.

NISS, THORVALD SIMEON
Danish School.
b. Assens 1842 (7th May). d. Hillerod 1905 (11th May).
Pupil of O. Bache and Copenhagen Academy.
Painted flowers, marines and landscapes.
*exhib.* Munich; Hamburg; Berlin; Vienna; Paris 1882, Gold
Medal; Universal Exhibition 1889 and 1900, Silver
Medal.

NISSL, *or* NIZI, RUDOLF
Austrian School.
b. Fugen 1870 (13th April).
Painted still-life and genre.
*coll.* Munich.
*exhib.* Universal Exhibition 1900, Hon. Mention.

NIXON, J. F.
British School.
*op.* 1864.
Tonbridge address.
*exhib.* Suffolk Street (1), fruit.

NIXON, MRS.
British School.
*op.* 1865.
Tonbridge address.
*exhib.* R.A. (2), fruit.

NOACK, HELENE
German School.
*op.* 1864-1895.
Working at Dresden, teacher of design. Painted flowers and
fruit.

NOAKES, CHARLES G.
British School.
*op.* 1885-1888.
Sydenham address.
*exhib.* N.W.C.S. (2), flowers.

NODE-SAINT-ANGE, CHARLES
French School.
19th century (*see* Vol. 3, Part I, p. 61).

NOLDE, EMIL HANSEN
German School.
b. Tonden 1867 (7th August), d. 1956 (15th April).
Painted flowers and still-life, engraved and was a sculptor.
*coll.* Essen; Halle; Mannheim; Nolde-Museum, Seebull.
*exhib.* Cologne.

NORBYE, ANNA
Danish School.
b. Copenhagen 1851 (22nd November).
Painted flowers.

NORMAN, MRS. CAROLINE H. (THE HON. MRS. NORMAN
(CAROLINE) GROSVENOR)
British School.
*op.* 1874-1891.
Devonport address as for Mrs. Caroline Norman. London
address for The Hon. Mrs. Norman Grosvenor.
*exhib.* as Mrs. Norman: R.A. (9); Suffolk Street (2);
N.W.C.S. (8), flowers; as Hon. Mrs. Grosvenor
1889-1893: R.A. (5); N.G. (10); V.E. (10), mini-
atures.

NOTHER, ADOLF
German School.
b. Dresden 1855 (9th December).
Painted flowers and landscapes.
*coll.* Bautzen; Dresden.

NOWLAN, MISS CARLOTTA
British School.
*op.* 1885-1891.
London address.
*exhib.* R.A. (3); N.W.C.S. (2), flowers.

NOY, MRS. R.
British School.
*op.* 1871.
Norwich address.
*exhib.* Suffolk Street (1), fruit.

NOYES, H. J.
British School.
*op.* 1873-1874.
Shrewsbury address.
*exhib.* R.A. (1); Suffolk Street (2), flowers.

NUNN, J. W.
British School.
*op.* 1865.
London address.
*exhib.* Suffolk Street (1), fruit.

NUTI, GUILIA-SIGNORA MARINI
Italian School.
19th century (*see* Vol. 3, Part I, p. 61).

NUTTER, MISS KATHERINE M.
British School.
*op.* 1883–1890.
London address.
*exhib.* R.A. (5); Suffolk Street (1); N.W.C.S. (2), flowers.

NYL-FROSCH, MARIE
German School.
b. Munich 1857 (12th January), d. there 1914 (9th November).
Painted flowers.
*coll.* Bucharest.

OAKES, MARIO
American School.
b. New York 1847.
Painted still-life, portraits and genre.

OBBARD, MISS C.
British School.
*op.* 1867.
Blackheath address.
*exhib.* R.A. (1), fruit.

OBERTEUFFER, HENRIETTE AMIARD
American School.
b. Havre 1878.
Wife of George Oberteuffer, American painter. Pupil of Laurens and B. Constant. Painted still-life and landscapes.
*exhib.* Salon.

O'CONNOR, CARLOS
Spanish School.
b. Almeira, d. Paris 1879 (14th January).
Painted still-life and landscapes.

O'CONNOR, RODERICK
British School.
19th century.
Painted still-life, fruit, and flowers.
*exhib.* Salon des Independants 1890.
*auct.* Sotheby's 10.4.1962.

OESTERLEY, MARIA *or* MARIE
German School.
b. Gottingen 1842 (1st October), d. Hanover 1916.
Daughter and pupil of K. W. F. Oesterley.
Painted flowers and landscapes.

OFFORD, GERTRUDE E.
British School.
*op.* 1895–1900.
Norwich address.
*exhib.* R.A. (2), flowers.

OGDEN, MISS JANE
British School.
*op.* 1879–1882.
London address.
*exhib.* R.A. (5); Suffolk Street (2), flowers.

O'KEEFFE, *or* O'KEEFE, GEORGIA
American School.
b. 1887.
Pupil of Chase, Vanderpoel and Dow.
Painted still-life.
*coll.* Brooklyn, Cleveland.
*exhib.* Philadelphia Museum, *World of Flowers*, 1963.

OLAVIDE, RAMON
Spanish School.
d. Madrid 1877.
Painted flowers and still-life.

OLBRICHT, ALEXANDER
German School.
b. Breslau 1876 (5th June).
Pupil of C. E. Morgenstern and Th. Hagen. Professor at Weimar. Painted flowers and landscapes and engraved.

OLEFFE, AUGUSTE
Flemish School.
b. St. Josse-ten-Noode (Brussels) 1867 (17th April), d. Uccle 1931 (Wilenski), d. Auderghem 1932 (Benezit).
Worked at Nieuwpoort. Painted still-life, portraits, genre and landscapes.
*coll.* Brussels.

OLIVER, MRS. C. N.
British School.
*op.* 1866—1868
London address.
*exhib.* Suffolk Street (3), flowers.

OLIVER, MISS
British School.
*op.* 1867.
Watford address.
*exhib.* Suffolk Street (3), still-life.

OLIVIERO, CAMMILLA
Italian School.
b. Turin 1844 (22nd December).
Painted flowers and still-life.


OPPENOORTH, WILLEM JOHANNES
Dutch School.
b. Amsterdam 1847 (2nd October), d. Utrecht 1905 (19th May).
Studied Amsterdam Academy. Painted still-life and landscape.


OPPERMANN, JOHANNA LOUISE, MME BERG
Danish School.
b. Frederikborg 1860 (28th February).
Painted flowers and on porcelain.


OPSOMER, ISIDORE
Flemish School.
b. Lierre 1878 (19th February).
Studied Antwerp. In London and Holland during 1914-18 War. Visited Italy and Spain. Painted still-life, religious, marine, landscapes and portraits.
coll.    Ghent; Paris, Mus. d'Art Moderne.


ORTGIES, VIDA
Swiss School.
b. Zurich 1858 (23rd May).
Pupil of J. Stadler, Lehmann and Gattiker.
Painted landscapes, etc.


OSIECK, BETSY
Dutch School.
b. Amsterdam 1880 (29th December).
Pupil of L. Ansingh, Dake and V. Derkinderen. Painted still-life and portraits.


OTTMANN, HENRI
French School.
b. Ancenis 1877 (10th April), d. Vernon 1927 (1st June).
Painted still-life, landscapes and genre.


OVERBURY, MISS L.
British School.
op. 1874.
London address.
exhib. Suffolk Street (1), flowers.


OYENS, DAVID
Flemish School.
b. Amsterdam 1842 (29th July), d. Brussels 1902.
Pupil of Portaels. Painted still-life, interiors, portraits and genre.
coll.    Amsterdam.
exhib. Ghent 1880, Medal; Universal Exhibition, Paris 1889; Munich.


PAERELS, WILLEM
Flemish School.
b. Delft 1878 (15th July).
Studied Brussels and Paris. Painted still-life and figures.

PALMER, HARRY SUTTON, R.B.A.
British School.
b. Plymouth, d. 1933.
Painted landscapes and still-life.
exhib. R.A. (6); Suffolk Street (11); V.E. (16), 'Landscapes' 1870-1893.

PALMER, JOHN
British School.
op. 1877-1887.
London address.
exhib. R.A. (1); Suffolk Street (1), still-life.

PALMER, MRS. W. J.
British School.
op. 1872-1879.
London address.
Wife of William James Palmer, an artist.
exhib. Suffolk Street (9), flowers.

PALMIER, CHARLES JOH.
German School.
b. Aschersleben 1863 (22nd October), d. Munich 1911 (15th July).
Studied Dresden Academy and in Munich; Painted still-life and landscapes.

PANKIEWICZ, JOSEPH
Polish School.
b. Lublin 1866 (29th November), d. Paris 1943.
Painted still-life and portraits; engraved and produced lithographs.
coll.    Varsovie.
exhib. Universal Exhibition Paris 1900, Silver Medal.
repr.    Bouquet, p. 23.

PANTAZIS, PERICLES                    (*see* PLATE 34)
Flemish School.
b. Athens 1849, d. Brussels 1884.
Pupil of G. Courbet and A. Chintreuil in Paris. Went to
Brussels. Painted still-life, genre, landscapes, marines and
interiors.
*coll.*    Brussels.


PARENT, ROGER
Flemish School.
b. Paris 1881 (21st August).
Settled in Brussels. Painted still-life and interiors.
*coll.*    Brussels.


PARIS, EDOUARD
Swiss School.
b. Colombier 1870 (16th May).
Pupil of Merson in Paris. Painted flowers and landscapes.


PARISSOT, ALBERT GEORGES
French School.
19th century.
Painted flowers and fruit. Working in Paris.
*exhib.* Salon 1879.


PARISY, EUGENE FERDINAND
French School.
19th century (*see* Vol. 3, Part I, p. 63).


PARK, STUART
British School.
b. Kidderminster 1862, d. Kilmarnock 1933.
Studied Glasgow School of Art and in Paris under Lefebvre,
Corman and Boulanger. Worked in Glasgow till 1896 then
removed to Kilmarnock. Painted flowers and portraits.
*coll.*    Glasgow (2), flowers.
*repr.*    *Colour Magazine*, Sept. 1918.
*auct.*    Glasgow 2.2.1945, flowers.


PARKE, R.
British School.
*op.* 1876.
Painted still-life.


PARKER, MISS ELLEN GRACE
British School.
*op.* 1875–1893.
London address.
*exhib.* R.A. (6); Suffolk Street (18); V.E. (16), flowers.


PARKER, JOHN
British School.
19th century (*see* Vol. 3, Part I, p. 63).


PARKINSON, MISS AMELIA
British School.
*op.* 1872–1873.
London address.
*exhib.* Suffolk Street (2), flowers.


PARKYN, JOHN H.
British School.
*op.* 1884–1905.
Bristol and Kingston-on-Hull addresses.
Painted flowers.
*exhib.* R.A. and N.W.C.S.


PARRA, JOSE FELIPE
Spanish School.
19th century (*see* Vol. 3, Part I, p. 63).


PARSONS, ALFRED, R.A., R.I., R.W.S., R.O.I.
British School.
b. Beckington, Somerset, 1847 (2nd December), d. Broad-
way, Worcs., 1920 (16th January).
Studied, South Kensington. Painted landscapes, particularly
orchards and blossom and still-life.
*coll.*    Bristol; Cardiff, flowers; London, Tate Gallery;
           Wolverhampton.
*exhib.* R.A. (39); Suffolk Street (9); N.W.C.S. (20);
           G.G. (15); N.G. (14); V.E. (104); Paris 1884, Hon.
           Mention; Universal Exhibition 1889 and 1900,
           Gold and Silver Medals; National Book League,
           Flower Books 1950.
*repr.*    *The Genus Rosa* by Ellen Willmott, London 1910.
*lit.*     Blunt.


PARSONS, MISS LETITIA MARGARET
British School.
*op.* 1877–1887.
Frome address.
*exhib.* R.A. (9); Suffolk Street (1); N.W.C.S. (6); G.G. (2);
           V.E. (25), flowers.


PARTON, H.
British School.
*op.* 1885.
London address.
*exhib.* R.A. (1), flowers.

PASMORE, EMILY
British School.
*op.* 1881–1884.
London address.
*exhib.* Suffolk Street (4), flowers.

PASTOUR, LOUIS
French School.
b. Cannes 1876 (27th June).
Painted flowers and marines.
*auct.* Paris, 4.11.1946, flowers.

PATISSOU, JACQUES                    (*see* PLATE 35)
French School.
b. Nantes 1880 (9th March), d. Paris 1925 (25th February).
Pupil of Cormon. Painted still-life, portraits and genre.
*coll.* Nantes Museum.

PAULUS, PIERRE
Flemish School.
b. Chatelet 1881 (16th March).
Painted flowers, figures, portraits, landscapes and lithographer.

PAULY *or* BOGDANFFY PAULY, ERICH *or* ERIK
Hungarian School.
19th century (*see* Vol. 3, Part I, p. 64).

PAULY, VICTOR
French School.
19th century.
Pupil of Lequien. Painted still-life and landscapes.
*exhib.* Salon 1879.

PAYNE, MISS FLORENCE
British School.
*op.* 1885–1886.
Oxford address.
*exhib.* R.A. (1); N.W.C.S. (1), flowers.

PEARCE, C. MARESCO
British School.
b. London 1874.
Pupil of Augustus John, Orpen, J. E. Blanchi and Sickert.
Painted still-life and figures.

PECHSTEIN, MAX HERMANN M.            (*see* PLATE 35)
German School.
b. Zwickau/Sachsen 1881 (31st December), d. Berlin 1955.
Pupil of Otto Gussmann. Visited Italy 1907. In Berlin 1908.
Member Berlin Academy 1923.
*coll.* Berlin, Erfurst; Mannheim; Wiesbaden.
*repr.* *Dekorative Vorbilder*, XVI, pl.4.

PEEL, ANNIE
British School.
*op.* 1882.
Clitheroe address.
Painted flowers.

PEEL, MISS J. MAUD
British School.
*op.* 1878–1885.
Clitheroe address.
*exhib.* R.A. (2); Suffolk Street (3); N.W.C.S. (1), flowers.

PELHAM, EMILY
British School.
*op.* 1867–1879.
Liverpool address.
*exhib.* Suffolk Street (4), fruit.

PELT, G. TH. M. VAN
Dutch School.
b. Antwerp 1873 (17th January).
Painted flowers and engraved.

PEMBERTON, SOPHIA T.
British School.
*op.* 1897.
London address.
*exhib.* R.A. (1), flowers.

PEPLOE, S. J., R.S.A.                (*see* PLATE 36)
British School.
b. Edinburgh 1871, d. 1935.
Painted flowers and still-life. Peploe's friend, J. D. Ferguson, painted stylistically very close to Peploe.
*coll.* Birmingham; Glasgow (2); Newcastle.
*exhib.* R.S.A. Centenary Exhibition 1926.
*repr.* *Bouquet*, pl. 30; *Colour Magazine*.
*auct.* London, 31.4.1946, flowers and fruit.

PEQUIN, CHARLES ETIENNE
French School.
b. Nantes 1879.
Studied in Paris. Painted still-life and landscapes.
*exhib.* Salon des Artistes Francais; Independants and d'Automne.

PERALTA, DEL CAMPO, FRANCISCO
Spanish School.
d. Rome 1897.
Pupil of E. Cano. Painted still-life and portraits.

PERRACHON, ANDRE
French School.
19th century (*see* Vol. 3, Part I, p. 65).

PERRELET, PAUL
Swiss School.
b. Geneva 1872 (17th September).
Studied Geneva, Paris, Florence, Munich, Madrid and
Venice. Painted still-life, portraits and landscapes.
*exhib.* Paris 1897, Silver Medal.

PERRIN, GABRIEL
French School.
19th century.
Studied at Lyon School of Art. Painted flowers.
*exhib.* Salon 1869–1896.

PERRIN-MAXENCE, HENRI
French School.
b. St. Etienne 19th century.
Painted flowers, still-life and landscapes.
*exhib.* Salon des Independants 1909.

PERSIN, MARIE
French School.
19th century.
Pupil of Cogniet and Mme Nicolas. Working in Paris.
Painted fruit and genre.
*exhib.* Salon 1870.

PETERS, ANNA
German School.
b. Mannheim 1843 (28th February), d. Sonneberg 1926.
Daughter and pupil of Pieter Francis Peters. Visited Stuttgart,
Paris, Rome, Holland, Bavaria and Switzerland.
Painted flowers.
*coll.* Munich.
*exhib.* Vienna 1873, Medal; London 1874; Munich;
Antwerp; Madrid, Hon. Mention.

PETIT, ALFRED
French School.
d. 1895.
Painted still-life and genre. Working in Paris.
*exhib.* Salon 1880.

PETIT, SOLANGE (*née* POIRSON)
French School.
19th century.
Pupil of Mme Demoulin. Painted flowers.
*exhib.* Salon 1878.

PETITJEAN, C.
German School.
19th century (*see* Vol. 3, Part I, p. 65).

PETO, JOHN FREDERICK
American School.
b. Philadelphia 1854 (21st May), d. Island Heights, New
Jersey 1907 (23rd November).
Son of Thomas Hope Peto a gilder and picture framer.
Lived in Philadelphia till 1889 then Cincinnati. Moved to
Island Heights in 1889. Married Christine Pearl Smith in
1887. Painted still-life.
*repr.* *After the Hunt*, Frankenstein 1953, pls. 6, 21, 45, 73,
83–92; *Antiques* (December 1962), p. 587, advert;
(February 1963), p. 153.
*lit.* Frankenstein.

PETRASCHEK-LANGE, HELENE
German School.
b. Dresden 1875 (25th May).
Painted flowers and lithographer.

PETTIE, MARION
British School.
*op.* 1874.
Painted flowers.

PEYRANE, LEOPOLD
French School.
19th century (*see* Vol. 3, Part I, p. 65).

PFAFF, MARGARETE
German School.
b. Chemnitz 1863 (26th June).
Studied Dresden and Munich. Painted still-life and landscapes.

PFLUGER, LOUIS
Swiss School.
b. Lausanne 1847 (19th April), d. there 1893 (18th April).
Pupil of Joseph Geisser, Gilbaut and V. Leclaire in Paris.
Painted flowers.

PHILIP, MISS CONSTANCE B. (*see* MRS. CECIL LAWSON)

PHILIPARD, CHARLES
French School.
19th century.
Working at Auxerre. Pupil of L. de Beauregard. Painted
flowers, fruit and portraits.
*exhib.* Salon 1863–1868.

PHILLIPS, MISS M. A.
British School.
*op.* 1872.
London address.
*exhib.* Suffolk Street (1), flowers.

PHILPOT, LEONARD, D.                    (*see* PLATE 37)
British School.
b. 1877.
Painted flowers and fruit.
*coll.*    Preston, Harris Museum and Art Gallery.
*exhib.* R.A. (12), 1929–1951

PICARD, AUGUSTINE
French School.
19th century (*see* Vol. 3, Part I, p. 66).

PICART LE DOUX, CHARLES ALEXANDRE
French School.
b. Paris 1881 (12th July).
Painted flowers, landscapes etc.
*coll.*    Algiers.

PICASSO, PABLO RUIZ Y
Spanish School.
b. Malaga 1881 (25th October)
Son of a drawing master. In 1895 the family moved to
Barcelona where the father had been appointed to the School
of Fine Arts.
The young Picasso studied there and later at the School of
Fine Arts in Madrid. He returned to Barcelona in 1898.
Went to Paris for short visit 1900 and then to Madrid and
Paris again. In 1902 returned to Barcelona. Settled in Paris
in 1904. Since the War he has lived chiefly in South of France.
*exhib.* London, Tate Gallery, Arts Council Exhibition,
    July–September 1960.
*repr.*    22 plates in catalogue of Tate Gallery Exhibition 1960.
*auct.*    Sotheby's 6.12.1961, still-life illustrated in catalogue.

PICK, EMME
German School.
b. Breslau 1882 (4th January).
Studied Breslau, Berlin, Munich and Paris. Painted flowers
and landscapes.

PICKARD, LOUISE
British School.
b. 1865 (6th June), d. London 1928.
Studied London and Paris. Painted still-life, portraits and
landscapes.
*coll.*    London, Tate Gallery, still-life.

PIEPER, OTTO
German School.
b. Altona 1881 (25th March).
Pupil of Potzelberger and Grethe. Painted still-life, genre
etc.

PIEPHO, KARL JOHANN NIKOLAUS
German School.
b. Frankfurt 1869 (25th March), d. Munich 1920 (23rd May).
Studied Karlsruhe and in Paris. Painted still-life, portraits
and landscapes.
*coll.*    Munich.

PIERDRON, ALPHONSE
French School.
19th century.
Painted fruit and landscape. In London for a time.
*exhib.* Salon 1876.

PIERRE-FOREST, JEAN ANTOINE
French School.
b. Nice 1883 (21st November).
Pupil of Forest-Fleury. Painted flowers, portraits and marines.

PIERREPONT, MISS C. CONSTANCE
British School.
*op.* 1877–1879.
London address.
*exhib.* Suffolk Street (2), flowers.

PINAZO, MARTINEZ JOSE IGNACIO
Spanish School.
19th century.
Working at Valencia. In Rome 1879. Painted still-life,
portraits and figures.
*exhib.* Salon; Universal Exhibition 1900, Silver Medal.

PINERA Y PEREZ, JUAN
Spanish School.
b. Seville, d. Canfranc 1878 (26th January).
Pupil of E. Cano. Painted flowers and genre.

PIRAMOWICZ, MLLE SOPHIE
Polish School.
19th century (*see* Vol. 3, Part I, p. 66).

PISSARRO, LUCIEN
French School.
b. Paris 1863 (20th February), d. Hewood, Somerset 1944.
Eldest son of Camille Pissarro. Original member of the Salon
des Independants. Settled in England about 1893 and founded
the Eragny Press. Painted landscapes, portraits and flowers
and still-life.
*exhib.* Salon des Independants 1886–1894; Venice, Bienale
1928.

PISTILLI, ENRICO
Italian School.
b. Naples 1854 (4th March).
Pupil of D. Morelli. Painted flowers, fruit and landscapes.

PITCAIRN, MISS CONSTANCE
British School.
*op.* 1881–1886.
*exhib.* R.A. (2); Suffolk Street (1), flowers.

PITCAIRN-KNOWLES, JAMES
British School.
b. Rotterdam (Scottish parents) 1864 (27th September).
Studied Munich and Paris. Painted flowers, portraits and landscapes.

PITMAN, JANETTA R. À.
British School.
*op.* 1880–1901.
Nottingham address.
Painted flowers, still-life and genre.
*exhib.* R.A. (16); Suffolk Street (2); N.W.C.S. (9); G.G. (1).

PITTARD, CHARLES WILLIAM
British School.
*op.* 1878–1891.
*exhib.* R.A. (8); Suffolk Street (7), still-life.

PITTS, MRS.
British School.
*op.* 1864.
London address.
*exhib.* Suffolk Street (1), flowers.

PLA Y GALLARDO, CECILIO
Spanish School.
b. Valencia 1860 (22nd November).
Pupil of E. Sala. Went to Madrid.
Painted still-life, portraits and figures.
*exhib.* Universal Exhibition 1900, Bronze Medal.

PLETSER, G.
Dutch School.
b. Rotterdam 1871 (25th June).
Painted still-life.

POLLEXFEN, J.
British School.
*op.* 1882.
London address.
*exhib.* Suffolk Street (1), flowers.

PONTEN, JULIA (*née* VON BROICH)
German School.
b. Aix-la-Chapelle 1880 (9th September).
Wife of Josef Ponten. Pupil of Mor, Heymann and L. Vorkonig. Painted still-life, portraits and landscapes.

POPE, ALEXANDER                    (*see* PLATE 38)
American School.
b. Dorchester, Massachusetts 1849 (25th March), d. Hingham, Boston 1924 (9th September).
Studied sculpture for a time. Lived in Boston.
Painted still-life.
*coll.* Sheffield, Graves Art Gallery.
*repr.* *After the Hunt*, Frankenstein 1953, pls. 72, 117 and 118.
*lit.* Frankenstein.

PORSCHE, OTTO MARIA
German School.
b. Gabel 1858 (18th June), d. Munich 1931 (11th June).
Studied Prague and Munich. Painted still-life and figures.

PORTAIL, AMIDEE LOUIS
French School.
19th century.
Working in Paris. Painted flowers and lithographer.
*exhib.* Salon 1865–1874.

PORTER, MISS IDA
British School.
*op.* 1885–1886.
London address.
*exhib.* Suffolk Street (1); N.W.C.S. (1), flowers.

POTTEN, MISS
British School.
*op.* 1875.
London address.
*exhib.* Suffolk Street (1), fruit.

POTTIER, CONSTANCE
French School.
19th century.
Pupil of A. Bonheur. Painted flowers.
*exhib.* Salon 1864.

POULTON, MISS A.
British School.
*op.* 1868–1869.
London address.
*exhib.* Suffolk Street (2), fruit.

POWELL, MISS C. J.
British School.
*op.* 1874–1877.
Charlton address.
*exhib.* R.A. (2), flowers.

POY, DALMAU EMILIO
Spanish School.
19th century (*see* Vol. 3, Part I, p. 67).

POYNTER, JAMES
British School.
*op.* 1880.
London address.
*exhib.* V.E. (2), still-life.

PRAETERE (PRATER) JULES DE          (*see* PLATE 38)
Flemish School.
b. Ghent 1879 (21st January).
Taught in Krefeld, Dusseldorf and Zurich. Returned to
Belgium in 1921. Studied Ghent Academy. Painted flowers.
*coll.* Brussels.

PRATI, GIULIO CESARE
Italian School.
b. Caldonazzo 1860 (19th December).
Studied at Milan Academy. Brother of Romualdo Prati.
Painted still-life, portraits and genre.

PRATI, ROMUALDO
Italian School.
b. Caldonazzo 1874 (3rd February).
Studied Venice Academy and in Paris.
Painted portraits, genre and fruit.

PRATT, CLAUDE, R.B.A.
British School.
*op.* 1887–1892.
Birmingham address.
Son of Jonathan Pratt.
*coll.* Birmingham, still-life signed and dated 1887.
*exhib.* N.W.C.S. (2); V.E. (4), Graves says 'Domestic'.

PRATT, JOHN
British School.
*op.* 1882–1889.
Leeds address.
*exhib.* R.A. (9), flowers.

PRATT, RALPH
British School.
*op.* 1881–1893. d. 1909.
Leeds address.
*coll.* Leeds, still-life.
*exhib.* R.A. (9), fruit.

PRATTEN, MRS.
British School.
*op.* 1875.
Haslemere address.
Painted flowers.

PREHN, ELISE
German School.
b. Altona 1848.
Working at Kiel. Painted flowers and still-life.

PRENDERGAST, MAURICE BRAZIL
American School.
b. Boston 1861 (October), d. New York 1924 (1st February).
Studied Julian Academy in Paris and under J. P. Laurens. In
Boston 1916 and New York.
Painted still-life, figures and landscapes.
*coll.* Boston; Cleveland; Detroit; New York, Museum
Modern Art.

PREUSCHEN, HERMIONE VON, FRAU SCHMIDT *then* FRAU
PREUSCHEN-TELMANN
German School.
b. Darmstadt 1854 (7th August), d. Lichtenrode (Berlin)
1898 (12th December).
Pupil of F. Keller at Kalrsruhe. Visited Italy, Holland and
France. Married Dr. Oswald Schmidt at Munich and later
Konrad Telmann the writer. Painted flowers and still-life.
*coll.* Halle.
*exhib.* Munich R.A. (1), still-life.

PREYER, PAUL
German School.
b. Dusseldorf 1847 (24th March), d. there 1931 (18th
December).
Son and pupil of Johann Wilhelm Preyer and studied
Dusseldorf Academy. Painted still-life, landscapes, portraits
and figures.
*coll.* Elberfeld.

PRICE, MISS GRACE
British School.
*op.* 1861–1862.
Old Charlton address.
*exhib.* Suffolk Street (2), fruit.

PRICE, LYDIA—MRS. FRANK CORBYN (Graves)—MRS. BILL-
INGSHURST (Benezit).
British School.
*op.* 1890–1894.
London address.
Painted domestic and flowers.
*exhib.* R.A. (3); N.W.C.S. (5).

PRICE, MATHILDE JULIANE ENGELINE
Danish School.
b. Copenhagen 1849 (6th April).
Pupil of V. Kyhn, O. D. Ottesen and C. Bloch.
Painted flowers and portraits.

PRIEUR, GEORGES ETIENNE
French School.
19th century (*see* Vol. 3, Part I, p. 68).

PRINGLE, JOHN QUINTON
British School.
b. Glasgow 1864 (13th December), d. Tollcross 1925.
Painted landscape, portraits and a number of still-life subjects.
*coll.* Glasgow; Kirkcaldy.
*repr.* *Scottish Art Review*, Vol. 9, No. 2, 1963.

PRITCHARD, MISS MARY E.
British School.
*op.* 1893–1895.
London address.
*exhib.* R.A. (2); Suffolk Street (1), fruit.

PROCTOR, JESSY
British School.
*op.* 1869.
Painted still-life in London.

PROSCHWITZKY, FRANK
British School.
*op.* 1883–1889.
London address.
*exhib.* R.A. (2), still-life.

PROUT, MARY
British School.
*op.* 1869.
London address.
*exhib.* Suffolk Street (1), still-life.

PUCCINI, MARIO
Italian School.
b. Livourne 1869 (28th June), d. Florence 1920 (18th June).
Studied Florence Academy. Painted flowers, still-life, landscapes and marines.
*coll.* Florence; Rome.

PUCKLE, MISS ETHEL M.
British School.
*op.* 1885.
Sutton address.
*exhib.* R.A. (1), flowers.

PULVERMACHER, MISS ANNA
British School.
*op.* 1882–1887.
London address.
*exhib.* R.A. (2); Suffolk Street (3), still-life.

PURVES, MISS C. J.
British School.
*op.* 1881–1885.
London address.
*exhib.* G.G. (2), flowers.

PURY, MARIE AMELIE MATHILDE DE (*née* WAGNIERE)
Swiss School.
19th century (*see* Vol. 3, Part I, p. 68).

QUARTREMAINE, G. W.
British School.
*op.* 1881–1882.
Stratford-on-Avon address.
*exhib.* V.E. (2), game.

QUEVREMONT, HENRI
French School.
d. 1892.
Pupil of Isabey and Ph. Rousseau. Working in Rouen.
Painted still-life and genre.
*exhib.* Salon 1865–1867.

QUIZET, ALPHONSE LEON
French School.
b. Paris 1885 (13th March).
Painted flowers and landscapes. Chevalier of the Legion of
Honour.
*exhib.* Salon des Independants; Salon d'Automne.
*auct.* Sotheby's, 6.7.1961, flowers.

QUOST, ERNEST
French School.
b. Avallon 1844, d. 1931 (24th March).
Painted flowers, fruit and still-life. Chevalier of the Legion of Honour 1883, Officer 1903.
coll.  Bernay; Castres; Gray; Luxembourg; Nancy; Paris.
exhib.  Salon 1866; Universal Exhibition 1880, 1882, 1889 and 1900, Medal.

RADLER, FRIEDRICH VON
Austrian School.
b. Znaim 1876 (29th September).
Studied Vienna Academy. Painted flowers and portraits.
coll.  Vienna.

RADLMACHER, KARL
Austrian School.
19th century (see Vol. 3, Part I, p. 68).

RAFFAELLI, JEAN FRANCOIS                    (see PLATE 39)
French School.
b. Paris 1850 (20th April), d. there 1924 (29th February).
Pupil of Gerome. Painted flowers, portraits, landscapes and engraved.
exhib.  Cologne.
auct.  London, 15.2.1950, flowers; Paris, 24.4.1947, flowers.

RAGOT, JULES FELIX
French School.
19th century (see Vol. 3, Part I, p. 68).

RAINER, JOHANN JOSEPH
Austrian School.
19th century (see Vol. 3, Part I, p. 68).

RAM, MISS JANE A.
British School.
op. 1892–1895.
Norwood and London addresses.
A sculptor and painted flowers.
exhib.  R.A. (1); Suffolk Street (2); V.E. (2).

RAMGE, HUGO
German School.
b. Hof 1866 (24th October).
Studied Munich Academy. Painted still-life, figures and landscapes.

RAMSDEN, THOMAS
British School.
op. 1883–1893.
Leeds address.
exhib.  R.A. (1); Suffolk Street (7), flowers.

RAMSEY, MILNE
American School.
b. Philadelphia 1846, d. there 1915 (15th March).
Studied Pennsylvania Academy and Paris.
Painted still-life of metal work.
repr.  After the Hunt, Frankenstein, 1953, pl. 130.
lit.  Frankenstein.

RANDALL, THOMAS MARTIN
British School.
b. Broseley, d. Shallowford 1859.
Apprenticed at Caughley. Went to Coalport, Madeley, Shelton, Derby and Pinxton Potteries. Went to London and had a business at Islington, decorating white Nantgarw porcelain in Sevres style.
lit.  Chaffers, 767, 773–4, 956, 1035.

RANDOLE, FREDERICK W.
British School.
b. London 1847, d. Liverpool 1880.
Visited America in 1860 and worked in Philadelphia. Painted still-life.

RANKEN, WILLIAM BRUCE ELLIS              (see PLATE 40)
British School.
b. Edinburgh 1881 (11th April).
Studied Slade School. Painted still-life, portraits and landscapes.
exhib.  R.I., etc.
repr.  Colour Magazine, May 1915.

RAPHAEL, W.
British School.
op. 1877.
Manchester address.
exhib.  Suffolk Street (1), still-life.

RASMUSSEN, NIELS PETER
Danish School.
b. Odense 1847 (1st December), d. Copenhagen 1891 (17th September).
Studied Copenhagen Academy. Teacher at Technical School 1878–1891. Painted flowers, animals and landscapes.

RASTOUK, JULES GASPARD
French School.
19th century.
Pupil of Numa Boucoiran. Working at Nimes. Painted some flowers but mostly religious subjects for churches.
*coll.*   Musee de Bagnols-sur-Ceze had a vase of flowers but it was destroyed by fire in 1924.
*exhib.*  Salon 1878. Salon des Artistes Francais 1883. Hon. mention 1910, Silver Medal.

RATHJENS, WILLIAM
British School.
*op.* 1879–1881.
Withington address.
*exhib.*  R.A. (2), flowers.

RATHONYI, PETER
Hungarian School.
b. Kokonyosd 1859 (22nd July), d. Balatonfured 1922 (3rd June).
Studied at Budapest. Painted still-life.

RAYMOND-WOOG
French School.
19th century (*see* Vol. 3, Part I, p. 68).

RAYNER, MRS. ROSA
British School.
*op.* 1885.
Hanwell address.
*exhib.*  R.A. (1), flowers.

READ, G. A.
British School.
*op.* 1876.
Nottingham address.
*exhib.*  R.A. (1), fruit.

READING, MISS C. R.
British School.
*op.* 1874.
London address.
*exhib.*  Suffolk Street (2), fruit.

REDMOND, FRIEDA (*née* VOLTER)
Swiss School.
b. Thun 1857 (6th February).
Married John Redmond of New York in 1888. Painted flowers.

REDON, GEORGES
French School.
b. Paris 1869 (16th November), d. 1943.
Painted flowers and lithographer.

REED, MISS KATE
British School.
*op.* 1873–1882.
Tunbridge Wells address.
*exhib.*  Suffolk Street (9), still-life.

REES, MISS M. R.
British School.
*op.* 1865–1872.
London address.
*exhib.*  R.A. (1); Suffolk Street (2), fruit.

REGNIER, LUDOVIC
French School.
b. Paris 1851 (2nd July), d. 1930.
Pupil of J. Pils. Painted flowers, landscapes and interiors.
*exhib.*  Salon 1877; Salon des Artistes Francais 1888.

REISER, CARL
German School.
b. Partenkirchen 1877 (5th June).
Studied at Munich Academy. Painted still-life, portraits and architecture.

RENNER
German School.
19th century (*see* Vol. 3, Part I, p. 69).

RENOIR, PIERRE AUGUSTE           (*see* PLATE 39)
French School.
b. Limoges 1841 (25th February), d. Cagnes 1919 (17th December).
Pupil of Gleyre. Worked at 13 years of age as a painter in a porcelain factory. Visited North Africa in 1879 and 1882 and Guernsey in 1880. Italy in 1881–1882. Also visited London, Holland, Spain and Germany. In 1906 settled in Cagnes. Crippled with arthritis. Last pictures painted with brushes strapped to his wrist. Painted about 6,000 pictures.
*coll.*   Berlin; Breme; Cambridge, Mass. Fogg Museum; Glasgow; Rouen.
*repr.*  *Flower Painting*, Marcus (Collins), 1961, pls. 21, 22 and 23.
*auct.*   Paris, 29.3.1962, rose in a vase; 5.7.1951, 30.5.1951; Sotheby's, 11.4.1962, fish; 14.6.1962, fruit, illus. in catalogue.

RENOUF, MRS.
British School.
*op.* 1883.
London address.
*exhib.* Suffolk Street (2), still-life.


REYNOLDS, APOLLONIA
British School.
*op.* 1882.
Guildford address.
*exhib.* Suffolk Street (1), still-life.


RHODES, HENRY J.
British School.
*op.* 1869–1882.
London address.
*exhib.* R.A. (4); Suffolk Street (2), flowers.
Graves also gives H. RHODES, 1869–1871, exhibiting R.A. and Suffolk Street—flower paintings. Possibly same as above.


RIBARZ, RUDOLF
Austrian School.
b. Vienna 1848 (30th May), d. there 1904 (12th November).
Studied Vienna Academy. Visited Brussels and Paris 1875.
Painted flowers and landscapes.
*exhib.* Berlin; Dresden; Paris, Universal Exhibition 1889, Silver Medal.


RICHARDS, THOMAS
British School.
19th century (*see* Vol. 3, Part I, p. 70).


RICHARDS, WILLIAM
British School.
19th century (*see* Vol. 3, Part I, p. 70).


RICHEBE, HORACE
French School.
b. Algiers 1871 (23rd November).
Pupil of Gerome. Painted flowers, fruit and genre. Chevalier of the Legion of Honour.
*exhib.* Salon 1907; Silver Medal 1924.


RICHMOND, JULIA
British School.
*op.* 1866.
London address.
Painted flowers.


RICHTER, HERBERT DAVIS, V.P.R.O.I., R.I., R.S.W., R.B.C.
British School.                            (*see* PLATE 41)
b. Brighton 1874, d. London 1955.

In practice at Bath as designer and architect 1895–1906.
Gold and Silver Medals Paris Exhibition 1900 for British-made cabinet work; Society of Arts Medal 1897. Director, Bath Cabinet Makers Co., Ltd. Studied painting with the late John Swann, R.A., and Sir Frank Brangwyn, R.A. First exhibited R.A. 1906, and regularly thereafter at the principal London exhibitions. Member N.W.C.S. Pastel Society, Ridley Art Club, etc.
Painted flowers, still-life, interiors and landscapes.
*exhib.* International Exhibition, Paris, 1937, Silver Medal; London, Fine Art Society, Memorial Exhibition, November–December 1956.
*repr.* *British Water Colour Painting Today*, pl. 17, 1921
*Floral Art-Decoration and Design*, 1932.
Hardie, *Flower Paintings*, 1947.
*lit.* *Art of H. D. Richter*, by H. Granville Fell, 1935.


RICHTER, MAX
German School.
b. Magdeburg 1860 (19th August).
Working in Berlin. Studied Berlin Academy. Painted still-life and landscapes.


RICHTER, ROBERT
German School.
b. Gumbinnen 1860 (11th January).
Painted still-life, portraits and landscapes.
*coll.* Charlottenburg; Wiesbaden.


RICO Y CEJUDO, JOSE
Spanish School.
b. Seville 1864 (27th March).
Pupil of M. Ussel and J. Garcia Ramos.
Painted flowers, landscapes and portraits.


RIDGEWAY, MISS E.
British School.
*op.* 1874.
Penmaenmaur address.
*exhib.* Suffolk Street (1), flowers.


RIDLEY, MISS ANNIE
British School.
*op.* 1864–1870.
London address.
*exhib.* B.I. (1); Suffolk Street (1), flowers.

RIECK, HERMANN
German School.
b. Hamburg 1850 (27th November).
Studied Berlin and Weimar. Visited Dusseldorf, Dresden and Munich. Painted still-life and landscapes.

RILEY, J.
British School.
19th century (*see* Vol. 3, Part I, p. 70).

RIPPOZ, AUGUSTE FELIX
French School.
d. 1890.
Painted flowers and fruit.
*exhib.* Salon 1864.

RISCHGITZ, MISS MARY
British School.
*op.* 1882–1892.
London address.
*exhib.* R.A. (6); Suffolk Street (8); V.E. (3), flowers.

RISLER, HELENE
French School.
19th century.
Painted flowers. Working at Geneva.
*exhib.* Salon 1879.

RITLENG, GEORGES
German School.
b. Strasburg 1875 (6th December).
Studied Strasburg. Visited Paris and Munich. Painted flowers.
*coll.* Strasburg.
Benezit gives this artist as a flower painter. The authorities at Strasburg Museum say he was not a flower-painter.

RITSEMA, COBA (JACOBA)          (*see* PLATE 42)
Dutch School.
b. Haarlem 1876 (26th June), d. 1961.
Painted still-life.
*coll.* Amsterdam, Rijksmuseum; Haarlem, Teylers Museum.

RITTENBURG, HENRY R.
American School.
b. Libau (Russia) 1879 (2nd October).
Pupil of W. M. Chase in Philadelphia. Painted still-life and portraits.

RIVA-MUNOZ, MARIA LUISA DE LA
Spanish School.
b. Saragossa 1859, d. Madrid 1926.
Visited Paris. Painted flowers and fruit.
*coll.* Madrid.
*exhib.* Berlin; Paris; Munich 1895 and 1897, Silver and Bronze Medals.

RIVERS, MISS MAY
British School.
*op.* 1890.
*repr.* *The Fruit Growers' Guide*, 43 coloured plates, by J. Wright, 1890.

RIVES, CECILE MARTHE ELISE
French School.
b. Carcassonne 1880 (12th September).
Pupil of Antony Rives. Painted flowers, still-life and landscapes.

RIVIERE, MRS. BRITON (ALICE)
British School.
*op.* 1868–1872.
Bromley address.
Wife of Briton Riviere, R.A.
*exhib.* R.A. (3); V.E. (7), flowers.

RIVIERE, CHARLES
French School.
b. Orleans 1848 (12th October), d. Paris 1920 (18th January).
Pupil of Bergeret. Painted still-life and animals.
*coll.* Orleans Museum.
*exhib.* Universal Exhibition 1900, Bronze Medal.

RIVIERE, MRS. W.
British School.
*op.* 1871.
London address.
Wife of William Riviere, an artist.
*exhib.* Suffolk Street (3), fruit.

RIVOIRE, FRANCOIS
French School.
b. Lyon 1842 (16th April), d. Grand St. Leger 1919 (7th August).
Pupil of Regnier. Chevalier of the Legion of Honour 1906. Painted flowers.
*coll.* Amiens; Arras; Lyon; Luxembourg; Mulhouse: Paris; Rheims; St. Etienne; Valenciennes.
*exhib.* Salon 1866; Universal Exhibition 1900, Bronze Medal.
*auct.* Paris 1.6.1951, flowers; 28.2.1951, still-life.

ROBBINS, MISS ANNA
British School.
*op.* 1867.
Thetford address.
*exhib.* Suffolk Street (1), still-life.

ROBERTS, ELSIE
British School.
*op.* 1882.
Sheffield address.
Painted flowers.

ROBERTSON, HENRIETTA J.
British School.
19th century.
Working in Glasgow. Painted still-life.
*exhib.* Royal Glasgow Institute 1880.

ROBINSON, MISS A.
British School.
*op.* 1871.
London address.
*exhib.* Suffolk Street (1), flowers.

ROBINSON, F.
British School.
*op.* 1878.
*auct.* Sotheby's, 25.10.1961, flower painting dated 1878.

ROBINSON, MRS. H. H. (*née* M. D. WEBB)
British School.
*op.* 1885–1901.
Wife of Henry Harewood Robinson. Painted flowers and domestic.
*exhib.* R.A. (6).

ROBINSON, JOHN
British School.
*op.* 1867–1880.
Norwood address.
*exhib.* V.E. (12), flowers.

ROBINSON, JOSEPH
British School.
*op.* 1862–1872.
Norwood address.
*exhib.* R.A. (3); B.I. (2); Suffolk Street (2), fruit.

ROBINSON, WILLIAM
British School.
*op.* 1883.
*exhib.* National Book League, Flower Books, 1950.
*repr.* *The English Flower Garden*, London, 1883, wood engravings.
*lit.* Blunt.

ROBSON, MISS HENRIETTA
British School.
*op.* 1872–1881.
New Brighton address.
*exhib.* R.A. (2), flowers.

ROBSON, MISS J. S.
British School.
*op.* 1873.
Ripon address.
*exhib.* Suffolk Street (1), flowers.

ROCCO, LILY ROSALIA
Italian School.
b. Mazzara de Vallo 1869 (13th November).
Studied Naples. Painted flowers and landscapes.

ROELOFS, WILLEM ELISA
Dutch School.
b. The Hague 1874 (24th April).
Son and pupil of Willem Roelofs.
Painted still-life, landscapes, and engraved.
*coll.* Amsterdam, Rijks. Museum, fish; Haarlem; Rotterdam.

ROGERS, MISS KATE
British School.
*op.* 1884–1885.
London address.
*exhib.* Suffolk Street (1); N.W.C.S. (1), flowers.

ROGERS, MISS M.
British School.
*op.* 1876–1879.
Acton address.
*exhib.* R.A. (2); Suffolk Street (2), flowers.

ROGERS, M. J.
British School.
*op.* 1872.
Thame address.
*exhib.* V.E. (1), fruit.

ROHLFS, CHRISTIAN
German School.
b. Holstein 1849 (22nd December).
Painted flowers and landscapes.

RONNER, ALFRED
Flemish School.
b. 1852, d. Brussels 1901 (7th October).
Painted still-life.

RONNER, EMMA ALICE HENRIETTE     (*see* PLATE 43)
Belgian School.
b. Brussels 1857.
Daughter of Henriette Ronner (1821–1909), the well-known painter of cats. Painted flowers and still-life. Signed her work 'Alice Ronner'.
*repr.*   *Colour Magazine*, February 1917.

ROOFF, W. A.
British School.
*op.* 1879.
London address.
*exhib.*  Suffolk Street (1), flowers.

ROOK, EDWARD FRANCIS     (*see* PLATE 42)
American School.
b. New York 1870, d. Old Lyme, Connecticut, 1960.
Pupil of Constant and Laurens in Paris. Member of National Academy 1924. Painted flowers and landscapes.
*coll.*   Cincinnati Museum, flowers.
*exhib.*  Penna Academy, Gold Medal 1898; Pan American Exposition, Buffalo, 1901, Bronze Medal.

ROOSENBOOM, MARGUERETHA CORNELIA JOHANNA
HENRIETTA     (*see* PLATE 44)
Dutch School.
b. The Hague 1843 (24th October), d. Voorburg 1896 (26th December).
Studied under father, Nicolaas Roosenboom. Worked at The Hague and settled in 1892 at Voorburg, where married to painter J. G. Vogel. Painted flowers and fruit.
*coll.*   Amsterdam, Rijks. museum; Municipal Museum; Breslau; The Hague, Mesdag; Haarlem, Teylers Museum; Rotterdam.

ROSAHL, PAUL
German School.
b. Lettin 1884 (23rd September).
Painted still-life, landscapes, portraits and engraved.

ROSAM, WALTER ALFRED
German School.
b. Hamburg 1883 (26th October), d. 1916 (14th August).
Painted still-life, landscapes, portraits and interiors.

ROSELL, JOSE MARIANO
Spanish School.
19th century (*see* Vol. 3, Part I, p. 72).

ROUAULT, GEORGES
French School.
b. Paris 1871 (27th May), d. 1958.
Apprenticed to a stained glass window maker. At 20 years of age went to the Ecole des Beaux Arts and became pupil of Moreau. To begin with painted mostly in water-colour and returned to oils in 1918. Also produced etchings, coloured etchings, and lithographs. Painted religious subjects, landscapes and flowers. Made tapestry cartoons.
*exhib.*  Fauve Exhibition 1905.

ROUBY, ALFRED
French School.
b. Paris 1849 (21st November).
Pupil of Beyle. Painted flowers.
*coll.*   Sete Museum.
*auct.*   Paris, 20.6.1951, flowers.

ROUGE, JULIE BONABES DE
French School.
19th century (*see* Vol. 3, Part I, p. 72).

ROUND, FRANK HAROLD
British School.
b. 1879 (10th January), living at Gt. Bookham 1949.
Assistant drawing master at Charterhouse School.
*coll*   British Iris Society (album of 47 colour illustrations of irises, in the care of the Royal Horticultural Society).
*exhib.*  National Book League, Flower Books, 1950.
*repr.*   *The Genus Iris*, 1913, by W. R. Dyke.
*lit.*   Blunt.

ROUSSEAU, HENRI
French School.
b. 1844, d. 1910.
Known as a 'Sunday' painter. Was a regimental bandsman in Mexico 1861–1867, and a Sergeant in the Franco-Prussian War of 1870. Entered the Customs service and earned nickname 'le Douanier'. Began painting in 1880. Kept a school for teaching elocution, music and painting.
*coll.*   Albright Art Gallery, Buffalo.
*exhib.*  Independants from 1886.
*repr.*   *Flower Painting*, Marcus, 1961, pl. 25.

ROUX, HIPPOLYTE
French School.
b. St. Euphemie 1852 (16th December).
Painted flowers and landscapes.

ROWLEY, HON. H.
British School.
*op.* 1866.
London address.
*exhib.* R.A. (1), flowers.

ROXBY, C. W.
British School.
*op.* 1875–1890.
London address.
*exhib.* Suffolk Street (19), still-life.

RUFF, GEORGE JUNIOR
British School.
*op.* 1879–1880.
London address.
*exhib.* Suffolk Street (3), still-life.

RUMLEY, MISS ELIZABETH (*see* MRS. B. DAWSON)

RUSSELL, JAMES
British School.
*op.* 1878–1887.
Bath address.
Painted flowers.

RUYSCH, ALETTA JACOBA JOSEPHINE
Dutch School.
b. 1860 (6th August), d. 1931.
Visited England in 1879; France 1880.
Painted still-life. Signed her paintings 'Aletta van Thol-Ruysch'.
*coll.*    The Hague, Municipal Museum, 3 still-life.

RUYTINA, ALFRED
Flemish School.
b. Schaerbeck 1871 (18th April).
Pupil of P. Livemont. Painted flowers and still-life.

RYAN, CHARLES J.
British School.
19th century.
Painted flowers and possibly landscapes. Master at the School of Art, Leeds.
*coll.*    London, Victoria and Albert Museum, 8 flowers.
A Charles J. Ryan living at Ventnor 1885–1891 exhibited landscapes at the R.A. and N.W.C.S.

RYAN, CLAUDE
British School.
*op.* 1874–1883.
London address.
*exhib.* Suffolk Street (8), flowers.

RYLAND, HENRY
British School.
b. Biggleswade 1856, d. London 1924 (23rd November).
Pupil of Benjamin Constant, Boulanger, Lefebvre and Corman.
Painted flowers, fruit and figures.
*exhib.* R.A. (6); N.W.C.S. (18); G.G. (3); N.G. (9); V.E. (3).

SABBACH, GEORGES HANNA
French (Egyptian) School.
b. Alexandra 1877 (18th August), d. Paris 1951 (9th December).
Pupil of M. Denis and Vallotton.
Painted still-life, portraits and landscapes.
*exhib.* Amsterdam; Brussels; Geneva; London; Stockholm.

SADLER, MISS KATE
British School.
*op.* 1878–1893.
Horsham address.
*exhib.* R.A. (10); Suffolk Street (6); N.W.C.S. (26); V.E. (10), flowers.

SADLER, THOMAS
British School.
*op.* 1878–1886.
London address.
*exhib.* R.A. (1); Suffolk Street (3); V.E. (4), flowers.

SAENGER, LUCIE VON, MME MIRAM
German School.
b. Riga 1862 (1st December).
Studied Riga and Munich. Painted still-life and portraits.

SALISBURY, FRANK O., C.V.O., LL.D., R.P., R.I.
British School.
b. Harpenden 1874 (18th December), d. London 1962 (31st August).
Pupil of his brother, H. J. Salisbury, a stained-glass artist, and Heatherley's School. Scholarship to R.A. Schools. Won Landseer Scholarship and journeyed to Italy in 1896. Married Alice Maud Greenwood. Painted portraits, murals, state ceremonies and royal groups. Master of the Worshipful Company of Glaziers 1933–1934. Painted some landscapes and flowers.
*exhib.* R.A.; Paris; Salon; R.I. etc.
*lit.*    *The Art of Frank O. Salisbury*, 1936.
          *Portrait and Pageant*, 1944.
          *In Praise of Flowers* (1950), 16 colour plates.

SALMON, MISS HELEN R.
British School.
*op.* 1884–1890.
Glasgow address.
*exhib.* R.A. (6), flowers.

SALTER, MISS ANNE G.
British School.
*op.* 1869–1885.
Leamington address.
*exhib.* Suffolk Street (2), still-life.

SALTER, MRS.
British School.
*op.* 1879.
London address.
*exhib.* Suffolk Street (1), flowers.

SAMPSON, HERBERT
British School.
*op.* 1879.
London address.
*exhib.* Suffolk Street (2), still-life.

SANCHEZ, PICAZO PEDRO
Spanish School.
19th century (*see* Vol. 3, Part I, p. 73).

SANDONA, MATTEO
American School.
b. Schio, Italy, 1881 (15th April).
Pupil of Nani and Bianchi and Verona Academy. Painted flowers and portraits.
*coll.* Chicago; San Francisco, Golden Gate Park Memorial Museum; Washington.
*exhib.* Sacramento 1917, Silver Medal; Lewis & Clark Exposition, Portland 1905, Silver Medal.

SANSON, STELLA
French School.
19th century (*see* Vol. 3, Part I, p. 73).

SARGENT, LOUIS AUG.
British School.
b. London 1881 (14th October).
Painted flowers, still-life and marines.

SAUVAGE, ARSENE SYMPHORIEN
French School.
19th century.
Pupil of Gerome. Painted fruit, still-life and portraits.
*exhib.* Salon 1868.

SAVIDGE, JOSEPH T.
British School.
*op.* 1900.
London address.
*exhib.* R.A. (1), fruit.

SCAMPTON, MISS MARY
British School.
*op.* 1879–1882.
Coventry address.
*exhib.* Suffolk Street (4), flowers.

SCHARTMANN, EMIL ADALBERT
German School.
19th century (*see* Vol. 3, Part I, p. 74).

SCHENLEY, HERMIONE
British School.
*op.* 1885.
London address.
*exhib.* Suffolk Street (1), still-life.

SCHILLIG, JOSEPHINE
Swiss School.
b. Altdorf 1846 (19th July).
Pupil of X. Schwegler. Painted flowers and portraits.

SCHIRREN, FERDINAND
Flemish School.
b. Antwerp 1872 (8th November).
Pupil of J. B. Keyser. Painted still-life, figures and landscapes.

SCHLUMBERGER, EUGENE JACQUES
French School.
b. Mulhouse 1879 (9th March).
Painted flowers and landscapes.
*coll.* Clermont; Ferrand; Rotterdam.
*exhib.* International Exhibition 1930 and 1937, Silver Medal.

SCHMALZ, HEINRICH P. (*or* SCHMALTZ)
German School.
19th century (*see* Vol. 3, Part I, p. 74).

SCHMIDT, ELISABETH
German School.
b. Sophienberg 1882 (18th February).
Painted flowers and portraits.

SCHMIDT-ROTTILIFF, KARL (*or* ROTTLUFF)
German School.
b. Chemnitz 1884 (14th December).
Studied Dresden. Visited Italy and Dalmatia. Painter and sculptor.

SCHMITT, NATHANAEL                    (see PLATE 44)
German School.
b. Heidelberg 1847, d. Karlsruhe 1918.
Pupil of G. Phil. Painted still-life, portraits and landscapes.
Visited Rome.
*coll.*    Karlsruhe Museum, flowers.


SCHMURR, WILHELM
German School.
b. Hagen 1878 (1st March), d. Dusseldorf 1959 (16th February).
Pupil of E. von Gebhardt and C. Meyer. Professor of painting
at the Academy of Arts in Dusseldorf from 1927 to 1947.
Painted still-life, portraits and landscapes.
*coll.*    Dusseldorf Museum.


SCHOCHLIN-ROMER, BERTHA (*née* ROMER)
Swiss School.
b. Bienne 1860 (22nd September).
Pupil of A. Bachelin, P. Volmar and W. Benteli. Painted
flowers, still-life and landscapes. Visited Panama and Chile.


SCHOLE
Austrian School.
d. Prague 1866 (December).
Working at Prague. Painted flowers.


SCHON, LUISE
Austrian School.
b. Vienna 1848 (24th January).
Pupil of Fr. K. Ponninger and Geyling. Painted flowers, still-
life and portraits.


SCHOU, PETER ALFRED
Danish School.
b. Copenhagen 1844 (8th October), d. Frederikborg 1914
(21st November).
Studied Dresden Academy and under L. Bonnat in Paris.
Painted still-life, figures, interiors and portraits.
*coll.*    Copenhagen, Faaborg Museum, still-life.


SCHREIBER DE GRAHL, HANNAH
German School.
b. Wiefsdorf 1864 (23rd April).
Pupil of K. Hagemeister. Painted flowers and landscapes.
Working in Potsdam.
*coll.*    Potsdam Museum.


SCHROESTER, ADELINE
British School.
*op.* 1877.
*exhib.* R.A. (1), flowers.


SCHUCH, KARL *or* CHARLES            (see PLATE 45)
Austrian School.
b. Vienna 1846 (30th September), d. there 1903 (13th September).
Studied Vienna Academy. Visited Munich, Paris and Italy.
Painted still-life, genre, landscapes and flowers.
*coll.*    Aix - la - Chapelle; Berlin; Bremen; Breslau;
Cologne; Krefeld; Dresden; Dusseldorf; Halle;
Hanover; Magdeburg; Mannheim; Munich;
Nuremburg; Stettin; Stuttgart; Vienna; Zurich.
*repr.*    Munich Catalogue.


SCHULTHEISS, NATALIE (*née* HAMPEL)
Austrian School.
b. Vienna 1865.
Studied Munich. Painted still-life.
*coll.*    Stuttgart, fish.


SCOTT, MISS FANNY C.
British School.
*op.* 1868–1871.
London address.
*exhib.* R.A. (1); Suffolk Street (2), fruit.


SCOTT, J.
British School.
*op.* 1863.
London address.
*exhib.* R.A. (1), flowers.


SCOTT, MISS KATHERINE
British School.
*op.* 1872–1892.
Streatham address.
*exhib.* R.A. (4); Suffolk Street (6); N.W.C.S. (15), flowers.


SEARLE, F.
British School.
*op.* 1877.
Redhill address.
*exhib.* Suffolk Street (1), fruit.


SEEMAN, RICHARD
German School.
b. Stuttgart 1857 (15th February).
Pupil of Herterich, Igler and Haug. Painted still-life and
figures.


SEGHERS, FRANCOIS *or* FRANZ
Flemish School.
b. Brussels 1849 (29th March), d. 1939 (19th March).
Studied Brussels Academy and under J. P. Laurens in Paris.
Painted flowers.
*coll.*    Ixelles Museum (azaleas).

SEGONZAC (*see* DUNOYER DE SEGONZAC, ANDRE)

SEGUIM, EDOUARD
French School.
19th century.
Pupil of L. Mouchet. Working in Paris. Painted flowers and fruit.
*exhib.* Salon 1877.

SEIFERT, ANNIE
German School.
b. Dresden 1863 (28th June), d. there 1913 (26th January).
Pupil of W. Claudius at Dresden and H. von Habermann and Th. Hummel in Munich. Painted flowers and landscapes.

SEIFFERT-WARTENBERG, RICHARD
German School.
b. Brunswick 1874 (23rd January).
Painted still-life, portraits and landscapes.

SELIGER, MAX
German School.
b. Bublitz 1865 (12th May), d. Leipzig 1920 (10th May).
Pupil of M. Koch and E. Doepler. Painted flowers and executed mosaics and frescoes.
*repr.* *Dekorative Vorbilder*, Stuttgart.

SEON, ALEXANDRE
French School.
b. Chazelles-sur-Lyon, d. Paris 1917 (7th May).
Pupil of Lehmann and Puvis de Chavannes. Painted flowers, fruit and portraits.
*exhib.* Salon 1879. Universal Exhibition 1889, Silver Medal.

SERAPHINE DE SELIS, SENLIS
French School.
b. Assy 1864 (2nd September), d. Clermont 1942 (11th December).
Painter of flowers and made designs for tapestry.
*repr.* Benezit VII, 24.

SERLE, MISS H.
British School.
*op.* 1874.
London address.
*exhib.* Suffolk Street (1), fruit.

SERRALUNGA, LUIGI
Italian School.
19th century.
In Turin 1880. Pupil of G. Grosso. Painted still-life and portraits.

SERUSIER, LOUIS PAUL HENRI
French School.
b. Paris 1865, d. Morlaix 1927 (6th October).
Painted fruit and still-life.

SERVANT, ANDRE
French School.
19th century.
Pupil of N. S. Cornu. Working at Lyon. Painted still-life, portraits and genre.
*exhib.* Salon 1867.

SETON-TAIT, ADELA
British School.
*op.* 1897–1900.
London address.
*exhib.* R.A. (3), flowers and fruit.

SEVERINI, GINO
Italian School.
b. Cortona 1883 (7th April).
Studied in Rome and Paris. Decorated churches in Switzerland with frescoes and mosaics. Painted still-life and portraits.
*repr.* *Encyclopedia of Painting*, Myers, p. 445.

SEYSSAUD, RENE
French School.
b. Marseilles 1867 (7th June), d. St. Chamas 1952 (26th September).
Officer of the Legion of Honour. Painted flowers, still-life, landscapes and marines.

SHAPLAND, ELLEN (MRS. A. F. TERRELL)
SHARPLAND (Graves)
British School.
*op.* 1883–1890.
Brighton address.
*exhib.* R.A. (4). Graves says 'still-life' 1888 exhibit was flowers, 1889 fish, and the name SHARPLAND, ELLEN.

SHEPHERD, FANNY
British School.
*op.* 1863.
Manchester address.
*exhib.* Suffolk Street (1), fruit.

SHEPPARD, EMMA
British School.
*op.* 1897.
Northampton address.
*exhib.* R.A. (1), flowers.

SHERINGHAM, GEORGE
British School.
b. London 1884, d. Hampstead 1937.
Pupil of Harry Becker. Painted flowers and still-life. Studied at Slade School and in Paris. Decorative painter, theatrical designer, illustrator and textile designer. Awarded 1925 the Paris Grand Prix. 1936 received degree of R.D.I. by Royal Society of Arts.
*coll.*    Birmingham.
*repr.*    Hardie; *Bouquet*, pls. 10 and 11.
          Richter, *Floral Art*.

SHINN, JOHN MARION
American School.
b. Dubuque, Iowa, 1849 (25th October), d. Mount Vernon 1936 (15th October).
Studied art at St. Louis. In New York 1872.
Painted still-life.
*repr.*    *After the Hunt*, Frankenstein, 1953, pl. 70.
*lit.*     Frankenstein.

SHRIMPTON, ADA M (MRS. WILLIAM GILES)
British School.
*op.* 1889–1897.
London address.
Painted flowers and domestic and engraved.
*exhib.*   R.A. (4);  Suffolk Street (7);  N.W.C.S. (5).

SHUBROOK, MISS LAURA A.
British School.
*op.* 1889–1893.
London address.
*exhib.*   R.A. (2);  Suffolk Street (10);  V.E. (5), flowers.

SHUBROOK, MINNIE J.
British School.
*op.* 1885–1899.
London address.
*exhib.*   R.A. (17);  Suffolk Street (14);  N.W.C.S. (3);  V.E. (5), flowers.

SICKERT, WALTER RICHARD, A.R.A.
British School.
b. Munich 1860 (31st May), d. 1942 (22nd January).
Naturalized Englishman. Son of Adalbert Sickert. Pupil of Whistler. Founded Camden Town Group in 1911. Member London Group and New English Art Club. Head of the Westminster Art School prior to 1914. Painted music hall scenes, landscapes—town views, not open country, portraits, flowers, fruit and still-life. In 1928 began to sign his work Richard Sickert. Well-known etcher.
*coll.*    Bedford, Cecil Higgins Museum (still-life).
*exhib.*   R.A.;  Suffolk Street (21);  N.W.C.S.;  N.E.A.C.
*lit.*     *Modern Masterpieces* by Frank Rutter.

SIKA, JUTTA
Austrian School.
b. Linz 1877 (17th September).
Painted flowers and landscapes.

SILAS, LOUIS F.
British School.
19th century. *op.* 1900–1932.
London address.
Painted flowers and decorative artist.
*repr.*    *Floral Art* (H. D. Richter).

SIMKIN, J.
British School.
*op.* 1875.
Lambeth address.
*exhib.*   Suffolk Street (2), fruit.

SIMONET, PAUL LEON
French School.
19th century.
Pupil of Bin and Lavastre. Working at Versailles. Painted fruit.
*exhib.*   Salon 1876.

SIMONS, FRANS *or* JAN FRANS
Flemish School.
b. Antwerp 1855, d. Brasschaet 1919 (21st February).
Painted still-life, portraits, genre and landscapes.
Studied Antwerp Academy.
*exhib.*   Universal Exhibition 1889, Bronze Medal.

SIMONSON, ANNA
British School.
*op.* 1895.
London address.
*exhib.*   R.A. (1), flowers.

SIMONSSON, BIRGER JORGEN
Swedish School.
b. Uddevalla 1883 (3rd March), d. 1938.
Pupil of Zahirtmann in Copenhagen and Matisse in Paris.
Painted still-life, portraits and landscapes.
*coll.*    Stockholm, National Museum.

SIMPSON, ALICE M.
British School.
*op.* 1885.
London address.
*exhib.*   Suffolk Street (1), flowers.

SIMPSON, MISS EUGENIE
British School.
*op.* 1883–1888.
Hackney address.
*exhib.* R.A. (7); Suffolk Street (2); V.E. (4), flowers.

SITTMANN, MATHILDE
German School.
b. Darmstadt 1878 (7th December).
Pupil of Wilhelm Bader. Painted flowers and portraits.

SKEATS, THOMAS
British School.
*op.* 1875–1882.
Southampton address.
*exhib.* Suffolk Street (13), flowers.

SKINNER, MISS V. M.
British School.
*op.* 1870.
Saxmundham address.
*exhib.* Suffolk Street (1), still-life.

SLADER, SAMUEL ERNEST
British School.
*op.* 1876–1879.
London address.
*exhib.* R.A. (1); Suffolk Street (1), fruit.

SLAGER, JEANNETTE
Dutch School.
b. Bois-le-Duc 1881 (14th July).
Pupil of Petrus Marinus. Painted flowers and still-life.

SLATER, C. H.
British School.
*op.* 1867.
Manchester address.
*exhib.* Suffolk Street (1), fruit.

SLAVICEK, ANTONIN
Czech School.
b. Prague 1870 (16th May), d. there 1910 (1st February).
Painted still-life.
*coll.* Pilsen; Prague; Raudnitz.
*exhib.* Universal Exhibition 1900, Bronze Medal.

SLEVOGT, MAX FRANZ THEODOR
German School.
b. Landshut 1868 (8th October), d. 1932.
Painted still-life and fruit.
*exhib.* Munich; Cologne.
*repr.* Cologne Catalogue.

SLOCOMBE, ALFRED, R.C.A.
British School.
*op.* 1862–1887.
London address.
*exhib.* R.A. (6); B.I. (2); Suffolk Street (4); N.W.C.S.
     (1); V.E. (5), flowers.

SMALL, FLORENCE VERU HARDY
British School.
19th century (*see* Vol. 3, Part I, p. 77).

SMART, CHARLES J.
British School.
*op.* 1867–1891.
London address.
*exhib.* Suffolk Street (2); N.W.C.S. (2), still-life.

SMET, GUSTAVE DE
Flemish School.
b. Ghent 1877, d. Deurle 1943.
Pupil at Ghent Academy. In Holland 1914–1918.
Painted still-life, figures and landscapes.
*coll.*     Amsterdam; Antwerp; Ghent.

SMET, LEON DE
Flemish School.
b. Ghent 1881.
Brother of Gustave de Smet. Studied Ghent Academy.
Visited France, Italy and England (1914–1918). Painted still-life, nudes, portraits, and landscapes.
*coll.*     Antwerp; Brussels; Ghent.
*repr.*     Colour Magazine (Nov. 1922), still-life.

SMITH, MISS ELIZA A.
British School.
*op.* 1865–1867.
London address.
*exhib.* B.I. (1), fruit.

SMITH, MISS FREDERICA J.
British School.
*op.* 1862–1863.
London address.
*exhib.* Suffolk Street (3), fruit.

SMITH, KATE ALICE
British School.
*op.* 1879.
London address.
*exhib.* Suffolk Street (1), flowers.

SMITH, SIR MATTHEW, C.B.E.       (*see* PLATE 46)
British School.
b. Halifax 1879 (22nd October), d. London 1959 (29th September).
Studied at Manchester School of Art. At 26 went to London and studied at the Slade School. In 1908 went to Pont Aven, Brittany, 1909 Dieppe, and 1910 Etaples and Paris. Returned to England 1912. Married Gwen Salmond, daughter of General Sir W. Salmond. Went again to Brittany until 1922. Paris 1930, South of France and London 1938–1939, Venice 1958, Tenerife 1959.

*coll.*     Birmingham; Bristol; Bradford; Leeds; London, Tate Gallery, Arts Council; Nottingham; Newcastle.
*exhib.*     Salon des Independants 1911 and 1912; London, Mayor Gallery, 1926; Reid & Lefevre 1927; Tooths 1929; R.A. Memorial Exhibition 1960; Tate Gallery Retrospective Exhibition 1953; Manchester, Works of Art from Private Collections, 1960, Nos. 216 and 217.
*repr.*     *Bouquet*, pls. 1, 2, 3, 4.

SMITH, MISS OLIVE WHEELER
British School.
*op.* 1878–1883.
Addiscombe address.
*exhib.* R.A. (2); Suffolk Street (2); V.E. (2), flowers.

SMITH, MRS. R. CATTERSON
British School.
*op.* 1882.
London address.
Painted flowers.

SMITH, MISS ROSA M.
British School.
*op.* 1883–1893.
London address.
*exhib.* R.A. (1); Suffolk Street (5), flowers.

SMITH, MISS T. W.
British School.
*op.* 1865.
London address.
*exhib.* R.A. (1), flowers.

SMITH, WILLIAM H.
British School.
*op.* 1863–1880.
London address.
*exhib.* R.A. (6); B.I. (8); Suffolk Street (17); V.E. (3); fruit

SNELLING, LILIAN
British School.
19th century, b. 1879 (?).
*coll.*     Royal Horticultural Society.
*exhib.* National Book League, Flower Books, 1950.
*repr.*     *The Genus Paeonia*, by Col. F. G. Stern, 1946.
*lit.*     Blunt.

SNOW, HELENA
British School.
*op.* 1879.
Dalston address.
*exhib.* Suffolk Street (1), fruit.

SODE, CHARLOTTE *or* CAROLINE CHARLOTTE
Danish School.
b. Vavergaard 1859 (16th April), d. Copenhagen 1931 (5th December).
Painted flowers, genre and portraits.

SODEN, MISS SUSANNAH
British School.
*op.* 1866–1890.
London address.
*exhib.* R.A. (4); Suffolk Street (4); N.W.C.S. (1); V.E. (7); flowers.

SOEBORG, AXEL
Danish School.
b. Viborg 1872 (22nd November).
Studied Copenhagen Academy. Painted still-life, portraits and landscapes.
*coll.*     Aabenraa; Aalborg.

SOGARO, OSCAR
Italian School.
19th century (*see* Vol. 3, Part I, p. 78).

SOHNGEN, ANDREAS BERNHARD
German School.
b. Oberlahnstein 1864 (14th February), d. Frankfurt 1920.
Pupil of Ed. von Steinle. Painted still-life and landscapes.

SOILLEUX, FREDERICK
British School.
*op.* 1870–1871.
London address.
*exhib.* Suffolk Street (2), fruit.

SOUTHBY, CLAUDIA
British School.
*op.* 1869–1874.
London address.
*exhib.* Suffolk Street (1); V.E. (2), flowers.

SOWDEN, JOHN
British School.
*op.* 1863–1892.
Bradford address.
*exhib.* R.A.(5); N.W.C.S.(1); G.G.(2); N.G.(1), flowers, etc

SPAANJAARD-SPANJAARD, R.
Dutch School.
b. Borne 1866 (5th December).
Pupil of J. Geerlings. Painted flowers and portraits.

SPEICH, MARY (*née* GALAY)
Swiss School.
b. Geneva 1869.
Pupil of J. Mittey and F. Gillet. Painted flowers and portraits.

SPEICHER, EUGENE E.
American School.
b. Buffalo 1883 (5th April).
Studied Buffalo, New York, and Europe. Painted still-life, flowers, portraits and landscapes.

SPENCER, MARGARET FULTON
American School.
b. Philadelphia 1882 (26th September), d. 1923.
Wife of Robert Spencer. Pupil of Mary Spencer, Birge and A. Harrison. Painted flowers and portraits.
*coll.* Cincinnati Art Museum, fruit; Detroit; St. Louis.

SPENDER, MRS.
British School.
*op.* 1861.
London address.
Painted flowers.

SPIHLER, PAUL
French School.
19th century.
Pupil of Baron Liebegott. Painted flowers and fruit.
*exhib.* Salon 1879.

SPILLER, W. H.
British School.
*op.* 1884–1886.
London address.
*exhib.* V.E. (3), still-life.

SPILLIAERT, LEON
Flemish School.
b. Ostend 1881, d. Brussels 1946.
Painted still-life, marines, landscapes and interiors.

SPIRO, EUGEN
German School.
b. Breslau 1874 (18th April).
Visited Munich, Paris and Italy. Painted still-life, portraits and landscapes.

SQUIRE, MISS EMMA
British School.
*op.* 1862–1891.
London address.
*exhib.* R.A. (9); Suffolk Street (11); V.E. (14), still-life.

SQUIRES, H.
British School.
*op.* 1864–1875.
Stratford address.
*exhib.* R.A. (2); B.I. (7); Suffolk Street (18), flowers.

STADE, MISS H.
British School.
*op.* 1868.
Finchley address.
*exhib.* R.A. (1), flowers.

STAIGER, EDMOND
French School.
19th century (*see* Vol. 3, Part I, p. 78).

STAMPER, JAMES WILLIAM
British School.
b. Birmingham 1873 (19th October).
Painted still-life.

STANNARD, LILIAN (MRS. W. B. SILAS)
British School.
b. Foxfield, Woburn, Beds., 1877 (24th March), d. Black-heath 1944 (24th November).
Second daughter of Henry Stannard, R.B.A., of Bedford. Married Dr. Walter B. Silas. Her sisters, Emily and Ivy, and her two brothers, Henry Sylvester and A. Molyneux Stannard, were all painters.
Painted flowers, but mostly flower gardens.
*exhib.* R.A. 1902–1930; R.I.; Norwich Castle Museum 1934, Stannard Exhibition; Ackermann Gallery; Mendoza Gallery 1906; Henry Graves & Co.

STANTON, EMILY R.
British School.
*op.* 1872–1893.
Stroud address.
*exhib.* R.A. (3); V.E. (12), flowers.
Graves gives Emily R. and Rose Emily separately. Possibly
the same artist.

STANTON, MISS ROSE EMILY
British School.
*op.* 1872–1892.
Stroud address.
*exhib.* R.A. (7); N.W.C.S. (4); V.E. (9), still-life.

STAPLES, MRS. JOHN C (*see* MRS. JOHN FREER *and* MISS MARY
ELLEN EDWARDS)

STAPLETON, MRS. GEORGE
British School.
*op.* 1880–1885.
London address.
*exhib.* N.W.C.S. (1); V.E. (2), still-life.

STARK, MRS. A. J. (R. ISABELLA)
British School.
*op.* 1880–1889.
London address.
*exhib.* N.W.C.S. (1); V.E. (1), still-life.

STARKE, JOHANN
German School.
19th century (*see* Vol. 3, Part I, p. 79).

STARLING, MISS MARION A.
British School.
*op.* 1883.
Brighton address.
*exhib.* R.A. (1), flowers.

STAUFFACHER, JOHANNES
Swiss School.
b. Nesslau 1850 (27th July), d. St. Gall 1916.
Studied St. Gall and Paris. Painted flowers.

STEBEL-RUDIN, ELISE
Swiss School.
b. St. Gall 1864.
Pupil of E. Jon in Paris and P. Muller in Munich. Painted
flowers and landscapes.

STEELE, HORATIO
British School.
d. 1874.
Flower painter at Derby Porcelain Manufactory. Also
painted mostly blue vetches, on Davenport china.
*lit.*    Gilhespy.

STEELE, THOMAS SEDGWICK
American School.
b. Hartford 1845 (11th June), d. Swampscott 1903 (10th
September).
Pupil of P. Marius Simons. Painted still-life.

STEGLER, ALBERT LORENTZEN
Danish School.
b. Fuglebjerg 1884 (10th September).
Studied Copenhagen Academy, Dresden and Berlin.
Painted flowers, portraits and landscapes.

STEINHEIL, ADOLPHE CHARLES EDOUARD
French School.
b. Paris 1850 (10th March), d. there 1908 (31st May).
Son and pupil of Louis Charles Auguste Steinheil.
Painted flowers and history. Chevalier of the Legion of
Honour.
*coll.*    Mulhouse, still-life.
*exhib.* Salon 1870; Universal Exhibition 1889, Bronze
          Medal.

STEINLEN, ALEXANDRE THEOPHILE          (*see* PLATE 46)
French School.
b. Lausanne 1859 (10th November), d. Paris 1923 (14th
December).
Painted genre, etc.; lithographer and sculptor.
*coll.*    Durban, South Africa, Museum and Art Gallery,
          flowers.

STEPHENSON, MISS ISOBEL H.
British School.
*op.* 1883–1887.
London address.
*exhib.* Suffolk Street (6), flowers.

STERCKMANS, MICHEL
Flemish School.
b. Schaerbeck 1883 (22nd April).
Painted still-life and portraits.

STERNE, MAURICE
American School.
b. Libau 1877.
Working in New York. Visited Europe and Paris. Painted
still-life, figures and portraits, and a sculptor.

STETTER, LINA
Swiss School.
b. Zurich 1869 (26th June).
Pupil of M. Dasio and Azbe. Painted still-life, landscapes and engraved.

STEVENS, GUSTAVE MAX
Flemish School.
b. Brussels 1871.
Pupil of J. Portaels in Brussels and F. Cormon in Paris. Painted flowers, figures, portraits and landscapes.

STEWART, MISS FLORENCE
British School.
op. 1884–1886.
London address.
exhib. R.A.(1); G.G.(2), flowers.

STIEFEL, MARIE
Swiss School.
b. Zurich 1879.
Studied Zurich and Paris. Painted flowers, interiors and landscapes.

STIFTER, MORITZ
Austrian School.
b. 1857, d. 1905 (23rd May).
Studied Munich Academy. Painted still-life and genre.

STIKEMAN, MISS ANNIE
British School.
op. 1882–1884.
Blackheath address.
exhib. Suffolk Street (2); N.W.C.S. (1), flowers.

STIRLING, MISS NINA
British School.
op. 1885–1888.
London address.
exhib. R.A. (2); Suffolk Street (2), flowers.

STOCK, MISS EDITH A.
British School.
op. 1880–1889.
Richmond address.
exhib. R.A. (3); Suffolk Street (3); N.W.C.S. (2); V.E. (3), flowers.

STOCKS, BERNARD O.
British School.
op. 1881–1890.
London address.
exhib. R.A. (3); N.W.C.S. (3), still-life.

STOCKS, MISS KATHARINE M.
British School.
op. 1877–1889.
London address.
coll.    London, Victoria and Albert Museum, flowers.
exhib. R.A. (6); N.W.C.S. (10); V.E. (14).

STOMPS, B. H.
Dutch School.
b. Gouda 1867 (6th January).
Pupil of J. F. Schutz and F. Oldewelt. Painted still-life.

STONE, ADA
British School.
op. 1879–1888.
London address.
exhib. Suffolk Street (3), still-life.

STONE, MISS ELIZABETH (see MRS. WILLIAM LAWSON, Vol. 3, Part I, p. 50)

STONES, MISS EMILY R.
British School.
op. 1882–1889.
London address.
exhib. R.A.(1); Suffolk Street (12); N.W.C.S. (6), flowers.

STONEY, CHARLES B.
British School.
op. 1879–1893.
London address.
exhib. R.A. (25); Suffolk Street (3); N.G. (2); V.E. (12), flowers.

STORM VAN 'S GRAVESANDE, CHARLES (see PLATE 22)
Dutch School.
b. Breda 1841 (21st January), d. The Hague 1924 (7th February).
Pupil of Roelofs and Rops. Painted landscapes, marines, etc., and produced lithographs.
coll.    Haarlem, Teylers Museum.
exhib. Paris, Universal Exhibition 1900.

STORY, MISS BLANCHE
British School.
op. 1881–1888.
exhib. G.G. (9), flowers.

STORY, MISS MARY L. S.
British School.
op. 1880–1886.
Nottingham address.
exhib. R.A. (2); G.G. (5), flowers.

STREBELLE, RODOLPHE
Flemish School.
b. Tournai 1880.
Studied Brussels Academy. Painted still-life, portraits,
decorative, designed tapestries.

STRETTON, MISS HESBA D.
British School.
op. 1884–1886.
Lee address.
exhib. R.A. (1); Suffolk Street (1), flowers.

STRYDONCK, GUILLAUME VAN
Flemish School.
b. Namos, Norway, 1861, d. Brussels 1937.
Studied Brussels Academy and pupil of L. Gerome in Paris.
Visited Holland, Italy, West Indies, Florida and England.
Teacher, Brussels Academy. Painted still-life, religious,
genre, portraits and landscapes.

STUART, J. E.
British School.
op. 1876.
Greenwich address.
exhib. Suffolk Street (1), fruit.

STUBBS, WOODHOUSE J.
British School.
op. 1893.
Painted flowers. Working in Sunderland.
exhib. R.A. (1).

STUHR, HERMANN
German School.
b. Schonberg 1870 (7th April).
Studied Berlin Academy. Painted flowers and landscapes.

STUHR, WILLIAM
Danish School.
b. Aalborg 1882 (10th February).
Studied Copenhagen. Visited Spain, Paris and the Bahamas.
Painted flowers, figures and landscapes.

STURGEON, KATE
British School.
op. 1882–1895.
London address.
exhib. R.A. (4); Suffolk Street (7); G.G. (9).

STURTEVANT, CHARLES T.
British School.
op. 1866.
Taunton address.
exhib. B.I. (2), fruit.

SUCHARDA, ANNA
Czecho-Slovakian School.
b. Nova Paka 1870 (23rd October).
Working in Prague. Painted flowers.

SUDDARDS, FRANK
British School.
op. 1884.
Bournemouth address.
exhib. N.W.C.S. (1), flowers.

SUGARS, FANNY
British School.
op. 1889–1898.
Manchester address.
exhib. R.A. (3), flowers.

SUGGATE, F. W.
British School.
op. 1878–1882.
London address.
exhib. R.A. (1); Suffolk Street (2), flowers.

SURVAGE, LEOPOLD
French School.
b. Moscow or in Finland 1879 (12th August).
In Paris in 1908. Painted landscapes and still-life and engraved.
coll. Athens; Chicago; Moscow; Paris; San Francisco.

SUTCLIFFE, MRS. L. T.
British School.
op. 1893–1895.
Whitby address.
exhib. R.A. (3), flowers.

SUTHERS, W.
British School.
op. 1878–1887.
London address.
exhib. R.A. (5); Suffolk Street (12); N.W.C.S. (1), flowers.

SUTTON, G. M.
British School.
op. 1875.
Worcester address.
exhib. Suffolk Street (1), still-life.

SUTTON, T.
British School.
op. 1868.
exhib. R.A. (1), fish.

SWAFFIELD, HELENA M.
British School.
*op.* 1891–1895.
Sevenoaks and London addresses.
*exhib.* R.A. (1); Suffolk Street (3); V.E. (1).

SWALLOW, MISS JANE F.
British School.
*op.* 1864–1869.
London address.
*exhib.* R.A. (1); Suffolk Street (5); V.E. (9), fruit.

SWAN, MISS ALICE MACALLAN
British School.
*op.* 1882–1890.
Cork address.
*exhib.* R.A. (8); N.W.C.S. (2), flowers.

SWINGLER, JOHN FRANK
British School.
*op.* 1886–1899.
London address.
*exhib.* R.A. (13); Suffolk Street (5); V.E. (7), still-life.

SWINSTEAD, ELIZA L. J.
British School.
*op.* 1881.
Dalston address.
*exhib.* Suffolk Street (1), flowers.

TAILLEUR, GERMAINE MELANIE MARIE
French School.
b. Besancon 1881 (22nd December).
Pupil of Madeleine Lemaire. Painted flowers and landscapes.

TARGETT, THOMAS G.
British School.
*op.* 1869.
Salisbury address.
Painted game.

TARNOCZY, TARNOCZY-SPRINZENBERG, BERTHA VON
Austrian School.
b. Innsbruck 1846 (1st April), d. Vienna 1936 (6th March).
Studied Munich and Vienna. Painted still-life, portraits and landscapes.

TASTEMAIN, PIERRE MAURICE EUGENE
French School.
b. Caen 1878 (6th September).
Chevalier of the Legion of Honour 1938. Painted still-life and portraits.
*coll.* Arles; Caen.
*exhib.* International Exhibition 1937, Bronze Medal.

TAVERNIER, HIPPOLYTE JEAN
French School.
b. Francheville 1884 (26th August).
Painted still-life and landscapes.

TAYLER, MISS KATE
British School.
*op.* 1872–1893.
London address.
*exhib.* R.A. (2); N.W.C.S. (2), flowers.

TAYLER, NORMAN E., A.R.W.S.
British School.
*op.* 1863–1893.
London address.
*exhib.* R.A. (13); B.I. (1); Suffolk Street (1); O.W.C.S. (90), flowers.

TAYLOR, MISS ADA E.
British School.
*op.* 1876–1881.
London address.
*exhib.* R.A. (1); Suffolk Street (1); V.E. (5), fruit.

TAYLOR, MISS CHARLOTTE
British School.
*op.* 1874–1884.
London address.
*exhib.* N.W.C.S. (2), still-life.

TAYLOR, ERNEST E.
British School.
*op.* 1882–1893.
London address.
*exhib.* Suffolk Street (1), flowers.

TAYLOR, J.
British School.
*op.* 1863–1865.
Plumstead address.
*exhib.* R.A. (2), fruit.

TAYLOR, MISS JANE
British School.
*op.* 1872–1874.
Rye address.
*exhib.* Suffolk Street (3), flowers.

TAYLOR, MISS PAULINE
British School.
*op.* 1868–1869.
Southport address.
*exhib.* Suffolk Street (4), still-life.

TAYLOR, SAMUEL C.
British School.
*op.* 1897.
Belfast address.
*exhib.* R.A. (1), still-life.

TENKOVIC, MILOS
Yugo-Slavian School.
b. Belgrade 1849 (8th April), d. there 1890.
Pupil of Stefan Todorvic and at Vienna Academy.
Painted still-life and portraits.
*coll.* Belgrade.

THAYER, EMMA (*née* BEACH)
American School.
b. 1850, d. 1924 (1st March).
Wife of Abbott Handerson Thayer. Painted flowers in oil and pastel.

THEVENET, LOUIS
Flemish School.
b. Bruges 1874, d. Brussels 1930.
Painted still-life.

THEVENET, PIERRE
Flemish School.
b. Bruges 1870 (1st March), d. Brussels 1937 (30th March).
Studied in Paris. Painted still-life, architecture and landscapes.

THOLEN, MARGO J.
Dutch School.
b. Kampen 1870, d. Apeldoorn 1911 (19th June).
Pupil of P. J. C. Gabriel and J. Voerman. Painted still-life and landscapes.
*coll.* The Hague, Municipal Museum.

THOLER, RAYMOND
French School.
b. Paris 1859 (19th November).
Pupil of Bergeret. Painted flowers and still-life.
*coll.* Niort Museum.
*exhib.* Salon 1877.

THOMA, CELLA (*née* BERTENEDER)          (*see* PLATE 47)
German School.
b. Munich 1858 (14th April), d. Constance 1901 (23rd November).
Wife and pupil of Hans Thoma.
Painted flowers and still-life.
*coll.* Karlsruhe; Frankfurt.

THOMAS, ANDRE FELIX
French School.
19th century.
Pupil of M. Starke. Working in Paris. Painted fruit and still-life.
*exhib.* Salon 1865.

THOMAS, MISS D. H.
British School.
*op.* 1878–1892.
Llandudno address.
*exhib.* N.W.C.S. (1), game.

THOMPSON, MISS E.
British School.
*op.* 1869.
Teignmouth address.
*exhib.* Suffolk Street (1), flowers.

THOMSON, MISS A. E.
British School.
*op.* 1884–1886.
Newstead address.
*exhib.* Suffolk Street (2), flowers.

THORBURN, ARCHIBALD
British School.
b. 1860 (31st May), d. Godalming 1935 (9th October).
Residing at Kelso in 1880. Painted flowers, birds and sporting subjects. Illustrated many works on natural history.
*coll.* Preston, H.M. and A.G., flowers.
*exhib.* R.A. (16); Suffolk Street (1).

THORNAM, EMMY MARIE CAROLINE
Danish School.
b. Horsens 1852 (10th March), d. Copenhagen 1935 (7th
January).
Pupil of Kyhn, and Bourgogne in Paris. Painted flowers.
*coll.* Aarhus Museum; Kolding; Vejle.

THORNHILL, PHILIP J.
British School.
*op.* 1895.
London address.
*exhib.* R.A. (1), flowers.

THORNYCROFT, HELEN
British School.
1864–1912.
London address. Daughter of Thomas Thornycroft, sculptor. Member of the Society of Lady Artists.
Painted scriptural subjects and flowers.
*exhib.* R.A. (20); Suffolk Street (4); N.W.C.S. (3); N.G.
(3); V.E. (60).

THORPE, JOHN HALL
British School.
b. Victoria, Australia, 1874 (29th April).
Painted flowers. Known as Hall Thorpe.
*repr.* Hardie, *Flower Paintings*, 1947.
Richter, *Floral Art*, 1932.

THORS, S.
British School.
*op.* 1880.
London address.
*exhib.* Suffolk Street (1), still-life.

THURNALL, HARRY J.
British School.
*op.* 1875–1893.
Royston address.
Painted flowers and game.
*exhib.* R.A. (4); Suffolk Street (7); N.W.C.S. (1).

THYSEBAERT, LOUIS
Flemish School.
b. Ghent 1879 (10th April).
Painted flowers, landscapes and interiors.

TIEMANN, WALTER
German School.
b. Delitzsch 1876 (29th January).
Studied Leipzig, Dresden and Paris. Painted still-life, portraits and landscapes.

TIFFIN, MISS LYDIA EMILY
British School.
*op.* 1863.
London address.
*exhib.* Suffolk Street (2), fruit.

TIRMAN, *or* TIRMON, JEANNE HENRIETTE
French School.
b. Charleville 1875, d. Sevres 1952 (30th October).
Painted flowers and still-life.
*exhib.* Salon des Artistes Francais 1889; Independants.

TISSOT, JAMES JACQUES JOSEPH
French School.
b. Nantes 1836 (15th October), d. Buillon (Nantes) 1902
(8th August).
Working in England after the Franco-Prussian war of 1870.
In Palestine for ten years engaged on pictures for a Life of
Christ. Painted history, genre, portraits, gardens, etc.
*auct.* A painting, 'Geranium', sold at Sotheby's, 6th
November 1963.

TITCOMB, WILLIAM HOLT YATES, R.B.A.
British School.
b. Cambridge 1858 (22nd February).
Studied South Kensington, and under Verlat at Antwerp,
Boulanger and Lefebvre in Paris and Herkomer at Bushey.
Working at Balham and St. Ives. Painted flowers and
domestic.
*exhib.* R.A. (8); Suffolk Street (12); V.E. (4); Paris 1890,
Medal, and Chicago 1893.

TODD, JOHN GEORGE
British School.
*op.* 1861–1892.
Ecouen address.
*exhib.* R.A. (10), flowers.

TODD, T.
British School.
*op.* 1874.
Ulverston address.
*exhib.* Suffolk Street (1), fruit.

TOLLES, SOPHIE MAPES
American School.
b. New York. *op.* 1864–1876.
Studied in Philadelphia, France and Italy. Painted flowers
and portraits.
*exhib.* National Academy 1876.

TOMSON, ARTHUR
British School.
b. 1858, d. Robertsbridge, Sussex, 1905 (14th June).
Painted flowers and landscapes.
*coll.* London, Victoria and Albert Museum, flowers.
*exhib.* R.A. (14); Suffolk Street (6); N.G. (10); G.G. (5); N.E.A.C. 1883-1902.

TOPHAM, MISS
British School.
*op.* 1868.
London address.
*exhib.* V.E. (3), fruit.

TOSI, ARTURO                 (*see* PLATE 47)
Italian School.
b. Busto Arsizio 1871 (25th July), d. Milano 1956 (31st January).
Painted flowers.
*coll.* Turin Museum.

TOUDOUZE, ISABELLE
French School.
19th century.
Painted flowers. Working in Paris.
*exhib.* Salon 1868-1875.

TOUDOUZE, MARIE ANNE
French School.
19th century.
Painted fruit. Working in Lyon.
*exhib.* Salon des Artistes Francais 1901-1904.

TOULMIN SMITH, MISS E.
British School.
*op.* 1868-1872.
London address. Taught design at Montpelier.
Painted flowers.
*coll.* Sete Museum.
*exhib.* Suffolk Street (6); V.E. (2). Graves says 'Domestic'.

TOURILLON, ALFRED EDOUARD
French School.
19th century (*see* Vol. 3, Part I, p. 83).

TOVO, PETRONILLA
Italian School.
19th century.
Painted flowers and landscapes.
*exhib.* Turin 1880-1898.

TOWERS, SAMUEL, R.C.A.
British School.
*op.* 1884-1894.
Bolton-le-Moors address.
*exhib.* R.A. (4), flowers.

TRIER, MRS. ADELINE
British School.
*op.* 1879-1893.
London address.
*exhib.* R.A. (5); Suffolk Street (4), flowers.

TRINQUIER, FERNAND
French School.
b. Montpelier 1863.
Pupil of Bideau. Painted flowers.
*coll.* Sete Museum.

TROIS, ENRICO GIULIO
Italian School.
b. Venice 1882 (1st February).
Painted flowers and landscapes.

TROUPEAU, FERDINAND
French School.
19th century.
Pupil of Pignot and Lambotti. Working in Bordeaux.
Painted flowers.
*exhib.* Salon 1880.
*repr.* *Dekorative Vorbilder*, Stuttgart.

TRUBNER, ALICE (*née* AUERBACH)
German School.
b. Bradford 1875 (24th August), d. Berlin 1916 (20th March).
Painted still-life, landscapes and portraits.
*coll.* Karlsruhe; Staedel; Frankfurt.

TRUBNER, WILHELM *or* HEINRICH WILHELM
German School.
b. Heidelberg 1851 (3rd February), d. Karlsruhe 1917 (21st December).
Pupil of Leibl at Munich. Professor at Frankfurt.
Painted still-life, portraits and landscapes.

TSCHUDI, RUDOLF
American School.
b. 1855 (27th April), d. Cincinnatti 1923 (23rd July).
Painted still-life, landscapes and portraits.
*coll.* Glanis Museum.

TULK, AUGUSTUS
British School.
*op.* 1877–1892.
Norwood address.
*exhib.* R.A. (3); Suffolk Street (11); V.E. (6), still-life.

TURNER, ANSELM
British School.
*op.* 1867–1871.
London address.
*exhib.* V.E. (7), fruit.

TURNER, HELEN M.
American School.
b. 1858 (?), d. 1958.
Pupil of Cox in New York. Member of the Federation of American Arts. Painted flowers, landscapes and portraits. Received teacher's diploma 1902.
*coll.* Detroit; New York, Metro.; Washington.

TYE, EDITH A.
British School.
*op.* 1894–1897.
London address.
*exhib.* R.A. (3), flowers.

UDVARLAKY, BELA
Hungarian School.
b. Vienna 1849, d. Budapest 1885.
Painted still-life.

ULM, EMILE
French School.
19th century.
Pupil of Gleyre. Working in Rochefort. Painted flowers and fruit.
*exhib.* Salon 1864–1866.

UMBRICHT, HONORE LOUIS
French School.
b. Obernai 1860 (17th January).
Pupil of Bonnat. Painted still-life, genre, landscapes and portraits.
*exhib.* Universal Exhibition 1900, Bronze Medal.

UNDERHILL, FREDERICK THOMAS
British School.
*op.* 1868–1890.
London address.
*exhib.* R.A. (3); Suffolk Street (5), fruit.

UNTHANK, GERTRUDE
American School.
b. Economy 1878 (26th October).
Pupil of J. E. Bechdy. Painted still-life.

URY, LESSER                                      (*see* PLATE 48)
German School.
b. Birnbaum 1861 (7th November), d. Berlin 1931 (18th October).
Studied at Antwerp, Brussels, Dusseldorf, Munich and Paris. Painted flowers.
*coll.* Berlin; Gratz Museum.

UYTTERSCHAUT, VICTOR
Flemish School.
b. Brussels 1847 (17th November), d. Boulogne 1917 (4th October).
Studied at Brussels Academy. Painted still-life, landscapes and marines.

VAES, WALTER                                     (*see* PLATE 48)
Flemish School.
b. Borgerhout 1882, d. 1958.
Pupil of his uncle, P. Verheart, and A. de Vriendt. Winner of Rome Prize and travelled in Italy, Spain, Central Europe, and Palestine. In Holland 1914–1918. Painted still-life, figures, landscapes, portraits, and engraved.
*coll.* Antwerp; Brussels; Utrecht.

VAL, VALENTINE SYNAVE NICOLAUD
Flemish School.
b. Brussels 1870, d. 1943.
Pupil of E. Carriere and Renoir. Painted flowers, still-life and landscapes.
*coll.* The Hague, Municipal Museum, flowers.
*exhib.* Salon 1913.

VALADON, MARIA, *or* MARIE VALENTINE SUZANNE
French School.
b. Bessines 1867 (23rd September), d. Paris 1938.
Painted flowers and still-life.
*coll.* Albi; Belgrade; Paris; Prague.

VALANTIN, PAUL
French School.
19th century (*see* Vol. 3, Part I, p. 84).

VALENTINE, ALBERT R., *or* VALENTIEN
American School.
b. Cincinnati 1862 (11th May), d. 1925 (5th August).
Studied Cincinnati Academy and under Duveneck in
Florence. Painted wild flowers and grasses.
*exhib.* Salon 1900.

VALENTINI, SALA IRENE
Italian School.
b. Milan 1864 (19th June).
Painted flowers, animals and genre.

VALK, MAURITS WILLEM VAN DER
Dutch School.
b. Amsterdam 1857 (16th December), d. 1935.
Pupil of A. Allebe. Painted fruit, still-life and landscapes.
*coll.*    Amsterdam, Municipal Museum, fruit.
*exhib.*  Universal Exhibition 1900, Silver Medal.

VALKEMA, HERMANN
Dutch School.
b. Soekamadjoe (Java) 1880 (18th April).
Pupil of L. Visser and The Hague Academy. Painted flowers
and portraits.

VALKER, AGNES
Hungarian School.
b. Gyor 1879 (17th October).
Pupil of Liezen-Mayer. Painted still-life.

VALLANCE, AYMER
British School.
*op.* 1880.
London address.
*exhib.*  Suffolk Street (2), flowers.

VALLENCE, MISS FANNY
British School.
*op.* 1876–1885.
London address.
*exhib.*  R.A. (1); Suffolk Street (1), fruit.

VALLOTTON, FELIX EDOUARD            (*see* PLATE 49)
Swiss School.
b. Lausanne 1865 (28th December), d. Paris 1925 (29th
December).
Naturalised Frenchman 1900.
Painter, sculptor and engraver.
*coll.*    Johannesburg; Lausanne; Neuchatel, all still-life;
          Zurich, flowers.

VALNAUD, LEONIE
French School.
19th century.
Pupil of Mme Trebuchet in Paris.
Painted flowers.
*exhib.* Salon 1879.

VALTAT, LOUIS
French School.
b. Dieppe 1869 (6th August), d. Paris 1952 (2nd January).
Painted flowers and landscapes.
*coll.*    Paris, Modern Art.

VAN HOORN, MDLLE C
Dutch School.
*op.* 1882.
Arnheim address.
*exhib.*  V.E. (1), flowers.

VAN HOUTEN, BARBARA ELISABETH
Dutch School.
b. Groningen 1862.
Painter and etcher.  Resident at The Hague.
*coll.*   The Hague, Mesdag Museum have etchings of
         flowers and still life.

VAN HOUTEN, MDME S. MESDAG
Dutch School.
b. Groningen 1834, d. The Hague 1909.
With her husband, Mr. H. W. Mesdag, the foundress of the
Mesdag Museum, The Hague. Painted landscapes, portraits,
flowers and fruits.
*coll.*    The Hague, Mesdag Museum.
*exhib.* G.G. (2), flowers.

VAQUEZ, EMILE MODESTE NICOLAS
French School.
b. Paris 1841, d. 1900.
Painted flowers in water-colour.
*exhib.* Salon 1873.

VARLEY, LUCY
British School.
*op.* 1886–1897.
London address.
*exhib.* R.A. (3); Suffolk Street (1); N.W.C.S. (5); V.E. (1).

VASSELON, MARIUS
French School.
Pupil of Dessurgey and Bonnat. Painted flowers, portraits,
        genre and landscapes.
*exhib.* Salon 1863–1880.

VENABLES, MISS ALICE
British School.
*op.* 1884.
Lincoln address.
*exhib.* Suffolk Street (1), flowers.

VERBOECKHOVEN, LOUIS THE YOUNGER
Flemish School.
19th century (*see* Vol. 3, Part I, p. 84).

VERHAEGEN, FERNAND
Flemish School.
b. Marchienne 1883 (27th July).
Painted flowers, still-life, landscapes and genre. Visited Paris and London.

VERHAEREN, ALFRED
Flemish School.
b. Brussels 1849 (8th October), d. Ixelles 1924 (10th February).
Pupil of L. Dubois. Painted still-life, interiors etc. Officer of the Legion of Honour
*coll.* Antwerp; Brussels; The Hague, Mesdag Museum; Paris, Louvre.
*exhib.* Universal Exhibition 1900, Silver Medal.

VERHEYDEN, ISIDORE
Flemish School.
b. Antwerp 1846 (24th January), d. Brussels 1905 (1st November).
Son of Francois Verheyden. Pupil of J. Quinaux and J. Portaels. Director Brussels Academy 1904. Painted still-life, landscapes and portraits.

VERHOEVEN, SERAPHIN ACHILLE
French School.
b. Tourcoing 1847, d. Dunkirk 1905.
Painted still-life.
*coll.* Tourcoing Museum.

VERNON, MISS MARY
British School.
*op.* 1871–1873.
Birmingham address.
*exhib.* Suffolk Street (5), flowers.

VERSTER, FLORIS HENDRIK                    (*see* PLATE 50)
Dutch School.
b. Leyden 1861 (9th June), d. there 1927 (February).
Pupil at The Hague Academy and under Breitner. Worked in Brussels and Leyden.
*coll.* Amsterdam, Rijks. Museum; Dordrecht; The Hague; Hamburg; Leyden; Rotterdam; Stedelijk Museum; Boymans Museum.

VESEY-HOLT, MISS A. JULIA
British School.
*op.* 1884.
London address.
*exhib.* R.A. (1), flowers.

VIDECOQ, LUCIE MARIE
French School.
19th century.
Pupil of Courtois. Working in Paris. Painted still-life and landscapes.
*exhib.* Salon 1878–1880.

VIGNE, EMMA DE
Flemish School.
b. Ghent 1850 (30th January), d. there 1898 (3rd June).
Pupil of uncle Felix Vigne. Painted flowers and fruit.

VILLERS, GASTON DE—GASTON BERNHEIM THE YOUNGER
Flemish School.
b. Brussels 1870 (20th December).
Painted flowers, still-life, interiors and portraits.

VINTER, MRS. C.
British School.
*op.* 1874.
Walton-on-Thames address.
*exhib.* Suffolk Street (1), flowers.

VINTER, MISS HARRIET EMILY
British School.
*op.* 1879–1880.
London address.
*exhib.* R.A. (1); Suffolk Street (1), still-life.

VIOLA, FERDINAND
French School.
19th century.
Painted fruit, still-life and genre.
*exhib.* Salon 1865.

VIOLA, RAOUL
French School.
19th century.
Pupil of G. Boulanger and Lefebvre.
Painted flowers and was a musician.
*exhib.* Salon 1880.

VIPAN, MISS E. M.
British School.
*op.* 1884–1885.
Brighton address.
*exhib.* Suffolk Street (1), flowers.

VIRET, FREDERIC
French School.
19th century (*see* Vol. 3, Part I, p. 85).

VISIEN, CHARLES ANTOINE DE
French School.
19th century.
Pupil of L. Cogniet and O. Mathieu. Painted flowers and still-life.
*exhib.* Salon 1867–1868.

VITTALY, JULES LOUIS
French School.
19th century.
At Langres, pupil of M. Baumann.
Known as Vitaly.
*exhib.* Salon 1879.

VLAANDEREN, JOHAN
Dutch School.
b. Kralingen 1867 (15th August).
Pupil of Schulman.
Painted flowers and landscapes.

VLAMINCK, MAURICE DE                    (*see* PLATE 51)
French School.
b. Paris 1876 (4th April) of Flemish parents, d. 1958
Self taught. Painted stormy landscapes and flowers. Was a racing cyclist, played the violin and wrote.
*repr.* Cologne Catalogue; *Bouquet*, pl. 47.
*auct.* Sotheby's 11.4.1962, still-life; flowers.

VLOORS, EMILE
Flemish School.
b. Borgerhout 1871 (31st August), d. 1952.
Pupil of A. de Vriendt in Antwerp and Leon Bonnat in Paris. Director of Antwerp Academy 1924. Painted still-life, interiors and portraits.
*coll.* Antwerp.

VOWE, PAUL GERHART
German School.
b. Elberfeld 1874 (16th May).
Studied Berlin and Munich Academies. Painted flowers, landscapes, portraits and figures.

VUILLARD, EDOUARD—JEAN EDOUARD        (*see* PLATE 52)
French School.
b. Cuiseaux 1868 (11th November), d. La Baule 1940 (21st June).
Pupil of Bouguereau and Gerome. Painted flowers, etc.
*coll.* Berlin; Boston; Cleveland; Glasgow; London, Tate Gallery; New York; Paris; Toronto; Washington.
*auct.* Sotheby's 14.6.1962, fruit.

WAAS, MORRIS ABRAHAM
American School.
b. 1843, d. 1927.
Philadelphia dentist and amateur painter. Painted still-life.
*lit.* Frankenstein *After the Hunt*, 1953.

WAGEMAN, M. JUNR.
British School.
*op.* 1866.
London address.
*exhib.* B.I. (1), still-life.

WAGEMANS, MAURICE
Flemish School.
b. Brussels 1877, d. Breedene-sur-mer 1927.
Pupil of J. Portaels and J. Stallaert. Painted still-life, landscapes, marines, portraits and genre.
*coll.* Antwerp.

WALFORD, H. LOUISA
British School.
*op.* 1891–1897.
Bushey address.
*exhib.* R.A. (1); N.W.C.S. (1), flowers.

WALKER, MISS ELIZABETH
British School.
*op.* 1877–1882.
London address.
*exhib.* R.A. (3), flowers.

WALKER, DAME ETHEL D.B.E., A.R.A.
British School.
b. Edinburgh 1867, d. 1951.
Studied Slade School. Member of the New English Art Club. Painted portraits, landscapes, marines, still-life, flowers and genre.
*exhib.* R.A.
*repr.* *Bouquet* pl. 13.
*lit.* *Modern English Painters*, Rothenstein 1952.

WALKER, PAULINE                    (*see* PLATE 53)
British School (Norwich).
*op.* 1870–1882, d. 1891 at Birkdale.
Southport address. Wife of James William Walker (1831–1898) an Art Teacher who painted landscapes.
*coll.* Norwich Museum.
*exhib.* R.A. (1); Suffolk Street (2); G.G. (2); V.E. (24), still-life; Victoria Hall Gallery, 1878 (2).

WALLER, C.
British School.
*op.* 1863–1865.
London address.
*exhib.* B.I. (2); Suffolk Street (2), flowers.

WALLIN, CARL E.                                    (*see* PLATE 53)
American School.
*op.* 1879.
Painted still-life.

WALLIS, ROSA
British School.
b. Stretton 1857 (5th March).
Studied Manchester.
Painted flowers in water colour.
*coll.*    London, Victoria and Albert Museum.
*exhib.* R.A. (5);  Suffolk Street (19);  N.W.C.S. (18);
        V.E. (10) 1878–1893 from London address.

WALTER, M. ALICE
British School.
*op.* 1880–1882.
Painted flowers.

WANN, PAUL
Austrian School.
b. Freudenthal 1869 (26th September).
Studied in Vienna. Painted flowers and still-life.

WARD, HERBERT
British School.
b. London 1863, d. Paris 1919 (7th August).
Painted still-life. Accompanied Stanley to Africa.
*exhib.* R.A. (1);  Salon des Artistes Francais.

WARD, MRS. KATHERINE M.
British School.
*op.* 1893–1894.
London address.
*exhib.* R.A. (2), flowers.

WARNER, MRS. A.
British School.
*op.* 1876.
Milford address.
Painted flowers.

WARNER, L.
British School.
*op.* 1878.
Aldershot address.
Painted flowers.

WARWICK, MISS EDITH C.
British School.
*op.* 1868.
London address.
*exhib.* Suffolk Street (1), flowers.

WARWICK, R. W.
British School.
*op.* 1876–1877.
London address.
*exhib.* Suffolk Street (2), fruit.

WASSE, ARTHUR
British School.
*op.* 1879–1895.
Manchester and London addresses.
Painted flowers and domestic.
*exhib.* R.A. (13);  Suffolk Street (1).

WATELET, EUGENIE SOPHIE
French School.
19th century.
Painted flowers.
*coll.*    Soissons Museum.
*exhib.* Salon 1869–1870.

WATERHOUSE, MRS. J. W.—ESTHER
British School.
*op.* 1884–1890.
London address.
Wife of John William Waterhouse, R.A.
*exhib.* R.A. (6);  N.W.C.S. (6);  N.G. (1), flowers

WATERLOW, SIR ERNEST ALBERT, R.A., R.W.S.
British School.
b. London 1850 (24th May), d. there 1919 (25th October).
Studied in London, Germany and Switzerland
Painted landscapes and flowers.
*exhib.* R.A. (45);  Suffolk Street (11);  O.W.C.S. (99);
        G.G (14);  N.G. (4);  V.E. (82).

WATSON, F. G.
British School.
*op.* 1882.
Witley address.
*exhib.* Suffolk Street (2), fruit.

WATSON, MRS.
British School.
*op.* 1881.
Witley address. Probably the wife of F. G. Watson.
*exhib.* Suffolk Street (2), flowers.

WAUGH, MISS NORA
British School.
*op.* 1884–1887.
London address.
*exhib.* Suffolk Street (2); N.W.C.S. (1); V.E. (3), flowers.

WAY, WILLIAM COSENS
British School.
19th century (*see* Vol. 3, Part I, p. 87).

WEIE, EDVAR *or* VIGGO THORVALD EDVARD
Danish School.
b. Copenhagen 1879 (18th November).
Painted still-life.

WEIR, JULIAN ALDEN
American School.
b. West Point 1852 (30th August), d. New York 1919 (8th December).
Son and pupil of Robert Walker Alden and of J. L. Gerome in Paris. Painted portraits, figures and still-life.
*coll.* Buffalo; Brooklyn; Chicago; Cincinnati; Cleveland; New York, Metropolitan Museum; Paris, Louvre; Philadelphia (none are flowers, fruit or still life).

WEISS, EMIL RUDOLF                     (*see* PLATE 54)
German School.
b. Lahr 1875 (12th October), d. Meersburg (7th November).
Pupil of Poltzelberger at Karlsruhe Academy. Worked in Paris and Baden. Painted flowers and fruit.
*coll.* Breme; Cologne; Dresden; Karlsruhe; Winterthur; Zurich.

WEISS, EMILE GEORGES
French School.
b. Strasburg 1861 (20th January).
Pupil of Bonnat and Grison. Painted fruit and landscapes.
*coll.* Nantes.
*exhib.* Salon 1880.

WELBY, MISS ROSE ELLEN
British School.
*op.* 1879–1897.
London address.
*exhib.* R.A. (4); Suffolk Street (6); N.W.C.S. (6); G.G. (1); N.G. (2); V.E. (12), flowers.

WENNERBERG, GUNNAR GUNNARSSON
Swedish School.
b. Shara 1863 (17th December), d. Paris 1911 (22nd April), National Museum, Stockholm, say 1914.
Pupil of H. Gervex and G. Courtois. Painted flowers. Mainly a ceramic designer.
*coll.* Stockholm, National Museum.

WEST, GERTRUDE
British School.
b. Birmingham 1872 (18th March).
Painted flowers.

WEST, MISS MAUD ASTLEY
British School.
*op.* 1880–1890.
Bedford Park address. Studied Bloomsbury School of Art.
Painted flowers.
*exhib.* N.W.C.S. (2); V.E. (1).

WESTON, ERNEST
British School.
*op.* 1884.
Woolwich address.
*exhib.* N.W.C.S. (1), still-life.

WEYHER, SUZANNE
French School.
b. Paris 1878, d. Lavandou 1924.
Wife of Jean Schlumberger.
Painted flowers and landscapes.

WHEELER, MISS ANNIE
British School.
*op.* 1868–1885.
London address.
*exhib.* Suffolk Street (6); N.W.C.S. (1), flowers.

WHEELER, MISS S. A.
British School.
*op.* 1863–1879.
London address.
*exhib.* R.A. (1); B.I. (1); Suffolk Street (8), fruit.

WHEELWRIGHT, ANNA
British School.
*op.* 1884.
London address.
*exhib.* Suffolk Street (1), flowers.

WHIPPLE, MRS. JOHN (AGNES)
British School.
*op.* 1881–1888.
London address.
*exhib.* R.A. (5); Suffolk Street (1), flowers.

WHITE, FLORENCE
British School.
*op.* 1881–1917.
London address. Painted flowers and domestic.
*exhib.* R.A. (7); Suffolk Street (5); G.G. (1); V.E. (8).

WHITE, MRS.
South African School.
*op.* 1870.
Wife of Samuel White, waggon maker of Grahamstown.
Painted flowers and birds.
*exhib.* Grahamstown May 1870.
*lit.*     *Pictorial Art in South Africa* by A. Gordon Brown 1952.

WHITEHEAD, MISS ELIZABETH
British School.
*op.* 1880–1900
Leamington address.
*exhib.* R.A. (8); Suffolk Street (3); V.E. (1), flowers.

WHITEHEAD, FREDERICK
British School.
*op.* 1870–1893
Leamington address.
*exhib.* R.A. (12); Suffolk Street (17); V.E. (6), still-life.

WHITFIELD, MRS. FLORENCE WESTWOOD
British School.
*op.* 1888.
Birmingham address.
*coll.*    Birmingham Art Gallery, flowers.
*exhib.* R.A. (1).

WHITLEY, MISS KATE MARY, R.I.
British School.
*op.* 1884–1893.
Leicester address.
*exhib.* R.A. (5); N.W.C.S. (26), still-life.

WHITTLE, MISS ELIZABETH
British School.
*op.* 1875–1879.
Croydon address.
*exhib.* Suffolk Street (2), fruit.

WHITTLE, T. S.
British School.
*op.* 1862.
Lewisham Address.
*exhib.* B.I. (1); Suffolk Street (1), fruit.

WHYTE, JOHN G.
British School.
*op.* 1877–1886.
Helensburgh address.
*exhib.* R.A. (5), flowers.

WIFFIN, H. H.
British School.
*op.* 1869.
Reigate address.
Painted flowers.

WIGNELL, MISS P. E.
British School.
*op.* 1872–1875.
Southsea address.
*exhib.* Suffolk Street (7), fruit.

WILKINSON, L. M.
British School.
*op.* 1881.
London address.
Painted flowers.

WILLEY, MISS H.
British School.
*op.* 1874.
Bristol address.
*exhib.* Suffolk Street (1), flowers.

WILLIAMS, BENJAMIN
British School.
b. Langley Green, Worcestershire 1868 (13th April), d.
Wolverhampton 1920 (13th December).
Studied at the School of Art, Birmingham. Taught art in
Birmingham where he lived from 1877. Authority on
musical instruments. Painted figure subjects and still-life.
*coll.*    Birmingham Art Gallery, 2 still-life; London, Victoria
          and Albert Museum, figure studies in water colour.
*lit.*     Catalogue of Water colours in Victoria and Albert
          Museum 1927.

WILLIAMS, CHRISTOPHER
British School.
b. Maesteg 1873 (7th January), d. 1935
Studied R.A. Schools. Painted flowers, portraits and history.

WILLIAMS, DEBORAH
British School.
19th century.
Dublin address. Daughter of Solomon Williams.
Painted flowers.

WILLIAMS, MISS EMILY
British School.
*op.* 1869–1889.
London address.
*exhib.* R.A. (5); Suffolk Street (1); V.E. (6), flowers.

WILLIAMS, POWNALL T. *or* POWNOLL
British School.
*op.* 1872–1897.
Hastings and London addresses.
*exhib.* R.A. (7); Suffolk Street (13); N.W.C.S. (1); G.G.
(3); V.E. (31).

WILLIAMS, MRS. SYDNEY
British School.
*op.* 1871.
Balham address.
Painted flowers.

WILLSHAW, J.
British School.
*op.* 1864–1866.
Newcastle-under-Lyne address.
*exhib.* B.L. (4), fruit.

WILSON, MISS FLORENCE E.
British School.
*op.* 1882–1890.
London address.
*exhib.* R.A. (2); Suffolk Street (3); N.W.C.S. (2), flowers.

WILSON, MISS KATE
British School.
*op.* 1878–1883.
London address.
*exhib.* Suffolk Street (2), flowers.

WILSON, STANLEY
British School.
*op.* 1878–1883.
London address.
*exhib.* Suffolk Street (1); V.E. (4), still-life.

WIMPERIS, MISS S. W.
British School.
*op.* 1868–1871.
Chester address.
*exhib.* Suffolk Street (5), flowers.

WING, MARY LOUISA
British School.
*op.* 1871.
London address.
*exhib.* Suffolk Street (1), flowers.

WIRGMAN, HELEN
British School.
*op.* 1879–1882.
London address.
*exhib.* V.E. (4), flowers.

WIRTH, ANNA MARIE
German School.
b. St. Petersburg 1846 (16th May).
Pupil of H. Canon at Vienna. Visited Munich, Painted still-life and genre.

WISINGER-FLORIAN, OLGA (*née* FLORIAN)
Austrian School.
b. Vienna 1844 (1st November), d. there 1926 (27th February).
Pupil of A. Schaeffer and E. Schindler at Vienna. Visited Paris. Painted flowers, landscape and genre.
*coll.*    Munich; Vienna.
*exhib.* Universal Exhibition 1900, Bronze Medal.

WITCHELL, MISS LUCY
British School.
*op.* 1883–1891.
Stroud address.
*exhib.* R.A. (3), still-life.

WITHERS, MISS MAUD
British School.
*op.* 1878–1880.
London address.
*exhib.* Suffolk Street (1); V.E. (3), flowers.

WITTE, ADRIEN DE
Flemish School.
b. Liege 1850 (2nd August), d. 1935.
Studied Liege Academy. Lived in Rome. Teacher and then Director of Liege Academy for a time. Painted still-life, genre, portraits and engraved.

WOESTYNE, GUSTAVE VAN DE
Flemish School.
b. Ghent 1881 (2nd August), d. Uccle 1947.
Studied at Ghent Academy. Lived in Brussels and Louvain 1909–1912. Visited Italy 1912. In England 1914–1918. Taught at Antwerp Higher Institute on return. Director Malines Academy.
*coll.*    Brussels, still-life.

WOLMARK, ALFRED AARON
British School.
b. Varsovje 1877 (28th December).
Painted flowers, portraits, etc.

WOOD, MISS CATHERINE M. (*see* MRS. R. H. WOOD)

WOOD, DANIEL
British School.
*op.* 1866.
Cambridge address.
*exhib.* B.I. (1), fruit.

WOOD, MISS ELEANOR STUART
British School.
*op.* 1876–1893.
Manchester address.
*exhib.* R.A. (11); N.W.C.S. (1); G.G. (11); N.G. (10)
fruit.

WOOD, MRS. R. H. (MISS CATHERINE M. WRIGHT)
British School.
*op.* 1880–1897.
London address. Wife of Richard Henry Wood (Benezit)
Graves gives Mrs. R. M. Wright. Painted figures, flowers
and still-life and views in Egypt, Italy, Greece and Switzerland.
*exhib.* As Miss C. M. Wright: R.A. (3); Suffolk Street.
(1); G.G. (2); N.G. (2); V.E. (4).
As Mrs. Wood: R.A. (24); Suffolk Street (26);
G.G. (1);1 V.E. (23).

WOOD, WILLIAM THOMAS                    (*see* PLATE 55)
British School.
b. Ipswich 1877 (17th June).
Painted flowers and landscapes.
*coll.*   Hull; Leeds; Manchester; Perth.
*exhib.* R.A. 1900.
*repr.*   Hardie, *Flower Paintings*, 1947.

WOODS, MISS ELLEN M.
British School.
*op.* 1874–1881.
Bristol address.
*exhib.* R.A. (1); V.E. (6), flowers.

WOOLLEY, MISS ALICE MARY
British School.
*op.* 1883–1892.
Sheffield address.
*exhib.* R.A. (4); Suffolk Street (5), flowers.

WOON, MISS R.
British School.
*op.* 1873.
London address.
*exhib.* R.A. (1), flowers.

WORMALD, FANNY
British School.
*op.* 1879.
Hertford address.
Painted flowers.

WORNUM, MISS CATHERINE AGNES
(MRS. FREDERICK PIERCY)
British School.
*op.* 1872–1877.
London address.
*exhib.* R.A. (1); Suffolk Street (1), fruit.

WORSDELL, MISS CLARA J.
British School.
*op.* 1884–1887.
Lancaster address.
*exhib.* R.A. (2), flowers.

WORSLEY, E. MARIA
British School.
*op.* 1874.
London address.
Painted fruit.

WOUTERS, RIK
Flemish School.
b. Malines 1882 (2nd August), d. Amsterdam 1916 (11th
July).
Studied Malines and Brussels Academies. In Paris 1912.
Painted still-life, figures, portraits, landscapes and interiors.
*coll.*   Antwerp; Brussels.

WRIGHT, ETHEL (MRS. BARCLAY)          (*see* PLATE 56)
British School.
*op.* 1887–1915.
London address.
Painted flowers and domestic.
*coll.*   Oldham.
*exhib.* R.A. (10); Suffolk Street (1); V.E. (13); Salon 1887.
*repr.*   *Colour Magazine*, December 1915, vase of flowers.

WRIGHT, F. P.
British School.
*op.* 1877–1883.
London address.
*exhib.* Suffolk Street (3), fruit.

WRIGHT, HELENA A.
British School.
*op.* 1883.
Nottingham address.
*exhib.* Suffolk Street (1), game.

WRIGHT, MRS. R. H. (*see* WOOD, MRS. R. H.)

WROE, MARY MCNICOLL
British School.
*op.* 1881–1891.
Manchester address.
*exhib.* Suffolk Street (1), flowers.

WYTSMAN, JULIETTE (*née* TRULEMANS)
Flemish School.
b. Brussels 1866 (14th July), d. there 1925 (8th March).
Pupil of P. Hendricks. Wife of Rodolphe Wytsman.
Painted flowers, landscape and genre.
*coll.* Brussels.
*exhib.* Liverpool 1909.

YON, MARGUERITE FREDERIQUE
French School.
d. 1898.
Pupil of M. J. Andre. Painted flowers and landscapes.
*exhib.* Salon 1869–1870.

ZANDLEVEN, JAN ADAM            (*see* PLATE 56)
Dutch School.
b. Koog 1868 (6th February), d. Rhenen 1923 (16th July).
Until 1902 in the colour-trade at Koog aan de Zaan, where his father had a colour-factory. In that year he broke with his father and the colour business and devoted himself exclusively to the art of painting (and drawing). Self-taught. Lived and worked successively at Beverwyck, Gorssel, Hengelow and Rhenen. Painted still-life, flower-pieces, landscapes, farm-houses, trees and toadstools.
*coll.* Dordrecht; The Hague.
*exhib.* Dordrecht Museum, 1962 (Zandleven Exhibition).
*lit.* Thieme-Becker, Kunstsler-Lexikon, 36, p. 402.
L. J. Bol, *Jan Adam Zandleven*, Exhibition cat. 1962, pp. 3–23.

ZANOBONI, ALFREDO
Italian School.
b. Empoli 1863 (4th October).
Studied Florence Academy. Visited Paris, London, Milan and Buenos Aires.
Painted still-life, landscapes, and was a sculptor.

ZELL, BEATRICE
British School.
*op.* 1880.
Manchester address.
*exhib.* Suffolk Street (1), fruit.

ZERLACHER, FERDINAND MATTHIAS
Austrian School.
b. Gratz 1877 (10th March), d. Salzburg 1923 (2nd January).
Studied Gratz Academy and Vienna. Painted still-life, portraits and landscapes.

ZEVENBERGEN, GEORGES ANTOINE VAN
Flemish School.
b. St. Jean Molenbeek 1877 (30th November).
Studied Molenbeek and Brussels Academies. Painted still-life and figures.
*coll.* Antwerp; Bergen.

ZILLHARDT, JENNY
French School.
b. St. Quentin 1857 (16th March).
Pupil of T. Robert Fleury. Painted still-life, genre and portraits. Chevalier of the Legion of Honour 1930.
*coll.* Langres; St. Quentin.
*exhib.* Salon 1878; Universal Exhibition 1926, **Silver Medal**; 1928, **Gold Medal**.

ZOLI, ALFREDO
Italian School.
b. Forli 1880 (2nd February).
Painted still-life and landscapes.

ZUBER, ANNA ELISE
French School.
b. Rixheim 1872 (13th July), d. 1932.
Painted flowers and landscapes.
*coll.* Mulhouse; Pontoise.

# SUPPLEMENT

BURNE-JONES, LADY (*see* MACDONALD, GEORGIANA)

CAMERON, KATHERINE
British School.
b. 1874.
Sister of Sir D. Y. Cameron, R.A. Studied Glasgow. Visited Italy. Painter and engraver.
*coll.* London, Tate Gallery, Mountain Fern, water-colour.
*exhib.* Berlin; Munich; Great Britain.

HARTRICK, MRS. A. S. (*see* BLATHERWICK, LILY)

HASERICK, ARTHUR AUGUSTUS
British School.
b. 1862, d. 1937.
Painted insects.
*coll.* London, Victoria and Albert Museum, (2), Moth and Butterfly.

INCE, EVELYN
British School.
b. c. 1886, d. 1941.
Painted flowers.
*coll.* London, Tate Gallery, flower piece.

LAWSON, CECIL GORDON
British School.
b. Salop 1849 (Cundall), b. Wellington, Shropshire (Benezit), b. 1851 (Victoria and Albert Museum Catalogue).
Son of W. Lawson, a portrait painter. Came to London 1861. Mostly self-taught. Painted landscapes in oil and water-colour and drew on wood for book illustrations.
*coll.* London, Victoria and Albert Museum (2), hollyhocks.
*exhib.* R.A. and G.G.

LEES, DERWENT
British School.
b. Melbourne, Australia 1885, d. 1951.
Studied at the Slade School, London. Visited Paris, Belgium, Germany, Italy and Russia.
*coll.* London, Tate Gallery, Pear tree in blossom.

MACDONALD, GEORGIANA—LADY BURNE-JONES
British School.
b. 1840, d. 1920.
Wife of Sir Edward Burne-Jones. Married at Manchester in 1860.
*coll.* London, Tate Gallery, water-colour, dead bird.

REICHELT, AUGUSTA WILHELMINE
German School.
b. Dresden 1840, d. 1907.
Painted flowers.
*coll.* Berlin, National Gallery, roses.
*exhib.* Berlin and Dresden.

RICH, ALFRED WILLIAM
British School.
b. Graveley, Sussex 1856 (4th March), d. Tewkesbury 1921 (7th September).
Painted landscapes and flowers in water-colour.
*coll.* London, Victoria and Albert Museum, anemones.

SICHEL, ERNEST LEOPOLD
British School.
b. 1862, d. 1941.
*coll.* London, Tate Gallery, musical instruments.

TYRWHITT, URSULA
British School.
b. 1878.
Wife of Walter Spencer Stanhope Tyrwhitt.
*coll.* London, Tate Gallery, flowers, water-colour.

# ILLUSTRATIONS

PLATE 1

Canvas     ANNA AIRY     50 × 30 in.
Signed

Canvas     ANNA AIRY     48 × 36 in.
Signed
Courtesy of Lt. Colonel J. G. Mackellar

Canvas     ALBERT ANDRE     18 × 21⅝ in.
Signed
Courtesy of Galerie Abels, Stadtwaldgurtel, Cologne

PLATE 2

Tempera             MAXWELL ARMFIELD, R.W.S.
                              Signed
                              P.W.U.

Canvas             ALFONS VAN BEURDEN             $38\frac{1}{2} \times 32\frac{5}{8}$ in.
                              Signed
        Courtesy of Koninklijk Museum voor Schone Kunsten, Antwerp

PLATE 3

Water-colour          GEOFFREY BIRKBECK          15 × 21½ in.
Signed
Courtesy of Durban Art Gallery

Canvas          BEATRICE E. BLAND          18 × 14 in.
P.W.U.

PLATE 4

Canvas                    PIERRE BONNARD             $19\frac{7}{8} \times 19\frac{3}{8}$ in.
Signed
Courtesy of Mr J. P. Durand-Matthiesen, Geneva

PLATE 5

Canvas

SIR FRANK BRANGWYN, R.A.
Signed & dated 1923
P.W.U.

PLATE 6

Canvas            MATILDA BROWNE (Mrs Frederick van Wyck)       36 × 30 in.
Signed
In the possession of Mrs Elsie F. Lewis

PLATE 7

ter-colour      MARY E. BUTLER      $11 \times 8\frac{3}{4}$ in.
Signed
Courtesy of the Victoria & Albert Museum, London

Canvas      CHARLES CAMOIN      $16\frac{1}{8} \times 13$ in.
Signed
Courtesy of Galerie Abels, Stadtwaldgurtel, Cologne

PLATE 8

Panel                           **EUGENE HENRI CAUCHOIS**           16 × 12 in.
Signed
Courtesy of Leggatt Brothers, London

PLATE 9

Water-colour    MARIAN EMMA CHASE, R.I.    $12\frac{1}{8} \times 9\frac{5}{8}$ in.
Signed & dated 1872
Courtesy of Victoria & Albert Museum, London

Oil on panel        WILLIAM A. CHASE        approx. $18 \times 14$ in.

PLATE 10

Canvas            WILLIAM MERRITT CHASE          $26\frac{7}{8} \times 44\frac{3}{4}$ in.
Signed
Courtesy National Gallery of Art, Washington D.C. (Chester Dale Coll.)

Canvas            WILLIAM MERRITT CHASE          $30 \times 36$ in.
Signed
Courtesy of Berry-Hill Galleries, New York City

PLATE 11

Canvas        ANTHONIE ELEANORE (ANTHONORE) CHRISTENSEN     48¾ × 37¾ in.
Signed & dated 1892
Courtesy of The Royal Museum of Fine Arts, Copenhagen

PLATE 12

Oil                    GEORGE CLARE                    22 × 18 in.
                              Signed
            Courtesy of Frost & Reed Ltd, Bristol & London

Oil                SIR GEORGE CLAUSEN, R.A.            14 × 16 in.
                              Signed
    Courtesy of The William Morris Gallery & Brangwyn Gift, Walthamstow. E17

PLATE 13

Canvas        PHILIP CONNARD, R.A.        30 × 25 in.
Courtesy Durban Art Gallery

Canvas        LOVIS CORINTH        20¾ × 33½ in.
Signed
Courtesy of Galerie Abels, Stadtwaldgurtel, Cologne

PLATE 14

Canvas                    KEES VAN DONGEN                    39⅜ × 31⅞ in.
                                Signed
                  Courtesy of Musées Municipaux, Amsterdam

PLATE 15

Water-colour             RAOUL DUFY             19¾ × 25⅝ in.
                            Signed
            Courtesy of Galerie Abels, Stadtwaldgurtel, Cologne

Canvas                   A. DURAN                16 × 20 in.
                     Signed and dated 1895
            Courtesy of Berry-Hill Galleries, New York City

PLATE 16

Water-colour CAROLINE H. EASTLAKE    $9\frac{3}{4} \times 8$ in.
Signed
Courtesy of Victoria & Albert Museum, London

Oil                    JAMES ENSOR                    $31 \times 38\frac{5}{8}$ in.
Signed
Courtesy of Koninklijk Museum voor Schone Kunsten, Antwerp

PLATE 17

Oil          GIUSEPPE FALCHETTI      $44\frac{7}{8} \times 25\frac{3}{8}$ in.  Oil       GIUSEPPE FALCHETTI     $25\frac{1}{2} \times 15\frac{3}{4}$ in.

Signed & dated 1898                           Signed & dated 1865

Courtesy of Museo Civico, Torino

PLATE 18

Water-colour                    ERNEST FILLIARD                    20½ × 18 in.
Signed
Courtesy of Durban Art Gallery

PLATE 19

Canvas                               CHARLES DANA GIBSON                     40 × 33½ in.
Signed
Courtesy of Berry-Hill Galleries, New York City

PLATE 20

Oil                SYLVIA GOSSE

Canvas                G. D. GRATAMA                21⅝ × 18⅛
Signed & dated 1903
Courtesy Teylers Museum, Haarlem

PLATE 21

Canvas        ORLANDO GREENWOOD        21 × 18 in.
Signed
Courtesy of Harris Museum & Art Gallery, Preston

PLATE 22

Canvas        STORM VAN 'S GRAVESANDE        21¼ × 14½ in.
Signed
Courtesy of Teylers Museum, Haarlem

Canvas        ANNA (HANNA) HALLER        31½ × 39⅜ in.
Courtesy of Berne Kunstmuseum

PLATE 23

Oil        W. M. HARNETT        46 × 38 in.
Dated 1886
Courtesy of Mr Paul Peralta-Ramos, New York

Canvas        CLAUDE RAGUET HIRST        10 × 14⅛ in.
Courtesy of Berry-Hill Galleries, New York City

PLATE 24

Canvas        HARALD MARTIN HANSEN HOLM        34¾ × 27½ in.
Signed & dated 1900
Courtesy of Royal Museum of Fine Arts, Copenhagen

Water-colour        FRANCIS EDWARD JAMES, R.W.S.        16 × 13½ i
Signed
Courtesy of Durban Art Gallery

PLATE 25

Canvas    ALEXEJ VON JAWLENSKI    $17\frac{7}{8} \times 22$ in.
Signed
Courtesy of Galerie Abels, Stadtwaldgurtel, Cologne

Canvas    MARCEL JEFFERYS
P.W.U.

PLATE 26

Water-colour

CATHERINA KLEIN
Signed
P.W.U.

PLATE 27

nvas        PIERRE LAPRADE      $17\frac{3}{4} \times 14\frac{1}{2}$ in.
Signed
Collection H.D., Paris

Canvas        HENRI LEBASQUE      $21\frac{5}{8} \times 18\frac{1}{4}$ in.
Signed
Courtesy of Galerie Abels, Stadtwaldgurtel, Cologne

PLATE 28

Canvas        HENRI LE-SIDANER        $36\frac{1}{4} \times 28\frac{3}{4}$ in.
Signed
Courtesy of Galerie Abels, Stadtwaldgurtel, Cologne

Canvas        GUSTAVE LOISEAU        $26 \times 21\frac{5}{8}$ in.
Signed
Courtesy of Galerie Abels, Stadtwaldgurtel, Cologne

PLATE 29

Oil            STEFAN LUCHIAN        $28 \times 10\frac{3}{4}$ in.
Signed
Courtesy of Art Museum of the Rumanian People's Republic, Bucharest

PLATE 30

Canvas        HENRI CHARLES MANGUIN        $19\frac{1}{2} \times 23\frac{5}{8}$ in.
Signed
Courtesy of Galerie Abels, Stadtwaldgurtel, Cologne

Black chalk        HENRI MATISSE        $17\frac{3}{4} \times 21\frac{3}{4}$ in.
Courtesy of Whitworth Art Gallery, University of Manchester

PLATE 31

Canvas       ROBERT MOLS       41⅝ × 33⅞ in.
Signed
Courtesy of Koninklijk Museum voor Schone Kunsten, Antwerp

Canvas       MAXIME E. L. MAUFRA       25⅜ × 17½ in.
Signed & dated 1911
Courtesy of Galerie Abels, Stadtwaldgurtel, Cologne

Panel       LUIGI MONTEVERDE       7⅞ × 5½ in.
Signed
Courtesy of Berne Kunst Museum

PLATE 32

Canvas                              F. MORTELMANS                    18⅞ × 30¾ in.
                                        Signed
                    Courtesy of Koninklijk Museum voor Schone Kunsten, Antwerp

Canvas                          MICHAEL LEIB MUNKÁCSY                18⅛ × 21⅝ in.
                              Signed & dated 5 Octobre 1879
                        Courtesy of Galerie Abels, Stadtwaldgurtel, Cologne

PLATE 33

Oil      ANNA MUNTHE-NORSTEDT    $26\frac{3}{4} \times 18\frac{7}{8}$ in.
Signed & dated 1908
Courtesy of National Museum, Stockholm

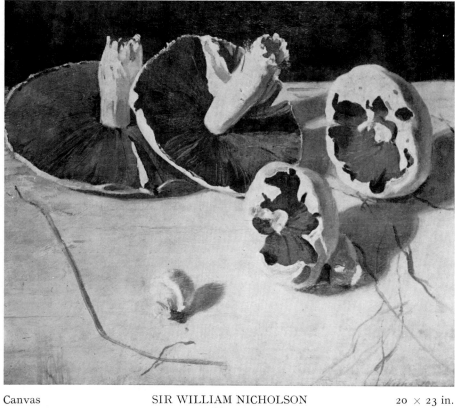

Canvas      SIR WILLIAM NICHOLSON    $20 \times 23$ in.
Signed
Courtesy of The Castle Museum & Art Gallery, Nottingham

PLATE 34

Canvas             PERICLES PANTAZIS           $45\frac{1}{8} \times 36\frac{5}{8}$ in.
Signed
Courtesy of Musées Royaux des Beaux-Arts, Brussels

PLATE 35

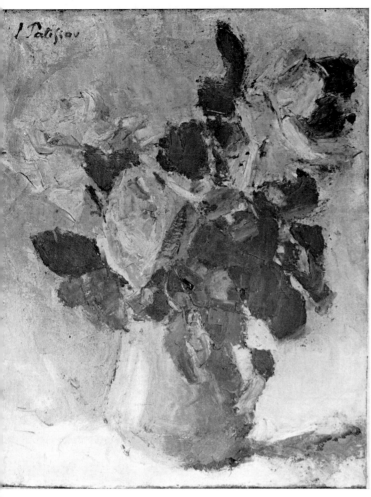

Canvas               JACQUES PATISSOU
Signed
Courtesy of Musée des Beaux Arts, Nantes

Canvas         MAX PECHSTEIN      $31\frac{7}{8} \times 27\frac{1}{2}$ in.
Signed
Courtesy of Stadt. Kunsthalle, Mannheim

Oil

S. J. PEPLOE
Signed

$19\frac{1}{2} \times 27\frac{1}{2}$ in.

PLATE 37

Canvas                            LEONARD D. PHILPOT                36 × 28 in.
Signed
Courtesy of Harris Museum & Art Gallery, Preston

PLATE 38

Canvas       ALEXANDER POPE       54 × 42 in.
Signed
Courtesy of Graves Art Gallery, Sheffield

Canvas       JULES DE PRAETERE       36 × 30 i
Courtesy of Musée Royaux des Beaux-Arts, Brussels

PLATE 39

Canvas JEAN FRANCOIS RAFFAËLLI $22\frac{3}{4} \times 18\frac{7}{8}$ in.
Signed
Courtesy of Galerie Abels, Stadtwaldgurtel, Cologne

Canvas AUGUSTE RENOIR $18 \times 21\frac{5}{8}$ in.
Signed
Courtesy of Mr J. P. Durand-Matthiesen, Geneva

PLATE 40

Canvas                                W. B. E. RANKEN

Signed

PLATE 41

Canvas

HERBERT DAVIS RICHTER, V.P.R.O.I.
Signed

PLATE 42

Canvas          COBA RITSEMA          39⅜ × 26⅜ in.
Signed
Courtesy of Teylers Museum, Haarlem

Oil          EDWARD F. ROOK          30 × 35 in.
Signed
Courtesy of Cincinnati Art Museum, U.S.A.

PLATE 43

Oil

ALICE RONNER
Signed & dated '09

PLATE 44

MARGUERETHA CORNELIA JOHANNA ROOSENBOOM
Canvas          Signed          $18\frac{7}{8} \times 13$ in.
Courtesy of Teylers Museum, Haarlem

Canvas          NATHANIEL SCHMITT          $28 \times 20\frac{1}{4}$ in.
Courtesy of Staatliche Kunsthalle, Karlsruhe

PLATE 45

Canvas             KARL SCHUCH          $14\frac{1}{2} \times 20\frac{1}{8}$ in.
Courtesy of Hallsborough Gallery, London

Water-colour       ANDRE A. M. DUNOYER DE SEGONZAC       $23 \times 31$ in.
Signed
Courtesy of The Reid Gallery, London

PLATE 46

Canvas       SIR MATTHEW SMITH      $22\frac{3}{8} \times 18\frac{1}{4}$ in.
Signed
By Courtesy of City Art Gallery, Bristol

Canvas      ALEXANDRE THEOPHILE STEINLEN    $18 \times 15$ in.
Courtesy of The Durban Art Gallery

PLATE 47

anvas          CELLA THOMA          $28\frac{1}{8} \times 19\frac{7}{8}$ in.
                    Signed
        Courtesy of Staatliche Kunsthalle, Karlsruhe

Oil          ARTURO TOSI
            Signed
    Courtesy of Museo Civico, Torino

PLATE 48

Canvas             LESSER URY        $40\frac{1}{8} \times 29\frac{1}{8}$ in.
Signed & dated 1921
Courtesy Galerie Abels, Stadtwaldgurtel, Cologne

Oil            WALTER VAES       $15\frac{3}{4} \times 14\frac{1}{2}$ in
Courtesy of Koninklijk Museum voor Schone Kunsten, Antwerp

PLATE 49

Canvas        FELIX VALLOTTON        $25\frac{1}{2} \times 21\frac{1}{2}$ in.
Signed & dated 1913
Courtesy of the Hallsborough Gallery, London

PLATE 50

Oil

FLORIS VERSTER
Signed
Courtesy of Musées Municipaux, Amsterdam

$53\frac{1}{8} \times 79\frac{1}{4}$ in.

PLATE 51

Canvas        MAURICE VLAMINCK        $36\frac{1}{4} \times 28\frac{3}{4}$ in.
Signed
Courtesy of Mr J. P. Durand-Matthiesen, Geneva

PLATE 52

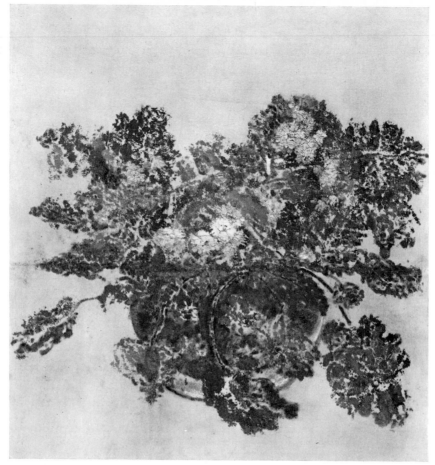

Tissue         EDOUARD VUILLARD         $24\frac{1}{8} \times 19\frac{1}{4}$ in.
Courtesy of Hallsborough Gallery, London

Canvas         EDOUARD VUILLARD         $13 \times 15\frac{3}{4}$ in.
Courtesy of Galerie Daber, Paris

PLATE 53

Water-colour  PAULINE WALKER  14⅛ × 12⅜ in.
Signed & dated 1878
Courtesy of Norwich Castle Museum

Oil  C. E. WALLIN  8½ × 12 in,
Courtesy of Berry-Hill Galleries, New York City

PLATE 54

Oil                            EMIL RUDOLF WEISS                     27 × 23¼ in.
Signed & dated 1901
Courtesy of Staatliche Kunsthalle, Karlsruhe

PLATE 55

Canvas                WILLIAM T. WOOD       46 × 36 in.
Signed
P.W.O.

PLATE 56

Oil                ETHEL WRIGHT
<br>Signed

Canvas         J. A. ZANDLEVEN       $21\frac{5}{8} \times 18\frac{1}{2}$ in.
<br>Signed & dated 1920
<br>Courtesy of Dordrecht Museum